Albert Augustus Gore

A Contribution to the Medical History of Our West African

Campaigns

Albert Augustus Gore

A Contribution to the Medical History of Our West African Campaigns

ISBN/EAN: 9783337308971

Printed in Europe, USA, Canada, Australia, Japan

Cover: Foto ©ninafisch / pixelio.de

More available books at **www.hansebooks.com**

A CONTRIBUTION

TO THE

MEDICAL HISTORY

OF OUR

WEST AFRICAN CAMPAIGNS.

BY

SURGEON-MAJOR ALBERT A. GORE, M.D.,

Late 34th Regiment.

SANITARY OFFICER ON THE STAFF OF THE QUARTER-MASTER GENERAL'S DEPARTMENT,
DURING THE ASHANTI WAR OF 1873.

"Facts are the Materials of Science."

LONDON:
BAILLIÈRE, TINDALL AND COX,
KING WILLIAM STREET, STRAND.
1876.

To the Memory

OF

AN AMIABLE AND ACCOMPLISHED

GENTLEMAN,

THE LATE

PROFESSOR EDMUND ARTHUR PARKES, F.R.S.,

THIS VOLUME

IS

AFFECTIONATELY DEDICATED,

BY

ONE OF HIS FIRST MILITARY PUPILS,

THE AUTHOR.

PREFACE.

The great charm in the writings of the older military surgeons was, that they were unpretending narratives of the campaigns in which they served, and of what they had heard and read of the wars to whose success they contributed not a little.

In the following pages I have endeavoured to follow their example, and to collect together in systematic order the many interesting facts bearing upon the health and efficiency of the soldier in a malarial climate, which lie scattered through the very voluminous literature of our West African Campaigns, adding in addition many personal notes and recollections. Of these wars the Ashanti campaign was undoubtedly the most important, as being the only one where a successful attempt had been made to conquer with European troops a great African kingdom, hitherto deemed to be impregnable. The volume I feel to be a very imperfect one, yet it may not prove the less interesting as a medical souvenir.

In conclusion, I must say I feel convinced that it is only by a repetition of similar independent literary ventures upon the part of others, that the quiet and useful profession to which I have the honour to belong will gain that status in the army which the great and varied experience of its executive officers in every clime so justly entitles it.

THE AUTHOR.

Dublin, *January 1st, 1876.*

TABLE OF CONTENTS.

	Page
PREFACE	v.

CHAPTER I.
EARLIER MEDICAL HISTORY . 1

CHAPTER II.
LATER MILITARY AND MEDICAL EVENTS . 19

CHAPTER III.
CLIMATE OF THE GOLD COAST . 51

CHAPTER IV.
COMPOSITION OF THE FORCE . 64

CHAPTER V.
DRESS, EQUIPMENT, AND WEIGHTS CARRIED . 70

CHAPTER VI.
FOOD SUPPLY; ITS EFFECT UPON HEALTH . 78

CHAPTER VII.
NON-ALCOHOLIC BEVERAGES . 88

CHAPTER VIII.
SPIRIT RATION: ITS USE AND ABUSE . 94

CHAPTER IX.
MEDICAL RESTORATIVES . 107

CHAPTER X.
TOBACCO IN THE FIELD . 108

CONTENTS.

CHAPTERS XI. AND XII.

	Page
WATER SUPPLY	109

CHAPTER XIII.

MARCHES IN AFRICAN WARFARE . . .	120

CHAPTER XIV.

HOUSING OF THE TROOPS	133

CHAPTER XV.

MEDICO-CHIRURGICAL LESSONS .	138

CHAPTER XVI.

WOUNDS AND INJURIES . .	183

CHAPTER XVII.

EXPEDITION AGAINST THE CONGO PIRATES	196

CHAPTER XVIII.

HISTORICAL SKETCH OF THE AFRICAN MEDICAL SERVICE . . .	202

ERRATA.

For "ebriositis," at page 105, read "ebriositas." In page 176, "arcola," read "areola."

CHAPTER I.

EARLIER HISTORY.

NEARLY every attempt to wage war in Western Africa in former years was unsuccessful, as much from the neglect of the most obvious hygienic precautions as from the admitted deadly nature of the climate. Either men were sent to Africa who should never have been allowed to garrison its forts and settlements, or where soldiers were required to operate against the enemy they had been obliged to fight or march under the most adverse sanitary conditions; the result very naturally under such circumstances, was death, disease, and subsequent inefficiency to an unprecedented extent. Scarcely could it be wondered then, that this *terra inhospita* was looked upon as the white man's grave.

Up to a comparatively recent period little was known of Western Africa outside a very limited circle, comprising the few *savants* who sought notoriety in endeavouring to penetrate its distant forest paths, men in search of mercantile adventures, and the small Colonial and Military Staff of the settlements, whose miserable banishment was the constant theme of their friends. To the physician its medical history was not uninteresting, as embracing the whole range of the most important of the tropical diseases—yellow fever, paludal remittents and intermittents, dysentery, cholera, splenetis, hepatitis, guinea-worm, lethargus, tropical ulcers, yaws, leprosy, elephantiasis græcorum, and a host of other affections whose etiology is still very much a matter of disputation among the learned of our ever speculative profession.

The earlier records of disease, or rather the brief glimpses we obtain of them, are very instructive. If, to commence, we turn back to the four years following the great European peace of 1815, when the effective and non-effective force serving in Western Africa was as below, we see in the brief record, at a glance, the influence of climate, want of attention to personal hygiene, and general insanitary conditions at that early date, causing a force of Europeans, equal in strength to an ordinary regiment of infantry, to die out and become inefficient in the short space of four years, in a ratio increasing directly with length of service on the Coast; while the native troops, serving side by side with their white comrades, lost only, on an average, 3·72 per cent. per annum during the same period.

YEAR.	Mean average effective.			Sick included.			Deaths.			Men.			Officers.	
	Europeans.	Blacks.	Total.	Europeans.	Blacks.	Total.	Europeans.	Blacks.	Total.	Invalided.	Average number present.	Died.		Invalided.
1816	540	538	1,078	55	22	77	115	17	132	32	45	6		6
1817	246	394	640	25	9	34	62	18	80	23	32	3		5
1818	102	326	428	7	6	13	38	10	48	10	21	2		2
1819	54	391	445	2	4	6	5	12	17	45	18	1		6

In other words, the ratio per cent. of invaliding and deaths among the European officers and men was:—

In 1816	.	.	Officers, 26·66	.	.	Men, 27·41
,, 1817	.	.	,, 25·00	.	.	,, 34·51
,, 1818	.	.	,, 19·05	.	.	,, 47·06
,, 1819	.	.	,, 33·88	.	.	,, 92·60

The native troops who were then serving on the coast of Africa had been originally embodied from slaves, procured by purchase in the West Indies; while on the Coast they were largely recruited from liberated Africans, who were being captured in increasing numbers, no less than 9,502 having been taken from slavers between the years 1819–26, inclusive, of which number 1,500 died before adjudication from previous ill treatment, unsuitable food, water, and overcrowding, a ratio of 15·78 per cent. of the whole.

Dysentery and diarrhœa accounted for a very large proportion of this mortality—attributed in part by some writers to the use of the meal of the bitter cassada *(Jatropha Manihot)*, which, in the absence of rice or corn, was shipped as food for the unfortunate beings cooped up between decks. This source of recruiting naturally ceased with the stoppage of the slave trade. The last recruits were obtained for the 2nd West India Regiment from a cargo of Congoes (liberated at Sierra Leone in 1861), in a very simple fashion: drawn up in line, such of them as were found of sufficient height, physique, and chest measurement by the adjutant and surgeon, were drafted at once into the ranks, and christened from the *Army List*, by which means many distinguished names have been handed down to subsequent generations, in a manner admitting of a double construction, which the original owners would, probably, have strongly objected to.

Now, upon first arrival, West Indian troops are alien to Africa; they consequently suffer more from climate than they would have done under the old system they, however, are not singular in this respect, as the Dutch at Elmina observed a similar result in their recruits brought from the interior to the swamps and alluvial shores of the seaboard, and an entirely different mode of life: up country was a still, dead heat; below, strong breezes, and much alternation of temperature, and a different diet.

Between 1819 and 1822, when the Ashantees invaded the Protectorate, there was little to note or particularize in West African military life: in the last year, desultory attacks commenced, which only ceased in 1827. During the continuance of these the native force was increased, and a batch of Europeans were sent out, the first detachment of a special corps of commuted-punishment men, raised in London from among military offenders, and styled the "Royal African Corps," a regiment composed of "the greatest rascals under the sun," and which, as a European one, had the short-lived existence of seven years—1823–30—after which date white drafts ceased to be sent to West Africa, and the corps, filled up by natives, merged into the "3rd West India Regiment," not long since disbanded. History repeating itself, the results observed between 1815–19 were, if anything, intensified in effect; between the years 1825–26 alone the death-rate averaged a ratio of:—

At Sierra Leone	. . .	65·0 per cent.
,, Isles de Los	. . .	60·0 ,,
,, Gambia	. . . .	150·0 ,,

During the whole of this frightful mortality at the Gambia, forty black soldiers had scarcely any sick in hospital, and only lost one man: but the contrast between the susceptibility of the white and black soldiers to the effects of climate is even better seen over a series of years.

In the seven years ending in 1833, while the native troops had

Treated to strength.	Deaths to strength.
1 to 1·321	1 to 40·84

the Europeans, in the three years ending 1829, had

Treated to strength.	Deaths to strength.
3·12 to 1	1 to 13·48

after which the numbers were too small to yield reliable data. The contrast is, however, sufficiently obvious.

The deaths and invaliding among the officers during the same interval was :—

In 1827	. . . .	36·3 per cent.
,, 1828	. . . .	42·6 ,,
,, 1829	. . . .	42·8 ,,

figures showing, conclusively, how superior was the old native corps to a European one upon economic, sanitary, and humanitarian grounds. The foregoing large mortality among the white troops was attributed to the fact of their being commuted-punishment men, and as such, reckless and dissipated. This was undoubtedly true of them as a class; but an interesting fact remains on record—that a detachment of recruits voluntarily enlisted at Chatham, and purposely separated by General Turner from their more depraved companions, by being quartered on the Isles de Los, three pretty volcanic islets, 60 miles north of Sierra Leone, suffered enormously, 62 dying out of 103 in a few months, principally from remittent fever. They had landed on the 25th February, 1825, two months before the setting in of the rains. Between the years 1822–29, 46·63 per cent., on an average, became inefficient among the officers annually from deaths and invaliding to England, very close upon half the number serving. The cause for this was not, however, purely climatic, as may be gleaned from the following description of the then daily life of Europeans in these colonies, noted by Dr. Nichol, at the time Deputy-Inspector of Hospitals in West Africa. In a report made to the Army Medical Department, he wrote: "In all the countries which I have visited, I never saw so much eating and drinking. Breakfast is taken at rising; at 11 A.M. they sit down to a relish, consisting of soups, meats, and the highest seasoned dishes; wine is drunk as at dinner, and afterwards saugaree, or brandy and water, which they too frequently continue sipping and drinking till late in the afternoon, sometimes to the dinner hour, 6 P.M." Such a course of life in a West African climate could produce no other result but disease, for the debility produced by the constant breathing of the malarial poison would be aggravated by a high temperature and a sedentary life, the three combined leading to engorgement of the viscera of the abdomen, which a more active life might, to some extent, have prevented, the excess of ingesta being in such a case worked off in replacing the more rapid metamorphosis of tissue which would naturally occur. Beyond the general fact that the mortality and sickness was much increased during the various military operations against the Ashantees—1822–27, and that we lost 42 men killed in action at the battle of Assamacou, 21st January, 1824, in addition to several officers, we have little left to study in the medical history of that unfortunate war. Before this had ended, General Turner had undertaken an expedition against some hostile chiefs at the Sherborough, 170 miles south of Sierra Leone, in the midst of the rainy season. Several of his European troops lost their lives from the effect of disease induced by their short trip up this pestilential river.

During the three years and a-half employed by Captain Owen in surveying the African coast from the Persian Gulf to the Gambia, 1821, 22, 23, the vessels under his command lost 38 officers and 85 per cent. of their crews, principally from malarial fevers.

On the Gold Coast the forts had been replaced under the management of the merchants in 1828, and garrisoned by a small local force of 80 men, scattered over seven stations: their diseases have not been handed down to posterity. They were dressed and armed in the military fashion of the day—scarlet tunics, yellow facings, and white trousers and shakos. In a few years this small force disappeared, to be ultimately replaced by another local levy, the "Gold Coast Corps," raised in 1851, recruited entirely from Fantees, who had European officers and non-commissioned officers, the former of whom obtained special advantages in the way of unattached promotion and retirement for service on the Coast. Two years before the regiments mutinied, its strength amounted to 279 non-commissioned officers and men, out of which were 162 admissions into hospital, and 7 deaths, a larger ratio than that of the West India Regiment then quartered at Sierra Leone, which corps, out of a strength of 363 non-commissioned officers and men, yielded 193 admissions and 5 deaths, showing the following ratio per 1,000:—

	Admissions.	Deaths.
Gold Coast Corps	580·64	25·09
W. I. Regiment (Sierra Leone)	531·68	13·77

Here the natives appeared to suffer more than the men brought originally from the West Indies; the latter were, however, somewhat acclimatized, as they had been already some years on the Coast, and were approaching the period of their relief; they also lived in better quarters, were under greater discipline, and more regularly and better fed: the Fantee private, on the other hand, receiving £1 per month, did, in respect to his messing, much as he liked—the striking points between the two corps being the comparative exemption of the Gold Coast Regiment from miasmatic and enthetic diseases, the prevalence amongst them of parasitic affections, and the low rate of mortality from tubercular disease, as may be seen below.

RATES PER 1,000.

	West Indian Regiment. Sierra Leone, 1859.		Gold Coast Corps. 1859.	
	Admitted.	Died.	Admitted.	Died.
Miasmatic	224·7	2·8	118·3	7·16
Enthetic	106·8	0·0	32·3	6·00
Parasitic	5·6	0·0	250·9	0·00
Tubercular	16·9	5·61	0·0	0·00
Nervous	0·0	0·0	10·8	0·00
Respiratory	39·3	0·0	21·5	0·00
Digestive	21·8	0·0	25·0	7·16
Urinary	5·6	5·6	7·1	0·00
Integumentary	53·4	0·0	75·3	0·00

The contrast between a period of peace and garrison life, and bush life preliminary to the operations of war upon the Gold Coast, is most marked in the more important affections.

	Gold Coast, 1859. Strength, 279.		Gold Coast, 1863. Strength, 546.	
	Admitted.	Died.	Admitted.	Died.
Miasmatic	118·3	7·6	609·9	40·29

During the last six months of 1863, the garrison, composed partly of acclimatized men, and partly of unacclimatized, and newly-arrived and enlisted young soldiers of the 4th West India Regiment, had been much exposed in the bush during preliminary preparations for a march to the Prah; while in 1859, a period of tranquility, there had been only one admission from acute dysentery (which ended fatally), two cases of intermittent, and four of remittent fever from among 279 men of the Gold Coast Corps; in 1863, under the circumstances already described, the admissions had increased to 25·28 and 78 respectively, from among 546 West Indians, showing the following ratio per cent:—

	Native Corps in Garrison.	West Indian Corps in Garrison and the Bush.
Dysentery	·37 per cent.	22·90 per cent.
Intermittent Fever	·71 ,,	5·12 ,,
Remittent do.	1·42 ,,	14·28 ,,

This large increase may be fairly ascribed to unacclimatization, unsuitable material, indifferent diet, exposure, and over work, as will be afterwards seen; but the great contrast between the local and alien corps is in the admissions for parasitic affections. Guinea-worm with the former was a fertile source of inefficiency, nearly every fourth man being, on an average, affected, as will be seen upon a perusal of the figures below:—

In 1859, a ratio of 25·09 per cent.
,, 1860,   ,,   24·58   ,,
,, 1861,   ,,   28·52   ,,

The admissions from this disease, confined almost entirely to the Gold Coast and Lagos, where it is evidently endemic, were:—

In 1859, out of 279 Men, 70, or 25·09 per cent.
,, 1860,   ,,   313   ,,   77   ,,   24·60   ,,
,, 1861,   ,,   315   ,,   87   ,,   27·94   ,,
,, 1862,   ,,   313   ,,   35   ,,   11·18   ,,
,, 1863,   ,,   546   ,,   7   ,,   1·28   ,,
,, 1864,   ,,   927   ,,   63   ,,   6·80   ,,
,, 1865,   ,,   654   ,,   33   ,,   5·05   ,,
,, 1866,   ,,   307   ,,   1   ,,   0·32   ,,
,, 1867,   ,,   238   ,,   1   ,,   0·42   ,,
,, 1868,   ,,   245   ,,   0   ,,   0·00   ,,
,, 1869,   ,,   285   ,,   1   ,,   0·35   ,,

The decrease in the admissions in 1862 may be explained by the reduction of the Gold Coast Corps in that year, and its replacement by a detachment of the 2nd West. The increase in 1864 by previous bush marching in the rains of 1863; the second decrease to the removal of the expeditionary regiments to the West Indies, the cases remaining being, probably, those already existing among the moiety left as a garrison until the arrival of the 3rd West India Regiment in 1865, since which period, with the exception of 31 cases occurring amongst the garrison of Lagos, in 1868, there were no admissions on the Gold Coast, dracunculus having almost disappeared from the returns forwarded from this portion of the Coast.

It will naturally be asked why was dracunculus so prevalent amongst the men of the Gold Coast Artillery, and why absent afterwards when the forts were garrisoned by men of a West Indian regiment, as long as the latter were not engaged in the bush? This question, of much interest, is difficult to answer in its entirety, but yet it may be touched upon. Four facts are well known with regard to this disease—

That it is endemic on the Gold Coast.

That the nature of the soil and water is favourable to its propagation and development.

That the natives are much marked from the ulcers resulting from its presence, especially on the lower limbs.

That it has always been most prevalent after previous bush marching during the rains.

It is more than probable that the Fantees, who composed the rank and file of the local regiment, brought in some instances the germs of the disease with them into the corps, in other cases contracted it afresh from living in much the same manner as the class from which they were originally drawn, and with whom they were constantly mixing. Like the natives, they would also probably cultivate farms in the neighbourhood, prepare them at the commencement of the rains, going and returning bare-legged through the muddy pools at a moment when the youthful *filaria* would be most active after their previous dry season's imprisonment. Their habit of daubing themselves all over with streaks of white clay, and swallowing the latter as a medicine, may also have had something to do with the introduction of the parasite: on the other hand, the men of the West India Regiment had nothing in common with the natives, did not adopt their customs, were messed by Government upon imported provisions, drank tank water, and constantly wore leggings, or other means of protection to the lower extremities, which rarely carried them beyond the streets of the town, where there was certainly no *nidus* for the parasite, presuming it came from without. Then, again, the men were more cleanly than the natives, had periodical bathing parades in sea water, and never disported themselves in the filthy pools in the vicinity of the town, as did their African brethren: facts of interest, as it is well known that proper clothing and personal cleanliness are the best preventatives in localities where guinea-worm is endemic. The immunity of the European officers, who always marched with well protected feet, and indulged in the luxury of a tub at the termination of a journey whenever practicable, points to a similar conclusion. The only case of dracunculus which came under my notice during the late military operations in Africa, occurred in a private of the 2nd West, who had contracted the disease at Lagos, long prior to admission into hospital.

Before reviewing the lessons of the Ashantee expedition of 1863-64, we must glance for a moment at the Medical History of the Baddaboo and Quiah wars, carried on, the first against the turbulent Mahomedan tribes of the Gambia, and the latter against the Timmanees, bordering upon the confines of Sierra Leone, two entirely distinct races in religion and manners; the first, followers of the Prophet; the latter believing in gri-gris and other charms against the machinations of an all-powerful evil spirit. The one living in villages, built upon extensive savannas, favourable to the operations of cavalry, in which they were particularly strong, their towns being protected by strong mud walls; the others upon the banks of rivers, or in the interior of a forest country, in villages composed of a number of circular mud huts, with high conical grass roofs, and protected by strong wooden stockades, which were defended with great bravery and obstinacy on every occasion when they were attacked.

In 1860 a mixed force, consisting of detachments of the 1st and 2nd West India Regiments, a battery of French Artillery from the Senegal, the Gambia militia, and a party of seamen and marines, forming a naval brigade, under Commodore Edmonstone, landed under cover of the guns of H.M.'s ship "Torch," at Swarraconda Creek, some miles up the River Gambia, to which the troops were conveyed by the colonial steamers and naval transports. After a variety of skirmishes, the enemy was encountered in force on the plains of Saba, on the 20th February, several miles inland; defeated after a smart action, and driven into his chief town, which he defended to the last, many being bayoneted in the works rather than surrender. The troops were about a month on shore in February, one of the winter months of the Gambia, and one of its driest and finest times, the Harmattan being at its maximum.

In the following November, December, and January, were undertaken the military operations against the King and chiefs of Quiah, who had been making frequent raids into the colony of Sierra Leone. The force employed against them consisted of a wing of the 2nd W. I. Regiment, the Sierra Leone Militia, and a large auxiliary force of Kossoos; and in the rivers and creeks, the boat's crews of H.M.'s ships "Falcon" and "Torch." During the period while these continued, the enemy was constantly harassed; his river villages, and those along the sea, bombarded and destroyed by parties landed from the boats of the squadron. Inland, the base of operations was pushed on to Waterloo on the frontier, this town being made the military Head Quarters, from which a road was afterwards made to Prince Alfred's Town, through a dense forest. Waterloo was especially convenient, as it was connected by water with Freetown, twenty miles distant, and by means of the Campbelltown Creek, with the sea, bordering upon the entrance to the Ribbee River, far away to the southward of the colony. From Waterloo, the interior stockaded towns of Madonkia, Robea, &c., were attacked, small mountain howitzers, and 6 pounder rocket-tubes being carried by Kroomen along the narrow roadways; the stretchers and other impedimenta were also carried by these hardy people. The troops bivouacked in the captured towns, making the last taken the base of operations against the next in advance. On one occasion, the troops were marching and engaging the enemy from 5 A.M. to 9 P.M., covering about twenty miles of country; very hard work for the officers in forage caps and white covers, for helmets were not worn in those days in Africa. On the march, the field ration consisted of navy pork, coffee, sugar, biscuit, and a gill of rum daily; at Waterloo, fresh meat was issued as often as possible, the cattle being brought up from Freetown. Pocket filters were not then available; the Jamaica spirit being thought a sufficiently powerful prophylactic against the water animalcules and other impurities.

Carried on during the dry season, when the men were not for a single day exposed to a tropical shower, these limited operations were chiefly of interest as proving the possibility of carrying on bush warfare with success during the dry season in Western Africa. For, although officers and soldiers were considerably exposed to the sun during the march, were several times up creeks and rivers, and on many occasions bivouacked in their blankets and greatcoats, round huge fires, they suffered little from disease; a few cases of pneumonia occurred at the Gambia, attributed to the Harmattan wind; the excessive evaporation on a perspiring surface, chilling the parietes of the chest, and causing the disease. In Quiah there were several men admitted for foot sore; and at the termination of the campaign, many officers and European non-commissioned officers suffered from attacks of ague, disappearing under suitable treatment. The men, when not marching in the bush, were well housed at Waterloo, where the military sick and wounded were distributed in hospital marquees and the houses of the town. Square iron slugs were the missiles chiefly used by the Timmanees, specimens of which are now in the Museum at Netley. They caused nasty wounds, and the slugs, when deep seated, were difficult to extract. Including the naval contingent, there were about 100 officers and men killed and wounded in these expeditions.

The next expedition of any importance was the one undertaken against the Ashantees on the Gold Coast, in 1863 and '64. It can scarcely be called a war, as an enemy was never seen, or a grain of powder expended; our troops were defeated by disease, much of which was preventable. In August of the former year, the right wing of the 4th West India Regiment landed at Cape Coast Castle. Preparations were at once commenced for the future advance. Stores were collected and paths cut, these operations lasting until December, during the continuance of which the men suffered much from dysentery, remittent and intermittent fever. On the 27th December a company of the 4th West was marched to Mansue, to guard the stores accumulated there; these had been carried up in parcels of 60 lbs. in weight. By the middle of January, three of five officers who had left with this detachment returned sick, one of the two left behind being very ill. The detachment of the 4th at Accra were in the meantime ordered to Swadro. On the 27th and 29th January, 1864, four companies of the 2nd and 4th West marched to the Prah at the rate of fourteen miles a-day. Half of the company which had been sent to Mansue in December were already sick. On the arrival of the Head Quarters at the Prah, to which a road had been cut wide enough to allow of a nine-pounder gun being dragged along it, it was found impracticable to send the sick down to Chamah by the river, in consequence of the numerous rocks which impeded the navigation. During the march up, the streams were found to be mostly dry, but much swollen when returning three or four months later. At this time (May and June), the forest, far and near, was a vast swamp; the Prah, on being reached in February, was found to be fordable, and the water clear. On arrival it was found necessary to pitch the *tentes d'abri* on ground damp and only partly cleared from plantations, upon which soil temporary huts were also erected. Numerous stumps of plantains were rotting all round. The floors of the huts were damp and unraised; the roofs leaked when it rained, the thatch not having been previously sun dried, as was the custom with the natives. These defects, with the living in the centre of a forest, close to the banks of a river and jungle growth, soon told on the men, who, in addition, had been subject to much fatigue in erecting huts, building stockades, and clearing their camp from *débris*.

In the first week in March the rains became very frequent and continuous, not like the seaboard, where they were irregular, the coast line being often dry when it was pouring in the bush, and where the wet season always commenced earlier. When the excitement and novelty wore off, great depression appeared among the men, so much so that by the middle of March more than fifty were in hospital, and several officers were attacked with fever. The rain was now falling in heavy squalls, thunder and lightning occurring every night. The heat increased daily as the sun entered its Northern course. The radiated heat was felt much; in addition, during the night, the damp chills caused by the rain and fogs were found very trying.

The thermometric reading was lowest when five feet distant from the ground, at which height, in the shade, from 9 A.M. to 11 A.M., it read 84° and 86°; 11 A.M. to 2 P.M., 90° to 96°; 8 P.M. to 9 P.M., 80° to 76°. Sometimes, during rain at night, the mercury fell as low as 72°, an average range of 20°, an extreme range of 24° in 24 hours. After sunset dense fogs rose from the river, hanging over the camp during the night, and becoming condensed on the surrounding trees during the morning, afterwards rising with the sun, thus rendering the nights chilly and the mornings foggy, from the effects of which climatic vicissitudes the seven sentries mounting guard on the confines of the camp were found to suffer much.

By the end of March, 90 men were in hospital out of 360—25 per cent. of the force—besides a large number who were sickly and weakly; nearly all the officers were sick, eleven having left for Cape Coast by the 1st April. The hospital in camp soon became overcrowded from men suffering from fever, dysentery, and diarrhœa. The streams had now become so swollen that canoes had to be sent up from Cape Coast for the purpose of admitting of their being crossed. Two companies and fifteen sick left for the Coast on the 12th April, reaching the Castle on the 18th, after a six days' march, during which the roads were found to be much under water, long detours being required to avoid the swollen streams. Enormous trees had been blown down by the previous tornadoes, impeding progress, and along the road there was no accommodation, and only bad drinking water could be obtained. The officers previously sent down from the bush were found stalking about the Castle like skeletons, gaunt and emaciated, the fresh arrivals suffering quite as severely as those who had been up country. The 1st West India Regiment, upon arrival on the 1st December, were obliged to send into hospital a number of old cases of chronic rheumatism. The left wing of the 4th, composed of a number of young men recently enlisted in the West Indies, suffered much on arrival from fever, owing to that want of habitual residence which appeared necessary to acclimatize the newly-arrived negro. By the middle of May all the members of the original force at Prashue were relieved. Eighteen officers and eighty men were in hospital at Cape Coast suffering from fever and dysentery, and a large number were convalescent or weakly. Several cases of chest affections admitted from on board the "Tamar," and caught in higher latitudes, in the trip across from the West Indies, contracted dysentery in hospital and died. While these results had followed the occupation of Prashue, the camp at Swadro had been much healthier, because the detachment of the 4th West sent there were picked men, the camp slightly elevated, not near the river, and the number occupying it smaller, better hutted, and during the greater part of the time able to obtain fresh vegetables and fruit from the Coast, conditions reversed on the banks of the Prah.

During this abortive expedition the 2nd West, who had lost all their weakly men before, and had been some time on the Coast, suffered least. The 4th West, composed of young and weakly recruits or old men, felt the effects of climate and exposure most, being attacked with fever and dysentery on arrival. Although recovered somewhat before December, the date of the first advance to Mansue, they were too weakly to go to the front. The 1st West on the other hand, composed of very old soldiers, half of them invalids with chronic rheumatism, or worn out, suffered much also. It was only natural that these several classes, when brought from the West Indies, where they had good barracks, water, and food, a climate their own, and duties not onerous, should suffer enormously on the change to the bad barrack accommodation, and exactly reversed conditions then prevalent on the Gold Coast. The actual casualties from the great camp diseases on that occasion are noted below:—

	1863 (strength, 546.)		1864 (strength, 927.)	
	Admissions.	Deaths.	Admissions.	Deaths.
Dysentery	125	20	210	32
Diarrhœa	46	0	214	5
Feb. Int.	28	0	618	3
,, Remit.	78	1	171	4
Rheumat., Ac.	20	0	32	1
,, Chr.	16	0	47	2
Bronchitis	10	0	112	8
Ulcers	73	0	122	0

The ratios per cent. of admissions from these several diseases, usually incidental to exposure, was:—

1st Phase, in 1863.		2nd Phase, in 1864.	
Admissions.	Deaths.	Admissions.	Deaths.
72·53	3·85	164·61	5·93

INCREASE IN 1864.

Admissions	.	.	.	92·08 per cent.
Deaths	.	.	.	2·08 ,,

Of 60 officers who served during these operations in the Protectorate, 21 or 35 per cent. succumbed to the effects of disease.

Taking, then, the Gold Coast in three epochs of its sanitary history, viz., 1859, a period of peace; 1863, of preliminary preparations in the bush; and 1864, the year during which this last was occupied, we have the opportunity of contrasting the effects of exposure upon our native and West Indian troops, with a sedentary garrison life. The rapid increase of mortality in the following ratio per 1,000 is striking:—

1859.	1863.	1864.
25·06	38·46	60·41

A year after the cessation of this bush camp work, viz., in 1865, the death rate had fallen to—

9·17 per 1,000 per annum.

While the average mortality per 1,000 per annum in the two years of quiet was 17·11, it had increased in the two years of activity, under conditions of mal-hygiene, to 49·43, an excess of—

32·32 per 1,000.

The ratio of sickness was of course much greater. The year previous to this great amount of sickness, Cape Coast Castle had been garrisoned for six weeks by 21 marines, with the loss of only one man from an accident; they had been carefully looked after, and not allowed to leave the precincts of the Fort between 9 A.M. and 4 P.M. As a contrast, it may be noted, in passing, that a man-of-war's crew landed up the Mellicore in 1865, to quell a disturbance among the natives, in which they perfectly succeeded, had upon re-embarking 105 out of 175 of the crew, or 30 per cent., at one time sick. Of this number 17 died, or 16·20 per cent. of those treated.

Before commenting upon the lessons taught by our latest war in these regions, let us for a moment glance at the teaching of the past. The foregoing brief history of disease, told us clearly, if it told anything, that—

The climate of Western Africa was especially enervating to the European constitution, and productive of disease; that the effects of climate *per se* were much aggravated by intemperance, an injudicious mode of life, and exposure. That the seven great predisposing causes to disease were a high temperature, excessive moisture, chills and great alternation of heat and cold, a heavy rain fall, much malarious emanations, a defective and unnutritious food supply, and indifferent water. That the rainy season was the period of the year when disease was most prevalent, and its effects most severely felt.

That good barrack accommodation during that particular period did away with much of its ill effects; practical experience teaching, in addition, that suitable clothing and food aided much the good effects of the former. That during all active operations, the prevailing diseases were of the miasmatic class, increasing over the admissions during a period of tranquility in a ratio of nearly 100 per cent.; the admissions to deaths in this particular class being in a proportion of about 15 to 1, pointing to a large amount of sickness, but a low rate of mortality.

That excessive eating and drinking, without adequate exercise, predisposed to diseases peculiar to the climate. That as exposure to the chills and damps of the rains increased the rate of sickness, and intensified its effects, the dry season was the only period when military operations could be undertaken with any prospect of success; and that as this season was very limited in duration, such operations should be necessarily short and to the point.

That sickness and mortality appeared to increase in a direct ratio with length of residence.

That a careful selection of the men to be employed in active operations was absolutely essential to success, as if too young, too old or infirm, they would only crowd the hospitals, and be useless for purposes of offence.

That good food, and vegetables of the anti-scorbutic class were scarce, and when the latter were obtainable, poor and watery.

That while the water was known to be as a rule bad, its exact chemical qualities and effect in the production of disease was not exactly made out; much disease, especially dysentery, being attributed to its use.

That salt rations, owing to their indigestibility and mode of preserving, predisposed to excessive thirst, scurvy, dysentery, and bowel affections in the West African climate.

That the judicious use of a spirit ration did not appear to predispose to disease.

That the large preponderance of affections of the malarial class in the returns pointed to the presence of paludal poisoning.

That animal transport was unknown in the country, hammocks and bearers being the usual mode of conveyance.

That parasitic affections of the class prevalent on the Gold Coast would not, owing to the period of incubation, affect the troops during the continuance of active operations.

That the evidence as to river expeditions was unsatisfactory, most of those undertaken ending in the production of much disease, especially during the wet season.

That the intermittent form of marsh fever was the prevailing variety, which would account for the low rate of mortality, in proportion to the large number of admissions.

It was further known that yellow fever was endemic in the Bights, epidemic about every seven years at Sierra Leone and the Gambia, and occasionally sporadic, but that it had never been prevalent at Lagos or the Gold Coast. That the remittent form of fever was much to be dreaded, especially in the rains.

That epidemic cholera had never come further south than the Island of Bulama, and that small-pox was the epidemic disease *par excellence* of the natives.

Such were the logical deductions on the facts passed in review in the foregoing part of this paper.

Before summarizing the lessons of the Ashantee war of 1873-74, the latest and most important of our military operations in Western Africa, we may glance with advantage at the *status in quo ante*. In the year previous to the outbreak of hostilities, the Gold Coast and Sierra Leone was garrisoned by a small force of the 2nd West India Regiment, which had been about three years in Africa. From among the 320 non-commissioned officers and men present, there were 625 admissions into hospital, and 5 deaths, or a ratio per cent. per annum of 195·3 and 1·6 respectively. The several diseases were in the following order of frequency of occurrence:—

Remittent Fever,	138 admissions.	Bronchitis,	15 admissions.
Intermittent Fever,	131 ,,	Orchitis,	15 ,,
Rheumatism,	49 ,,	Abscess,	14 ,,
Gonorrhœa,	42 ,,	Diarrhœa,	13 ,,
Accidental wounds	28 ,,	Conjunctivitis,	13 ,,
Ulcers,	22 ,,	Other affections,	98 ,,
Primary Syphilis,	18 ,,	Dracunculus,	*Nil* ,,
Dysentery,	16 ,,		

At Sierra Leone the men occupied good barracks. On the Gold Coast and Accra the prevailing diseases will be seen to have been those usually attributable to a malarial tropical climate, remittent and intermittent fevers, these two affections making up more than half of the total admissions.

With regard to the experiences of non-professional writers, that of Dupuis, noted down in a journey to Coomassie, undertaken fifty-six years before, turned out to be wonderfully exact. He was the first European to visit the capital of Ashantee. He thought the inland climate more salubrious and more pure, and the soil less humid and vaporous than that of Cape Coast Castle; the dry season the most healthy, and the water, with few exceptions, limpid and sweet flavoured. He mentions rain, a tornado, and heavy rain on the 10th February, causing the ground to become sodden, and the leaves to wet the bodies of the travellers, the general appearance of the sky indicating rain.

By the end of March and beginning of April the rains, up country, rendering the forest one sheet of water in many districts, and causing the rivers to become swollen into rapid torrents. (On the 14th of November,

1873, the Okee rose five and a-half feet in forty-eight hours.) He also mentions the fact of the rains commencing sooner up country, and the dry season commencing on the coast about the middle of November. He alludes to the fact of most of the capital towns of Ashantee being embosomed in impervious forests and thicket, which breaks off sixty miles N.E. of the capital. To the S.E. was a champaign land. The route to the Volta from Coomassie was reckoned eighteen journeys to the mouth of the river, lying over a hilly country, intersected by numerous water courses, the road from time to time being shut up by fallen trees and masses of vegetation, torn down by the force of the tornadoes at the break of the monsoon. The country from Cape Coast, commencing with dwarf shrubs and forest trees, blended together with detached patches of bamboo and dwarf palms, was followed in the second stage by dense forest, numerous creepers, and little animal life, exactly as our troops found it in after days.

The following rough memorandum, written for the information of the Director-General, 21st May, 1873, embodied my personal impressions, derived from previous service in Africa. "The expedition (small force of marines), will arrive on the Coast at the commencement of the rains, a season of the year when offensive operations are never carried on without serious risks to life. On this account it may be surmised the troops will remain on the defensive, or at most go not more than a day's march from the Coast. If the health of the troops is to be considered of primary importance, strict orders should be issued to defend our garrisons. An enemy cannot remain long before them without supplies, which are not obtainable without great difficulty on the Gold Coast, even at the best of times.

"In order to protect the town, out-posts will be probably placed on the heights, in the neighbourhood of the Castle. Tents will have therefore to be supplied. Hospital, or as more portable, officers' marquees should be supplied for this purpose. The Bell tent is unsuitable in the rains for anything like a permanent encampment. A plentiful supply of cork mattresses and waterproof sheeting will be required. Tentage should be calculated at the rate of one tent for every three or four men.

"White troops on arrival may be supposed to suffer from fever and dysentery. Black troops from similar affections if recently arrived from the West Indies, plus rheumatism and inflammatory lung diseases, especially pneumonia. Wounds may also be expected. These will be mostly inflicted by irregular iron slugs and bullets, difficult to extract, but will be found to heal if the constitution be not below par, by simple attention to cleanliness, water, and carbolic acid lotions. As slugs are difficult to extract, some additional extractors and strong forceps, well roughed at the points, will be required; small portable detachment cases will be found useful, better than larger ones for operations.

"On the Gold Coast there is no animal transport. The wounded will have to be carried in native grass hammocks, suspended to a long pole, resting on the shoulders of two men, or on stretchers which require four men. As natives always carry the poles on their heads or shoulders, any other form of conveyance for wounded or sick would be useless, as unsuitable to the country, the roads in which are mere narrow paths.

"I would suggest that by next mail orders should be sent to Sierra Leone to hire 50 Kroomen as sick bearers, and also to send with them a sufficient number of grass hammocks and bamboo poles, which may be obtained there for about a dollar each. Kroomen can be hired for about £2 10 0 a month. We found them most useful for this purpose during the Quiah war, carrying the sick and wounded and guns in the manner I have described.

"Medical comforts must be sent on. Arrowroot can be obtained in plenty at Sierra Leone, but not on the Gold Coast. It should be therefore sent on direct from England, also tapioca and Newsome's preserved sugar and milk. For bowel complaints, these and port wine will be found necessary.

"At the period of the year when the expedition will arrive the climate of the Gold Coast will be a wet or damp one, and it must be remembered that supplies of food are very deficient. This will render necessary the following precautions:—

"1. That the troops, native or European, be clothed in serge or flannel, wear flannel shirts and cholera belts and cloth waterproofs. No other clothing is suitable.

"2. To keep the men in health, large supplies of preserved provisions, potatoes and soups, must be forwarded. Orders should be sent out, directing steamers touching at Sierra Leone to carry down to Cape Coast live beef and fowls, neither of which can be obtained there. Rice should be sent from England for the use of black troops, as it is not easily obtained on the Gold Coast or the Coast, singular as it may appear; also, coffee, cocoa, and milk.

"3. Coffee and quinine should be taken by all troops the first thing on rising—a morning parade.

"4. Water may prove a difficulty if the rains are scanty: it should be condensed in steamers, or brought in casks from Sierra Leone, where it is very good.

"5. Frequent examinations should be made to detect incipient fever or dysentery: this is the best time for checking the last.

"6. The men should be kept from the common trade rum of the Coast, the use of which will prove most pernicious.

"To sum up: defensive operations, proper clothing, plenty of good, fresh food, and arrangements to supply it, will be the best preventives of disease.

"An officer proceeding to the Coast should take a light kit, serge suits, knickerbockers, merino or flannel underclothing, flannel shirts, a pair of long boots, a waterproof coat or cloak, leggings, a felt helmet, and a good umbrella.

"In the West Indies none but strong men should be embarked for the Gold Coast. If any weakly men should arrive, it would be more prudent to send them up to Sierra Leone, bringing down, in lieu, more seasoned men. Army Hospital Corps men, known to be temperate, might be sent out to superintend natives in nursing the sick. These last must be chiefly relied upon.

"Field panniers, a few field companions, water bottles, bandages, tourniquets, lint, old sheeting, flannel for stupes, &c., &c., should be forwarded.

"The foregoing comprise the principal points to be attended to."

CHAPTER II.

LATER EVENTS.

UPON the invasion of the Protectorate, in January, 1873, by the Ashantees, the detachment of the 2nd West India Regiment at Cape Coast Castle was reinforced from Sierra Leone as soon as possible, all available men being ultimately sent from there, the more weakly being returned with the women and children, in order to afford greater space for the garrison, and relieve the narrow limits of the Fort from overcrowding.

On the 21st March, a portion of the regiment was encamped under canvas at "Connor's Hill," being the first corps of regular troops to move out of barracks. The arrival of the Head Quarters (5 officers and 150 non-commissioned and men), on the 8th July, at Cape Coast Castle, raised the number of the 2nd West serving in Western Africa to about 600, all told. Of this number, at least a third were inefficient, either sick, convalescent, weakly, absent at Sierra Leone, or dead, at the close of the first phase of the war in December, 1873, during which detachments of the corps had been present in every engagement, and encamped or in the bush for a considerable portion of the time. That portion to which the subsequent figures refer, had its base in garrison at Cape Coast Castle, 50 non-commissioned officers and men at Fort Napoleon, a small encampment five miles distant, and overhanging the Sweet River. This detachment was relieved every six weeks, the road being patrolled daily by small parties. The men and officers were under canvas, eight of the former in each tent. Another detachment was under canvas at Connor's Hill, close to Cape Coast Castle. The remaining portion of the corps had its base at Elmina, and a detachment of 100 men at Camp Abbey, fourteen miles distant. Outlying parties occupied Accra, Dix Cove, and Axim.

The following table shows the effects of climate, duty, and exposure, upon the Cape Coast Castle or Head Quarter contingent, during a period of twenty-two weeks—4th April to 26th September—the month of July being omitted, owing to the return available having been incomplete :—

Month ending Friday.	Strength.	Nights in Bed.	Weather and Temperature.	Clothing, &c.	Rations and mode of preparation.	Water supply.	Duties.	Barrack accommodation, &c.	Total admissions.	Weekly percentage of sick to strength.	Ague.	Remittent Fever.	Dysentery.	Diarrhœa.	Rheumatism.	Chest Affections.	Ulcers.	Guinea-worm.	Wounds.	Other affections.
25th April (4 weeks)	185·25	3 & 4	*hot sun on cessation of rain: hot sun on cessation of: in shade 75 to 90°; in sun 100° to 156°, according to cloud.*	*In practice, duck smock frocks, flannel shirts, loose serge breeches, socks, white gaiters, shoes, red fez, great coat, blanket, waterproof sheet.*	*During each week — ¾ lb. of preserved meat one day; 1 lb. salt pork one day; 1 lb. salt beef one day; 1 lb. fresh meat four days; 1 lb. rice, 6 lbs. bread; quality of fresh meat indifferent; cooking, primitive, camp kettles, boilers; spirit ration in field.*	*Tanks at Cape Coast Castle and Connor's hill; source, rain; at Napoleon, water of Sweet River chiefly: 8 miles from Elmina; impregnated with organic matter.*	*Guards and fatigues at Cape Coast Castle, patrols to Napoleon, an occasional march to Elmina; operations against enemy, 13th June, 1873.*	*In Barracks at Cape Coast: about 300 cubic feet each, 30 feet superficial; 3 to 8 men in tents, on raised beds made of wattle; ventilation in barracks by opposite doors and windows; when sick, treated regimentally.*	22	2·98	5	1	..	1	5	1	..	2	2	5
30th May (5 weeks)	188·40	3 & 4							47	4·75	23	1	..	4	2	3	5	..	3	8
27th June (4 weeks)	185·00	3 & 4																		
29th Aug. (5 weeks)	248·00	4 & 5							80	6·53	53	..	6	7	2	2	1	..	..	9
26th Sept. (4 weeks)	227·25	2 & 3							48	5·23	20	2	7	3	1	6	2	..	..	6

During the twenty-two weeks this table refers to, intermittent fever was the prevailing disease; then diarrhœa, dysentery (which first shows itself after active operations in June, and the occupation of Camp Napoleon), and remittent fever. The large increase in August may be in part ascribed to increased strength, and the effect of climate upon new arrivals, several of the men having come shortly before from the West Indies. There is a remarkable absence of guinea-worm and syphilis; there were only three cases of gonorrhœa; the same exemption from enthetic diseases may be noticed in the returns of the old Gold Coast Corps. It is also worthy of notice, as illustrating the influence of vaccination, and the comparative isolation of the troops, that whereas small-pox was committing frightful ravages among the inhabitants of the town and neighbouring villages, especially one which gradually sprung up in the vicinity of Fort Napoleon (52 cases were under treatment in the Colonial Hospital on the 24th April), only one case occurred amongst the men in a month not included in the return.

On looking over the admissions on the sick list from among the staff, departmental, and regimental officers, previous to the commencement of more active operations in October, 1873 (1st January to 27th September, 1873), it was found that of 44 treated:—

Intermittent Fever accounted for		18 Admissions.
Remittent Fever	,,	13 ,,
Dysentery	,,	5 ,,
Albuminuria	,,	3 ,,
Diarrhœa	,,	1 ,,
Hæmorrhoids	,,	1 ,,
Purpura	,,	1 ,,
Asthenia	,,	1 ,,
Conjunctivitis	,,	1 ,,

Among the Europeans, as among the natives, the intermittent form of the malarial paroxysm appeared to be the prevailing disease on the Gold Coast.

With the end of September closed the defensive stage of the Ashantee War. During the previous nine months the enemy had gradually advanced from the Prah, burnt the Assin and Fanti villages, defeated the Protectorate forces at Yancoomassie, destroyed Dunquah, and debouched to the westward, towards the woods surrounding Elmina, against which last place they advanced on the evening of the 13th June, 1873. Being repulsed with a loss of two or three hundred men, who were buried in three long trenches in the plain beyond the garden wall, they retired and established themselves in a large camp at Mempon, drawing their supplies from the rebel villages Essiaman, Akimfoo, and Ampenee, and the surrounding country, and from their position threatening the scene of their late repulse, and Cape Coast, from each of which they were about 14 miles distant. Since the 6th August a patrol of 50 non-commissioned officers and men communicated daily with Napoleon; and Gordon, with a working party and two non-commissioned officers of the Royal Marine Artillery, protected by a company of Cape Coast Volunteers, had opened the road as far as Dunquah, twenty miles distant. The sick from Connor's Hill and Napoleon were sent into the Hospital at Cape Coast. On shore the weather was broken—either warm, cool, bright, or cloudy days, with light sea breezes commencing to blow about 10 A.M., or calm, oppressive ones, afterwards followed by showers or heavy rain. The temperature of evaporation ranged in the shade from 71° in the early morning to 76° at 3 P.M. The temperature of the air from 74° to 79°. Now and then a typical

Coast day between the wet and dry seasons occurred—an airless, cloudy, sultry, and hazy day, with an atmosphere highly charged with moisture, there being only two or three degrees between the wet and dry bulb readings. Up country the rains had little abated.

The average strength of the 2nd West at Cape Coast and its vicinity was 224·5.

Average daily sick during the month	16·26
Deaths (a case of dysentery contracted at Axim)	1
Number in Hospital on last day of September	16
Mean cubic space in barracks	354·3
,, superficial area	30·0

Fevers, dysentery, and diarrhœa were the prevailing diseases, 20 cases of the former, and 11 of the two latter named affections, out of a total of 51, a reduction on the previous month of 34 and 2 respectively. Our opponents had already suffered severely from an epidemic of small-pox, as they did now from dysentery and diarrhœa; in fact the enemy were exactly in the same predicament at this time, away from their, to them, comfortable homes, and regular and accustomed food, as our troops were in 1864, when encamped away from their barracks on the banks of the Prah. The exposure and errors of diet on each occasion led to nearly similar results. The history of the first detachment of Marines sent to the Gold Coast on the 13th May, 1873, which arrived at Cape Coast Castle on the 7th June following, the height of the rainy season, is also instructive. Six days after arrival, viz., 13th June, the men marched in the early morning to Elmina, eight miles distant, wading the Sweet River *en route*. Upon reaching their destination, they were employed in assisting to destroy the native town, and in repelling an attack of the Ashantees, who had come down from the neighbouring hills. The season was an unhealthy one, the rains unusually late and excessive, provisions scarce, and the natives crowded into the vicinity of the Fort. By the 26th of August 12 deaths had occurred, and 77 men were invalided, the Himalaya having arrived in England with that number on that date. Allowing twenty-three days as the usual duration of the voyage, these figures would show that of 110 officers and men, 12 had actually died, and 77 had become inefficient in the short space of 58 days on the Gold Coast, only 21 (4 officers and 17 men) remaining for duty; within a few weeks, 16 of the 17 had ceased to belong to the Gold Coast Squadron.

According to Dr. Donnet, of the 77 who arrived in England on the 26th August, 18 were discharged to duty, and 59 were admitted into hospital: of those admitted, 40 suffered from remittent fever, and 19 from dysentery. The appearance of the whole was stated to be that of men who had underwent much suffering and fatigue; their countenances were sallow and marked with depression; they all bore an anæmic look, and in manner were listless and apathetic; the colour of their skin was universally of a citron hue. Dr. Donnet partly attributes this excessive mortality and sickness to unsuitable provisions, inferior cooking, which was universally complained of, the provisions consisting at first of salt meat, rice, and bread, and, subsequently, of fresh beef of such inferior quality that loss of appetite was the result. To these defective dietetic arrangements were superadded the necessity of using offensive well water, dulness of life and inaction within a fort, the heavy tropical rains preventing outdoor exercise, to which might be added the necessity of sleeping in over-crowded and imperfectly ventilated rooms, use of unripe fruit and spirits, and the constant breathing of malaria.

Previous to their arrival, the principal sanitary precautions against disease had been the removal of the women and children from the town to the Castle, upon the outbreak of small-pox occurring among the natives; the relief of the detachment of the 2nd West, on Connor's Hill, by a party of Houssas; the employment of labourers to empty the latrines at Axim, and of extra water carriers, and the allowance of free rations to the Houssas and Cape Coast Volunteers, when employed in the field; the hiring of houses in the town, in anticipation of the arrival of the Marines in the Himalaya; and the formation of a special corps of 13 hands to man the surf boats. In May, 10 per cent. of hospital clothing for the whole force was sent out, camp kettles, blankets, waterproof sheets, 30 tents, 10 Norton's tube wells; and in July, hospital stores for 20 per cent. of the native troops, and 45 per cent. of the Europeans, with a reserve of 7 per cent. in the Simoom, as well as large supplies of food.

Subsequent to the arrival of the contingent of Marines and Royal Marine Artillery, in June, the following scale of rations was agreed upon for the use of European troops then lately joined, viz:—1 lb. of fresh or salt meat, $1\frac{1}{4}$ lb. of biscuit, or $1\frac{1}{2}$ lb. of bread, $\frac{1}{4}$ lb. of rice, or $\frac{1}{2}$ lb. of vegetables, or 1 oz. of lime juice, in lieu, 1 oz. of soluble cocoa or chocolate, $\frac{1}{4}$ oz. of tea, 1 oz. of sugar, $\frac{1}{2}$ gill of rum, or a ration of porter or beer, $\frac{1}{4}$ gill of vinegar, and $\frac{1}{4}$ oz. of salt, mustard, and pepper.

A suitable building was hired at Elmina for 50 sick, four hammock bearers and a hammock being allowed to convey the patients to hospital, upon the requisition of the senior medical officer. A morning meal of cocoa was directed to be issued to the men of the Royal Marines, when in garrison at Cape Coast, and a ration of lime juice. Four cooks and eight batmen were also allowed for their use. The ration issued to the men of the 2nd West was also increased by $\frac{1}{4}$ lb. rice daily, and 1 lb. instead of $\frac{3}{4}$ lb. of bread, when the latter was issued. Upon a case of small-pox being admitted into the regimental hospital on the 6th August, all *possible restrictions* were enforced to prevent intercourse between the men and inhabitants of the town. Two hammocks were to follow in rear of the daily patrol to Napoleon, each man carrying his field blanket and waterproof sheet. On the 9th August some of the men at Elmina were put under canvas at Fort St. Jago, to relieve the quarters, and prevent overcrowding. The guards were to be reduced, so as to give, if possible, at least four nights in bed in each week; and a sufficient supply of drinkable water was to be sent daily to Napoleon for the use of the officers and men (a Crease's filter had already been in operation at Cape Coast). On the 19th August the dry earth system replaced the ill-smelling latrines at Cape Coast Castle, some temporary wooden structures being erected upon the battlements in the vicinity of the latter, immediately to the eastward of Dalzel's Tower. Previously to this, the soil had fallen upon the foundation of the sea wall, from which it was washed into the sea. In the course of years the mass of dark gneiss had become completely impregnated with ill-smelling fœcal discharges. Four hammock bearers and a hammock were placed in charge of the medical officer at Camp Abbey and Napoleon, for the purpose of conveying the seriously sick to Elmina and Cape Coast respectively. On the 24th September the Control Department was ordered to furnish supplies for all auxiliary troops in the field; and on the 27th, Acroful was to be occupied by 150 of the 2nd W. I. Regiment, who were to take with them 16 bell tents, 1 canteen, 20 camp kettles, and 2 hammocks, and each private his field kit, consisting of 1 grey service blanket, 2 flannel shirts, 1 knife, fork, and spoon, the whole to be wrapped up in a waterproof sheet; they were also to carry their great coats, water bottles, haversacks, and canteens, a pretty fair load in the tropics, with rifle, accoutrements, clothing, and 70 rounds of ball cartridge. These men marched in their white serge jackets.

With the coming of the Ambriz, on the 2nd October, with Sir Garnet Wolseley and the Head Quarter Staff, was initiated the offensive stage of the Ashantee war of 1873–74. On that day the distribution of the garrison of the Gold Coast was as follows:—Cape Coast, 150 men of the 2nd W. I. Regiment; Elmina, 170; Secondee, 25; Dix Cove, 50; Axim, 48; Napoleon, 50; Abbey, 100; Acroful, 50; blockaded by an Ashantee army estimated at from 30,000 to 40,000 individuals.

In addition to the officers of the West India Regiment, there were 2 officers of the Royal Marine Artillery, Lieutenant-Colonel Festing and Captain Crease; Captain Thompson, of the Bays; Lieutenant Gordon, of the 98th; 3 Control Officers; and the following members of the Medical Staff:—

At Cape Coast—Deputy-Surgeon General Home, V.C., C.B., principal medical officer; the Author, and Surgeon-Major Rowe, Colonial surgeon.

,, Elmina—Surgeon-Major Mosse.

At Acroful—Surgeon-Major Fox.
„ Camp Abbey—Surgeon Ley.
„ Fort Napoleon—Visited twice a week from Cape Coast Castle.
„ Secondee—Surgeon Conelan.
„ Axim—Surgeon Goldsbury.
„ Dix Cove—Surgeon Horton.

In the Ambriz came the first addition to this small staff of Military Medical Officers, Surgeon-Major Jackson and Surgeon Atkins, followed towards the end of the month by Surgeons M'Nalty, Thornton, Moore, and Bennett, who, with the officers previously mentioned, saw the last of the Ashantees over the Prah. To their exertions the Major-General paid the following graceful tribute in his Despatch of the 15th December, 1873:—"The officers of the Control and Medical Departments have worked with the greatest zeal and energy."

The Protectorate phase of the Ashantee war of 1873, 74 commenced on the 2nd October, and ended on the 27th December following, when the Naval Brigade landed and made their onward march to the Prah, through a country which had been cleared of the enemy since the 1st instant, on which date the latter had crossed the boundary stream a harassed, dispirited, and defeated crowd of fugitives, driven from their hitherto impregnable forest fastnesses by a handful of officers and men skilfully led, and who, through rain and storm, an almost unknown jungle, and often without food or shelter, hung on to their foe until he no longer dared to resist them. Were it not for such devotion to duty as this a white regiment would never have reached the confines of the Protectorate, and the subsequent march to there have become "a pleasant picnic," as described by the historian of the war. During these few months took place the attack on the rebel villages beyond Elmina, Essiaman, Amquana, and Ampene, 14th October. Reconnaissance to Abracrampa on the 28th, *via* Assayboo. Surprise of the Ashantee Camp near Dunquah, 27th November. Defeat of the enemy at Iscabio, near the same place, on the 3rd November. Threatened attack on Cape Coast Castle. Reconnaissance from Beulah. Attack on Abracrampa, 4th November, and its relief on the 6th. Forward march of the 2nd West India Regiment to Mansue on the 1st November. Reconnaissance in rear of the retreating enemy from Quaman Attah, 17th November. Threatened attack on Mansue, 18th. Reconnaissance from Addawarra, 21st. Acrofroom, 23rd and 24th. Feeling the enemy as he retired to the West of the Prah, until he got in at Sutah. Stand of his rear-guard at Fassowa, 26th November, and his final retreat over the Prah five days afterwards. The departure of the Simoom for Ascension and St. Helena on the 20th with invalid officers and men completes the brief history. These several military operations were accomplished with the occasional aid of a small force of seamen and marines, at no time exceeding 300 in number; the available men of the 2nd West, Russell's and Wood's native regiments, a few Houssas and Fanti police, and a mob of badly disciplined auxiliaries. On the 14th November Amenquatia's Head Quarters were at Yanibobo, south-west of Wonkorsu and Mansue, and about ten miles west of Dunquah; his foragers and armed scouts were hanging about and feeling the road between there and Mansue, where were only 3 officers and 75 men of the 2nd West, 22 Houssas, 17 Police, 158 Cape Coast Volunteers, 463 Native Allies, 2 Officers of Engineers, 1 Officer of Marines, 2 Medical Officers, and 1 Control Officer, to oppose him, should he make a vigorous attempt to break in on the road. On the 9th December the Himalaya arrived off the coast. On the 10th the Tamar, and on the 18th the Sarmatian, with the 23rd, Rifle Brigade, 42nd, a battery of Artillery, company of Engineers, and a large contingent of medical officers. The greater portion of this force left for a man-of-war's cruise, to rendezvous 180 miles distant until the 31st.

While the enemy was being driven from the Protectorate, the road was gradually pushed on towards Prashue, which was occupied by the native regiments in December, and the preliminary preparations made for the future reception of the European troops; stores were collected and pushed on to the front, the native auxiliaries disarmed and turned into a very unwilling transport corps, the telegraph erected, road and stations improved, Crease's filters got up to Sutah, and basket filters beyond, and the road made so as to enable the men to march dry shod to the Prah; increased hospital accommodation provided, and the irregular regiments augmented in strength by Kossoos, Sierra Leone men, Opobos, Bonny men, and natives of Winnebah, the regular native forces being increased at the same time by the arrival of the 1st West India Regiment. Men-of-war were dispatched to the westward and leeward to impress carriers from the Coast villages; and on the 22nd December the Active, Encounter, and Merlin were sent to Chamah to co-operate with the Wassaws in an attack on the villages at the embouchure of the Prah, the scene of the former attack on the Commodore, while some of the transports went to collect Kroomen at Cape Palma, cattle and mules at Madeira and Teneriffe. On the 27th December, with the disembarkation of the Naval Brigade, commenced the concluding phase of the military operations. On the 7th January the Head Quarter Staff, Naval Brigade, Wood's and Russell's regiments, and the Head Quarters of the 2nd West were at Prashue; half battalion of the Rifle Brigade at Barraco and Assin Yancomassie; 42nd at Mansue and Yaucoomassie Fanti; right half battalion of the 23rd at Acroful. The hospital ship Victor Emanuel had arrived at 2 P.M. on the 1st January, 1874, and the Dromedary shortly afterwards.

On the 5th January was made the first advance beyond the Prah by a scouting party of Russell's regiment as far as Essiaman, thirteen miles distant, the main body entrenching themselves at Attobiassie, six miles from the Prah. On the 14th, 200 men of the 2nd West advanced across the River, followed on the 16th by the Artillery and 2nd Irregular Regiment, the Naval Brigade, Rifle Brigade, 42nd, and 100 men of the 23rd. Our men marched with little opposition through Essiaman, Acrofumu, over the Adansie hills, to Quesa (half way to Coomassie), Fomanah (half a mile distant), Dunpassie, Datchiassie, King Bossu, Amquassie, Insarfu (distant only two miles from Amoaful) where they first came in serious contact with the enemy on the morning of the 3rd January, exactly a month from the date of disembarkation of the white troops - - the villages of Quarman and Agginassie intervening between Insarfu and Amoaful. The action lasted five hours. At its termination the troops occupied Amoaful for the night. On the 1st February the men pushed on to Aquamemmu; on the 3rd to the Dah, on the 4th to Coomassie, constantly opposed by the enemy. On the 6th the return march to the Coast was commenced, halting at the Dah, Aquamemmu, Amoaful, Akinquassie, Fomanah, Acrofumu, Essiaman, Prashue, the latter place being reached by the Naval Brigade and 23rd on the 12th February; Rifle Brigade on the 13th, and 42nd on the 14th. On their return the road to the Coast was found in excellent condition; swampy places in thorough order, bridges repaired, extra huts erected at the camps, and 200 separate beds available at Prashue Hospital. The Dromedary started on the 16th with invalids, and on the 22nd February the last of the European troops had embarked, and left the Gold Coast for England after a sojourn on shore of fifty-five days.

The possibility of completing the work thus accomplished had been much canvassed. The general opinion was that during the rains, at least, it could not be successfully performed. Orders to this effect were issued by Lord Kimberley in August, when he directed that no operations should be then undertaken, which would expose the officers and men to the risk of climate. In the following month Mr. Cardwell seemed to be of the same opinion, for he wrote that if such operations became necessary during the rains they should be carried on by "Houssas or by native auxiliaries, or some other force indigenous to the country," and not carried on at all—

1. Unless the service was one of permanent importance to the main object of Sir Garnet Wolseley's mission.

2. Or unless it could be accomplished with a rapidity of execution which would render the exposure to the climate very short.

"For this reason," wrote Mr Cardwell, "if the employment of Europeans shall become a necessity, every preparation should be made in advance, and no European force should be landed on the Coast until the time for decisive action arrived." The Secretary-at-War further wrote, "The period when the risk of loss from climate is at its minimum appears to be that comprised within the months of December, January, February, and March." Ten days subsequent to his arrival in October, the Major-General wrote home to the effect that European troops might be employed without extraordinary risk, and landed again in England in March, provided every recognized sanitary precautions were taken, and that the longest time they would be required to remain in the country would be two months. The result justified in every respect the correctness of his views, for the white troops completed their object, were five days less than two months in the country, and were landed in England in March. From these brief remarks will be seen how important were held to be the preliminary sanitary preparations for the reception of the European regiments.

Upon Sir Garnet Wolseley's arrival, and the probable subsequent large influx of Europeans at Cape Coast, these sanitary measures claimed a large share of attention, as well as the necessity of pushing on the road, and selecting the halting places, clearing the sites, and erecting buildings and hospitals with the least possible delay; for the time was limited to a sharply defined date, and not to have these preparations ready for the advance, and the Protectorate cleared of the enemy, meant a total cessation of all offensive work until the termination of the succeeding rains, much loss of prestige, great additional expense, and the probable abortive ending of the whole expedition.

The condition of Cape Coast previous to the institution and labours of the Sanitary Committee is best told in the words of Sir Garnet Wolseley and his Military Secretary, Major Brackenbury. "It is impossible to describe," writes the General, " the foul stench which arose from the exposed heaps of ordure at the edges of the town, more especially those close to the ponds from which the natives drew their supplies of water by the side of the road to Dunquah. From the ditch known as the Cape Coast River, running through the town, from a foul stagnant pond in the town also, rose smells of the most nauseous description. It was scarcely possible to walk a hundred yards from Government House without being sickened." "The filthy habits of the natives made the town, its environs, and the beach one vast cesspit," wrote the latter officer. There was not the least exaggeration in these expressions; they were literally true: a more foul place I had never been in before. The causes were many. A large influx of natives, their crowding together in a limited area; the configuration of the ground rising into small eminences, with intervening hollows difficult to drain; the want of any form of sewer or running water to carry away the "soil;" the number of tumbledown and unoccupied houses impeding ventilation, which were little better than receptacles for filth; and the habit of throwing all liquid ordure into the streets and back lanes, and the non-cleansing of the pools and surface wells, as well as the neglected state of the graveyards; also the promiscuous use of the hills and beach by the natives for the purpose of relieving nature. To the beach, east and west of the Castle, and in the hollows between the hills, and on the outskirts of the town, were carried in pots and baskets all kinds of filth, where it was allowed to rot and putrefy under the influence of heat and moisture. The Sanitary Committee for the town, which some time earlier in the year had done a great deal of good work, had ceased to exist, and as a necessary result, evils had sprung up anew all around.

On the 16th October a Standing Sanitary Committee was appointed to meet at such times and places as might be deemed expedient.

President.
LIEUTENANT-COLONEL FESTING, R.M.A.

Members.
HON. CHARLES GRANT, Member of Council.
DR. O'REILLY, Acting Colonial Surgeon.
CAPTAIN CREASE, R.M.A., Acting Colonial Surveyor.
MR. IRVING, Collector of Customs.
The SANITARY OFFICER.

Upon the departure of Colonel Festing, shortly afterwards, I was directed to preside, and the Fort Adjutant was added to the number of members.

The orders of the General were to do something practical at once.

At the preliminary meetings of the Committee it was agreed upon unanimously, that the best course to pursue was to divide the town into three districts, two of the Committee being allocated to each; to hire a corps of 50 scavengers, and provide them with cutlasses, picks, shovels, and brooms; that the sanitary inspector should be directed to warn all householders that the nuisances ordinance would be put in force against all sanitary defaulters; that simple earth latrines should be dug, and as far as possible isolated in retired situations between and at the back of the hills; that all the heaps of ordure already accumulated should be buried and burnt; that the disused Krotakraba and other wells should be filled in, and those in use cleaned out; that the rivulet in the centre of the town should be cleared, its banks swept and cleaned, and a free exit made for it into the sea; and that the beach should be no longer used for its former offensive purpose; and the streets and lanes should be swept daily, and the refuse collected and destroyed; the habit of slaughtering bullocks on the beach under the walls of the Castle discontinued, and a proper abattoir and cattle pen erected at the Salt Pond. These measures received the approval of the General, and all the necessary expense connected with their carrying out was sanctioned through the Acting Colonial Secretary and Treasurer, Major Lanyon. At the same time a quarantine ordinance was drawn up at the suggestion of the principal medical officer, Dr. Horne, and a naval surgeon appointed health officer of the port, with the privilege of drawing the usual fees for visiting all steamers and vessels arriving in the roads, one of the houses in the town being extemporised into a lazaretto. The water supply had been already analyzed and reported upon to the Director-General and Quartermaster-General. Little more could be done in the short space of time, and with the limited amount of labour available. The meteorological instruments brought by me from England had been placed in the hospital compound, and an interesting record of the observations kept during the months of September, October, November, and December, at the base of operations.

Cape Coast Castle was vacated by the Head Quarters of the 2nd West India Regiment, and a site for their encampment selected by myself and Captain Buller, D.A.Q.G., on Connor's Hill, in rear of, and on the land side of the plateau, the bell tents being placed in *echelon* of three rows, each tent six paces apart, and so arranged as to catch the prevailing sea breeze, and allow of a free circulation of air between them; the openings faced the sea; water was rolled up in casks, and wood carried upon labourers' heads, as also the daily rations of provisions. The sick were sent to the General Hospital at Cape Coast.

The old Castle had hitherto afforded the accommodation shown below, where the cubic space, superficial area, and allotment are arranged at a view:—

WESTERN TRIANGULAR COURTYARD.

Base, Palaver Hall; *N. W. Boundary*, Battery containing rooms, 1, 2, 3, 4; *S. W. Boundary*, Battery containing casemates or storehouses, 5, 6, 7, 8, 9, 10, 11, 12. This triangle was termed the Spur Battery. The rooms are enumerated from the right of the entrance gate on the land side, going round to Dalzel's Tower.

	Cubic Space.	Superficial Area.	Remarks.
Prisoners' Room,	4001·60	250·10	
No. 1 Casemate,	4208·57	264·69	
,, 2 ,,	4263·33	268·15	
,, 3 ,,	4081·55	269·28	
,, 4 ,,	4208·57	264·69	
,, 5 ,,	1265·32	79·58	Occupied in Store-houses, Married or Soldiers' Quarters, according to the strength of the Garrison.
,, 6 ,,	3286·44	214·80	
,, 7 ,,	3176·28	207·60	
,, 8 ,,	3176·28	207·60	
,, 9 ,,	3176·28	207·60	
,, 10 ,,	2617·30	212·79	
,, 11 ,,	2691·11	175·89	
,, 12 ,,	2691·11	175·89	
,, 13 ,,	2691·11	175·89	
Guard-room,	4344·81	387·93	

Central range of building running North and South, forming base of Western and Eastern triangles, connected by an archway; range terminated at the town side by Maclean's Turret, on the sea front by Dalzel's Tower, contains Palaver Hall—three floors. First, or ground floor, rooms North and South of archway.

	Cubic Space.	Superficial Area.	Remarks.
No. 1 Room,	2868·79	253·84	Nos. 1, 2, 3. North of entrance; Nos. 4, 5, 6, South of it—rooms usually used as Married Quarters.
,, 2 ,,	4194·45	358·50	
,, 3 ,,	4351·34	371·91	
,, 4 ,,	4645·87	383·94	
,, 5 ,,	4576·62	383·44	
,, 6 ,,	4561·38	376·97	

Second floor above number 1, enumerated from sea to land extremity.

	Cubic Space.	Superficial Area.	Remarks.
No. 1 Room,	5030·45	415·74	Sergeants' Mess.
,, 2 ,,	4769·51	400·82	2 European Non-commissioned Officers.
,, 3 ,,	4669·40	403·38	Quartermaster Sergeant.
,, 4 ,,	3966·73	341·96	2 European Non-commissioned Officers.
,, 5 ,,	4510·08	388·80	Quartermaster's Store.
,, 6 ,,	4259·52	367·20	2 European Non-commissioned Officers.
,, 7 ,,	4816·32	415·20	Brigade Office.
,, 8 ,,	3063·06	340·34	Orderly Room.

Above this was the third floor, containing from North to South, or from the land towards the sea extremity:—Maclean's Turret, 2 stories; Officers' Quarters (2); Men's Room; Pantry; Officers' Quarters (2); Dalzel's Tower, also of 2 stories.

The land side of the Eastern Triangle consisted of English House, running almost due East and West. The ground floor was occupied as Store-rooms; the second floor, as Soldiers' Quarters, or Barrack Rooms; the upper, or third floor, as Officers' Quarters.

	Cubic Space.	Superficial Area.	Remarks.
No. 1 Room,	6760·00	520·00	Office.
„ 2 „	4108·00	316·00	Soldiers' Quarters.
„ 3 „	5434·90	391·00	Do.
„ 4 „	5861·70	651·30	Do.
„ 5 „	7507·60	585·20	Do.
„ 6 „	4939·20	352·00	Do.
„ 7 „	20023·17	1627·90	Long Room.
Cells situated to the left of the Town Gate,			Nos. 1, 2, 3, 4, 5.
each	406.89	40·68	In an enclosed yard.

The Castle is an irregular trapezium, or figure of four sides, with four bastions, one at each angle: the whole, in olden days, mounting eighty pieces of cannon; two-thirds of the walls are washed by the sea. Originally settled by the Portuguese, it was taken from them by the Dutch, who took great pains to strengthen the fortifications. It was captured by Admiral Holmes in 1661, who demolished the Citadel. It was confirmed to the British by the Treaty of Breda, and withstood the utmost endeavours of De Ruyter to destroy it in 1665, although attacked by thirteen men-of-war. The Company, who obtained a charter in 1672, added greatly to its strength by building additional bastions. In the middle of the 17th century, the garrison numbered 200 officers and men. When Cape Coast Castle was replaced under the management of the merchants, in 1828, the Fort was governed by a President and Council, £3,500 per annum being allowed for the maintenance and defence of the Settlements. At Cape Coast Castle were then residing the following employés:—

President of the Council, Treasurer, Warehouse-keeper, and Commander of the Troops, per annum.	£400
Secretary, Accountant, Assistant Warehouse-keeper, and Registrar	200
Captain of the Guard, Adjutant, Chief Engineer, and Surveyor	200
Surgeon and Superintendent of Schools	200
Schools	100
Eighty Men, at £12 a Man	960
Clothing for ditto, at £2 10 per Man	200
Labourers, Male and Female	400
Extraordinaries, including Ammunition, Repair of Forts, Presents, Stationery, Medicines, Canoe Hire, Funerals, Non-Commissioned Officers, Messengers, &c.	740
Total,	£3,400

A quaint and curious list, suggestive of the times, and to be admired for its frugality of administration.

In October the first steps were taken as to the selection of the proposed camping grounds. Captain Huyshe had made a preliminary survey as far as Mansue by the 30th, on which date he reported—

"I have inspected the proposed camping grounds—Inquabim, Acroful, Yaucoomassie, Mansue.

"Inquabim lies to the right of the road in Native Cassada Gardens, lying partly on flat and partly on sloping ground, between two small hills; distance from C. C., 7 miles.

"Acroful lies N. of the village 400 yards, on ground sloping down to the River Atchisimassoo, some 350 yards off. The ground appears favourable in every way; not yet cleared; distance from Inquabim, 7½ miles.

"Yaucoomassie lies N. of the River Quadoo, a clear, rapid stream (say about 300 yards N.); ground is already partially cleared and open, with a gentle slope down to the river. This spot will make a very good encamping ground; distance from Acroful, 10 miles.

"Mansue—A large tract has already been cleared; a palisaded fort with redoubt, constructed by Major Home. The ground is a flat plateau, of several acres in extent, water on three sides. To the south a stream 400 yards off. To the east the River Okee, 250 yards off; to the north, a muddy stream, crossing the road, 600 yards off.

"Of these four I consider Yaucoomassie the best, then Mansue, then Acroful. At Inquabim the water question has not yet been determined, but there is water in the low ground adjacent, and as soon as this has been settled by sinking a well or pump, the sanitary officer might inspect and report on the quality of the water at all four camping grounds."

To this memorandum the Commanding Royal Engineer, Major Home, appended the following remarks :—

"I could get a good deal gradually down to the camping grounds as opportunity offers, and I trust his Excellency will pardon my asking for his decision on those proposed, namely—

"Inquabim, three to four miles from Yamoranza.

"Acroful, near the stream and detached village.

"Yaucoomassie.

"Mansue.

"With native troops at Dunquah and a large croom two miles south of Mansue.

"I am strongly of opinion that these are the most suitable places. If his Excellency would desire them to be inspected by the sanitary officer, I could accompany him, so as to get at least the two first settled."

Sanitary Officer.

"1. Inquabim.

"Started to reach at 6.30 A.M., 1/11/73. Reached Cassada Gardens 9.15 A.M., two and a-half hours' smart walking, 120 paces to the minute.

"Site to right surrounded by hills on N.E., E., and S.E., low, level of road; receives drainage of hills; would be flooded in a tornado. Am of opinion site to left of road, twenty to forty feet above the other and nearly opposite and beyond the village, would be better; is partially cleared; ample space for 400 men.

"Water—From small pool to right of road, dry in hot season; water then obtained by natives by sinking; water passes nearly clear through Abyssinian pocket filter; contains very faint traces of aluminous earths, unimportant traces of lime salts and chlorine; none of organic matter. After filtration may be used; Norton's tube wells should be sunk for water.

"10 A.M.—Hygrometer in shade under a tree: dry bulb 86°; wet 79°; black bulb in sun 156°; Aneroid 29·45; no breeze.

"2. Acroful.

"Started to reach from Cassada Gardens 11 A.M., arrived at 1 P.M.

"Site selected by Captain Huyshe, D.A.Q.M.G., unobjectionable; requires levelling, filling up of holes, surface draining, &c.

"Water—Passed through Abyssinian pocket filter nearly clear; before filtration very impure; after filtration retains large amount of organic matter; only faint traces of lime salts and chlorine. This pool is said to flow E., and to be nearly dry in the hot season; water bad; pool might be cleared out for bathing purposes. Better water 30 minutes distant from Acroful on Dunquah road; a clear running stream, the 'Brooka,' flowing at the rate of three or four miles an hour over a sandy bed in an E. direction. Better water than that at Acroful, now used by officers; brought in barrels and filtered.

"Hygrometer in shade under a tree at 3 P.M.: dry bulb 83°; wet bulb 78°; black bulb in sun, 127° (clouded); Aneroid 29·72."

This short sketch will suffice to show how quickly, briefly, and accurately the salient hygienic and strategic points in each station were reported to the Assistant Adjutant and Quartermaster-General at Head Quarters, Major Baker. In a similar manner were those beyond reported upon and settled. At this early date the Ashantee General-in-Chief, Amenquatia, had just broken up his camp at Mempon, and made a movement in the direction of the road in our rear. In consequence of this and the alarming rumours flying about, it was with the utmost difficulty that our native carriers were kept together and got on to the stations further north, which were settled with the enemy still in our rear. A detailed report was afterwards made upon them to the Quartermaster-General, with recommendations as to their improvement and sanitary equipment, each being for 400 men.

On my return from the front I laid before Major Baker the following proposals for submission to his Excellency, the Major-General Commanding :—

FIELD SERVICE.

Cape Coast, *November 27th, 1873.*

SIR,

In view of the early arrival of European troops in this command, and in accordance with the instructions laid down in the Medical Regulations for the guidance of sanitary officers attached to the Quartermaster-General's department, it now becomes my duty to lay before you, for the favourable consideration of his Excellency the Major-General, the following sanitary memoranda bearing upon the health and physical efficiency of the officers, non-commissioned officers, and men about to march against the enemy.

1. I would respectfully recommend that the troops should not be permitted to disembark until the halting stations selected for the purpose, between Cape Coast Castle and the Prah, be ready for their reception, and all rivers and streams, as well as morasses along the road, bridged over and filled in. It is of the last importance that the men should reach the confines of the Protectorate with dry feet and in perfect health.

2. PREPARATIONS RECOMMENDED AT HALTING STATIONS PREVIOUS TO ARRIVAL OF TROOPS.

(*a*) For each station a number of cooks should be told off, in order that the meals of the men should be previously prepared and ready for use shortly after their arrival.

(*b*) Filters should be in operation from early morning and over night, with the view of having a plentiful supply of filtered water available. This should be taken from sources previously indicated. Every effort should be made to get up a Crease's filter to each station.

(*c*) For ablution and culinary purposes a supply of water should also be immediately available.

(*d*) A collection of dry wood should be made at each camping ground, and piled in proper proportions in rear of each hut and the kitchens, either to be used for lighting fires at night in the buildings or as may otherwise be required. Large fires should be kept burning from sunset to sunrise.

(*e*) The most perfect cleanliness and surface drainage should exist at the different stations previous to their occupation, and a small but efficient corps of sanitary police and scavengers, under a responsible officer, be formed, for the sole purpose of camp conservancy. Latrines should be carefully attended to, and all fouling of sources of water supply by natives carefully guarded against. At the intermediate halting places sheds should be erected (native fashion) as a protection against the rays of the sun.

3. DISEMBARKATION.

(*a*) The men should be directed to relieve themselves at the urinals and latrines on board previous to leaving the ship.

(*b*) Forty-five minutes previous to disembarkation a parade should be formed up, and in the presence of the medical officer in charge, each man should take four grains of quinine in solution, previously prepared; fifteen minutes afterwards, and half an hour previous to leaving the transport, a full meal of cocoa and a biscuit.

(c) The men should be again fallen-in, their canteens examined, and seen to be filled with tea, made shortly before; also that each individual wore his cholera belt and was in possession of his proper clothing. Boots and feet should be also carefully examined.

(d) Disembarkation should be concluded by 5.30. Immediately after the parade being formed the men should march for Inquabim.

4. PRECAUTIONS EN ROUTE.

(a) The men should move off at a moderate pace, to be gradually increased. On no account whatever should their strength be overtaxed. A halt of twenty minutes might take place midway to Inquabim, under *proper shade*, and occasional halts of five minutes duration if there are any stragglers.

(b) Men allowed to fall out upon permission of C. O. or M. O., should on no account be permitted to regain their former place in the column at a run; they should be directed to fall-in in the rear. Unless this precaution is adopted they will become much exhausted, and ultimately have to fall out again and be carried.

(c) A sufficient number of bearers with condensed or filtered water should follow in rear of the column, and at the first halt of twenty minutes, canteens be examined, and all requiring it filled.

(d) As each stream or pool is reached, a guard should fall-in at either side of the bridge or crossing, and no man should be permitted upon any pretence whatever either to walk through the water or to use it. This precaution is especially necessary in the case of West Indian troops : chilled feet are a fertile source of colic and diarrhœa.

(e) A liberal supply of hammocks should follow in rear.

(f) The men should march in their flannel shirts except in the raw of the early morning, carrying their jackets strapped across the shoulders, a proper proportion of carriers being told off for surplus clothing and remainder of the kit. Carriers attached to each company should wear a distinguishing mark, in order that the men may be able at once upon arrival at their destination to obtain a change of clothing.

(g) The men should never be allowed to lie upon the ground.

5. ARRIVAL AT CAMPS AND IMMEDIATE HALTING PLACES.

(a) In the case of the first two stations, half an hour after arrival a good meat breakfast should be served up to the men and officers. Where the marches are longer, this meal should be ready prepared at the intermediate halting places.

(b) Upon arrival in camp the men should be at once told off in sections, and marched to their respective huts, and no straggling in the sun or hanging about in cold draughts permitted.

(c) At these intermediate stations, where it is necessary to break the march by a halt more or less prolonged according to circumstances, sheds should be erected (country fashion) as a protection against the rays of the sun, and the men be not permitted to leave them. For this purpose the shade of large trees may also be made available, the space round the trunk having been cleared previously.

(d) When the men arrive early in camp, and are not to leave until the following day, they should remove clothes saturated with perspiration, and hang them upon rails (previously erected) in the sun. When dry and well brushed, they should be neatly folded and placed under cover. Before putting on other clothes the body should be dry-rubbed with a soft towel. Half an hour to an hour afterwards would be the proper time for a change. This should be immediate if wet by a thunder shower.

(e) After leaving the Coast, on no account should dry clothes be hung up at night in the huts : they should be folded and placed under the pillow, otherwise before morning they will have become thoroughly saturated with moisture. Boots should be at once rubbed dry and greased; the feet washed in a solution of alum and dried, and any signs of foot sore at once attended to. A large supply of alum should be provided at each station for the foregoing purposes, as well as for the purification of water containing clay in solution.

6. HOURS RECOMMENDED FOR MARCHING.

The two first marches might be completed in the early morning. The advantages are manifest. After arrival the men would have a long rest, and ample time and sun to dry all clothes and underclothing previously saturated with perspiration. As the distances between C. C. Castle and Inquabim, and the latter place and Acroful are short, there would be no danger from exposure to the sun ; the afternoon rains, if any, would also be avoided. The third march should be a morning and afternoon one. Starting from Acroful at 5.30 the men would arrive at Dunquah at 8.30, halt during the day, and proceed onwards to Yancoomassie at 4.30, arriving there at sunset. As after leaving Yancoomassie the forest becomes denser and the shade consequently greater, an advantage increasing *pari passu* with the advance, I am of opinion that by an early start Mansue may be reached in one march without any danger. Exclusive of halts, this has been gone over by troops in five hours. At Mansue the men should have one clear day to themselves. During this they will have an opportunity of washing underclothing if necessary, and of bathing in the River Okee. Here all the men should undergo a most careful and minute medical inspection. The ample hospital accommodation at this station will allow of any requiring it and unable to proceed onwards at once, being received for treatment. As the forest now becomes much denser, I think the remaining marches to the Prah might be completed in the morning without danger to health from exposure to the sun. Upon arrival in the vicinity of the River Prah, the men should have one or two days' rest before advancing to meet the enemy. Here, as at Mansue, a minute medical inspection should be made, and all men not likely to be effective left at the depôt, or forwarded to the rear.

7. MEALS.

Forty-five minutes before starting, and fifteen minutes before the morning cup of cocoa, the men should be paraded, and given, as previously recommended, four grains of quinine in solution, a strong cup of cocoa and a biscuit, before marching off; cold tea during the march and at its termination in the case of the first two marches, and at the intermediate halting places during the subsequent ones a meat breakfast, with tea and fresh bread ; dinner at the usual hour, with good soup, and as much fresh or preserved vegetables as possible ; tea in the evening, with bread and butter. Preserved lime juice should be forwarded on to all stations up to the Prah, and a ration issued daily to the men. There should be also a plentiful supply of port wine, preserved milk, and essence of beef. One of the most powerful and agreeable restoratives after a long march is a mixture of these three substances. The issue of a spirit ration will depend upon the recommendation of the medical officers. A supply of rum should be available for use at each station.

On no account should spirits be issued during a march; afterwards it may be occasionally necessary and useful. Salt pork should be used as sparingly as possible. In conclusion, I would respectfully recommend that every effort should be made to have a plentiful supply of live cattle, and fresh or preserved vegetables, and flour at the several depôts. Nothing can compensate for the issuing of a fresh meat ration, bread and vegetables. Without these in abundance the officers and men cannot reach the Prah in the best physical health. After crossing that River the general sanitary principles I have thus minutely laid before you should be adhered to as far as the exigencies of the war will permit, and all villages should be preserved from destruction during the advance.

I do myself the honour of remaining,
Your very obedient servant,
ALBERT A. GORE, M.D.,
Surgeon-Major,
Sanitary Officer.

Major Baker,
Assistant Adjutant-General,
Government House.

These suggestions were followed as far as practicable during the after march of the European troops to Coomassie.

Subsequently to the arrival of Sir Garnet Wolseley, in October, it was directed in General Orders that the men hired at Sierra Leone should receive sixpence a-day (afterwards increased to ninepence), subsistence money, in lieu of rations, and in addition to their pay; that officers should take immediate steps to complete their field kit; that artificers were to be treated in military hospitals; and the rum ration discontinued as an issue in the field, except upon the recommendation of a medical officer. The subsistence money allowed to Fanti levies was to be $4\frac{1}{2}d.$; and the men of the Carrier Corps in the field were to have $1\frac{1}{4}$ lb. of rice in addition to their pay. Officers of all ranks were directed to march on foot in the field, and were only to be carried when sick. The bush was to be cleared round the military posts established to a radius of 60 yards, and the men proceeding to them were to carry a week's supply of provisions. Filters were to be provided for each post, and when regular troops were on the march in the field for every ten men, and under, 1 hammock would accompany the column; for 25 men, 2 hammocks; 50 men, 3 hammocks; and so in proportion. Native troops were allowed 3 hammocks per cent. Special arrangements were to be made for other than ordinary marches. These hammocks were intended for the foot sore and sick of all ranks. Huts were sent on to Assayboo, Dunquah, and beyond; and in consequence of the great sickness prevailing in the Ashanti camp, no prisoners but those in a good state of health were to be sent to Cape Coast; those retained at the posts were to be kept separate from the garrisons. A portion of the ration issued on the previous night was to be made into soup for men marching early on the following morning, and the rations given to servants in the field were to be the same as those for native levies. Six bearers were allowed to each hammock, and one carrier for 50 lbs. weight of baggage. Standing bedsteads for all the men were to be made at the different posts, and personal cleanliness, and the ablution and conservancy arrangements attended to. All the sick and weakly men of the 2nd West India Regiment were to be sent to Sierra Leone, and on the march to the front the same ration was to be issued to the Naval Kroomen as to the native levies—$\frac{1}{2}$ oz. of cocoa being given on the march, in lieu of $\frac{1}{4}$ oz. of tea. It was also directed that the military mail was to leave for the Prah at 4.30 A.M. on the 21st December; the following day at 1.30 P.M.; the return mail, leaving Prashue at 5 P.M., was to reach Cape Coast Castle at 2.30 P.M. on the following day.

On the 20th December was issued the following General Order:—

"March to the Prah. Memorandum on arrangements for the move of the troops to the front on landing, 27th December. Head Quarters, 20th December, 1873.

"27th December, Naval Brigade, 13 officers and 25 men, land and march. 15 hammocks and 6 bearers each.

"30th December, 2nd W. I. Regiment leave Mansue, and reach the Prah 2nd January.

"1st January, 1st detachment of regular troops move to Prah, reaching on 8th; last will land and march on 6th, and reach on 13th.

"2nd January, Russell's Native Regiment move to the Prah.

"1st W. I. Regiment will be distributed between C. C. Castle and Elmina, ready at all times to take the field.

"Regular troops land by half battalions. Artillery and Engineers will land with one of the half battalions, and march with it to the Prah.

"Regimental baggage will be landed at 4.30 previous evening, removed by carriers from Castle 4.30 following morning.

"Each half battalion will consist of 15 officers and 330 N. C. officers and men, and will require 278 carriers.

"Royal Artillery, 3 officers and 50 men, 55 carriers. Royal Engineers, 2 officers and 48 men, 52 carriers.

"Kroomen into three parties, one to go with Head Quarters. Half battalion of each regiment to carry regimental reserve of S. C. ammunition.

"Arrangements will be made with 2nd W. I. Regiment by which a money payment will be made to men instead of European rations. The corps will receive rations according to scale laid down for native levies. This is done to relieve transport force to be taken beyond the Prah.

"200 2nd W. I. Regiment, 25 R. A. (England), to remain stationary in *tete de pont* on the Prah.

Manœuvring Column will consist of 3 Battalions of English Troops	. 2,046		2nd W. I. Regiment .	. 200
Naval Brigade	. 265		Rait's Artillery .	. 50
R. A. (English)	. 35		Wood's and Russell's Regiment	800
Engineers	. 50			
Rait's Artillery	. 9		Total drawing Native scale of rations	. 1,050
1st Regiment S. A. A.	. 7			
2nd West India Regiment	. 14			
Russell's Regiment	. 12			
Wood's do.	. 12			
Head Quarters and other Staff, including Departmental Officers	. 60		Labourers and Carriers, not including those for carriage of provisions, to draw rations according to scale laid down for Carriers and Labourers .	. 4,000
Total drawing European scale of rations .	. 2,510			

"Troops marching from the front will start for their halting places punctually at 5.0 o'clock each morning, and will receive before starting a ration of cocoa. Officers commanding are requested to see that the men reserve a small portion of the previous day's biscuit ration to eat before starting.

"By Order.

"G. R. GREAVES,

"*Chief of the Staff.*"

Upon the march to the front, Brigadier-General Sir Archibald Alison, who had arrived in the Sarmatian, assumed command of the Brigade of European troops and fighting column.

The arrangements made for the treatment and care of the sick by the principal medical officer of the expedition, Sir Anthony Home, were perfect in every detail. Previous to the arrival of the Special Service Officers, in October, the sick of the 2nd West India Regiment were treated in hospital at Cape Coast and Elmina, private houses having been transformed into hospitals for the purpose. In both cases the patients were subjected to the same stoppages and given the same diets as were allowed to sick soldiers at home. The diets were supplied by a native clerk in the hospital, or purveyor to the Control Department. The cook was a private of the 2nd West; the sick attendants, the Acting Hospital Sergeant and men of that corps, the general arrangements being exactly similar to those of a regimental hospital in England, with this exception—that the medical officer was a staff surgeon. As the number of irregular troops increased, more particularly after the arrival of Sir Garnet Wolseley, in October, the hospital accommodation proved wholly insufficient. The basement story of the building at Cape Coast was at first told off for men of the irregular regiments who reported sick, and required admission, an attempt not proving satisfactory, or that of enforcing an hospital stoppage from them. This last regulation was shortly discontinued, and a far simpler method introduced, viz., not issuing to them their subsistence money while under treatment, and while dieted in hospital. In a short time wooden huts were erected opposite to the hospital gate for the sick of the Houssas, irregular regiments, artificers, labourers, &c. In them the cots were arranged along only one (the land side) of the hut, leaving the space opposite the foot of the beds quite free. In one corner of each hut was a filter; at the centre of the unoccupied side, a table and form for the use of the medical officer and patients. These huts, which answered their purpose very well, had been made and numbered in England, so that a very short time sufficed to erect them, the ground being merely levelled to allow of the frame-work being put down. They were not raised on either brick-work or pillars, had boarded floors, and a wooden roof, covered with felt, which with the sides were whitewashed, in order to reflect the solar rays, and keep the interior cool. They were ventilated by means of large folding doors at either end, a ridge along the centre of the roof, and also openings beneath the projecting eaves. The interval between the projection of the eaves and ground was rather too little, one being obliged to stoop to enter. The temperature in the interior varied from 86° to 96° Fahr. at mid-day.

At Connor's Hill the long wooden convalescent hut was equipped with hospital beds, bedding, &c., for twelve patients, and two large hospital marquees were erected and furnished with six cots each. All Europeans coming from the front were, pending their being transferred to the Simoom or Victor Emanuel, sent up here, or accommodated in one of the town hospitals in the first instance. Subsequently to this, two or three wooden huts were erected on Connor's Hill, facing the sea. The officers', or convalescent hut, was equipped for four patients, and the church opposite the Castle gate re-roofed, whitewashed, cleaned, and converted into an hospital for 22 sick. Bellevue House, an old tumble-down building, on Macarthy's Hill, was converted into a yellow fever or contagious diseases hospital, capable of containing 10 beds. As the stations were gradually occupied along the coast, hospitals sprung up. At Acroful, the first on the route, the Methodist Chapel was converted into a repository for the sick. At Dunquah, two hospital marquees were pitched within the fort; and at Mansue, seven hospital bamboo huts were erected in *echelon* at the entrance to the station—one for officers, another for convalescent patients, and the remainder for non-commissioned officers and men—the whole accommodating in separate beds 65 patients. At Prashue was another large station hospital, capable of containing 100 sick, supplemented by hospital marquees. To this station 150 hammocks were sent on, and when not otherwise required, utilized in carrying on stores to the front. As the troops marched up, a portion of the barrack huts were set apart for the sick at each station. In this way Dr. Home's original idea, viz., that at every twenty miles should be available intermediary hospitals, and at every forty miles larger station hospitals, where the men more severely wounded, and seriously sick, could be treated, was in practice carried out. At the base of operations at Cape Coast was hospital accommodation to the extent of 66 beds for white troops, each individual being allowed 2,000 cubic feet of air space; 18 sick officers could also be received for treatment. Trifling cases of illness, lasting two to four days, were not to be sent away from the stations where they were admitted on the sick list. To these several establishments were attached trained orderlies of the Army Hospital Corps, and a fixed establishment of medical officers—usually a surgeon at the smaller, and a surgeon-major and number of surgeons proportionate to the wants of sick at the more important and larger stations.

Total Hospital Accommodation South of the Prah.

Cape Coast	18 Officers.
	66 Europeans, Non-Commissioned Officers and Men.
	40 West Indians.
	24 Irregulars.
In Harbour	240 on board Victor Emanuel.
	100 ,, Himalaya.
	100 ,, Tamar.
Mansue	. 66 Non-Commissioned Officers and Men.
Prashue	. 100 Non-Commissioned Officers and Men.

A total of some 554 beds, exclusive of the sick cots in reserve on board the steamers chartered by Government, and those available at the smaller stations, viz., Acroful, Dunquah, Assin Yaucoomassie, &c.

The Simoom when in the roads had been used as an hospital ship, and did good service in this capacity. She was afterwards despatched to Cape de Verde, as a receiving ship for invalids. At the camps established at Napoleon and Abbey, a hammock, with four bearers, was allowed for the purpose of conveying the sick to Cape Coast and Elmina respectively; and at each of the barracks a hammock and sick bearers were in readiness to convey any invalids to hospital. The smaller detachments while on the march were followed by a hammock to pick up stragglers—officers of all ranks being obliged to march on foot while in the field, being only carried when ill and unable to proceed. Boxes of medical comforts and some simple surgical dressings and appliances accompanied each column as it advanced. Field companions were found very useful and portable.

The manœuvring army which crossed the Prah amounted to 3,554, officers and men, for whom 300 hammocks and cots, with 1,200 bearers (about 10 per cent.) were available. The former were sent back to the front as quickly as they deposited their sick at the first field and station hospitals, so that a continuous stream of sick bearers was on the move going and returning. When the army reached Fomanah a large station hospital was established in the King's Palace, the nearest large medical base for the more immediate front. The hospital supplies and equipments were drawn on demand from the Control Department by the medical officers who managed and equipped the various station hospitals on the line of march with the aid of the Army Hospital Corps, large contingents of which were constantly arriving with the various batches of European troops, as well as abundant supplies of medical comforts, packed in small quantities for convenience of carriage. As carriers became more numerous, these were rapidly accumulated at the various stations in rear of the advancing troops.

Dr. Home's original idea, which a paucity of carriers to some extent modified, provided for 18 per cent. of carriage, which was sub-divided into—

1. Station Hospital.
2. Movable Transport with the Force.

Each day's journey was to average thirteen miles. Thirty-five cots or hammocks were to be available at each station, with six bearers each, which would allow of fifteen sick being passed down to the base every morning, and leave five cots to spare. The cots were to be returned to the stations from which they had been sent daily. Eighty-five cots or hammocks, with 540 bearers, were to have accompanied the column which advanced against the enemy, any choking up of transport after an action being met by diverting the sick to the hospitals at Prashue, Mansue, &c.

By the 1st January the medical establishment had reached the number of 96, all told. Of this number 10 were Surgeons-Major, the remainder Surgeons. There was also a Captain and Lieutenant of Orderlies, the latter on board the hospital ship, the former on shore. Five Medical Officers, a Surgeon-Major and four Surgeons had been attached to each of the European regiments on their departure from England: only two were retained with each corps after its arrival in Africa, the surplus officers being told off for general duty. The hospital tents and *personnel* followed in rear of the column for the temporary reception of the wounded and sick, pending their being transferred to the nearest fixed station hospital, *en route* to the base at Cape Coast and hospital ships in the offing, the Europeans going to the Victor Emanuel, the natives to the several hospitals on shore.

Previous to the action at Amoaful the baggage of the white troops and the Control stores were left at Insarfu, four miles in their rear. When the village of Akanquassie, two miles beyond Insarfu, was clcared of the enemy's scouts by the 42nd, the ammunition and hammocks were moved into a space cleared by the engineer labourers in rear of the village. This village, consisting of only five or six small huts, was the central spot to which three roads converged, and was the site of the first field hospital. The wounded were brought here from the action going on scarcely a mile in front, the preliminary dressings applied by the regimental surgeons in action removed, slugs extracted, bandages re-applied, and the more severely wounded prepared for transport to the fixed hospitals in the rear. As the sick bearers deposited their burdens they were started back again at once to the scene of conflict in the immediate front. When not thus employed, they were kept at work clearing the village. As the day was overcast, those present suffered little from heat or thirst. The first convoy of forty-one hammocks, conveying wounded, with twenty-one men capable of walking, escorted by a company of the Rifle Brigade, left Agginassie for Insarfu at 2.30 p.m. As they were entering Insarfu, the firing of the enemy attacking Quarman in the rear so alarmed the carriers that they flung down the hammocks and rushed into the village. One of the wounded officers only saved himself from being trampled upon by using his sword very freely. When leaving Agginassie a section of the 42nd was passed protecting one of their officers who had been severely wounded, without which precaution he would have probably been decapitated.

After all the actions of the war, the wounded and sick were carried in cots or hammocks to the rear along the main road at a rate of twenty miles a day. When a halt took place, food was cooked for the sick, the bearers at the same time preparing their own meals, and resting to recruit their strength. In the forest paths, hammocks and cots, especially the latter, were with difficulty carried, owing to the numerous obstructions. In such situations it was impossible to use hammocks with cross-pieces, as two men were unable to walk abreast, the native grass or country cloth hammocks, slung upon a single pole and supported upon the head of a bearer at either end, being alone of use. While these various methods had been adopted on shore, the most complete preparations had been made for the reception of the sick and wounded in the hospital ships, and for their subsequent transport to England. A health officer visited all the African steamers from the leeward ports in order to ward off by a preliminary quarantine any possible importation of contagious disease into the town or shipping. Upon the arrival of the Victor Emanuel on the 1st January, 1874, the Simoom, which had just before returned from a man-of-war's cruise of six or seven weeks duration, *via* St. Helena and Ascension, was again despatched to St. Vincent to act as a receiving ship for future invalids, this step becoming necessary owing to the refusal of the Portuguese authorities at Madeira to allow Dr. Makinnon to establish a sanitarium there or at St. Vincent, no one coming from the Gold Coast being allowed *pratique*. The Dromedary and other steamers were to leave every ten days for St. Vincent, with invalids, either to catch the Cape or Brazilian packets, which would convey them to England, where the invalids upon arrival would be transferred to Haslar or Netley, according to the branch of the service to which they belonged. While waiting the arrival of the vessels they were accommodated on board the Simoom. In this way the Victor Emanuel and auxiliary hospital ships were periodically relieved, and ample accommodation ready at all times for the sick and wounded coming from the front.

The military and medical officers on board the hospital ships were furnished with printed instructions for their guidance. The navy undertook the lodging, victualling, conveyance of sick, furnishing everything necessary for these purposes. A steam launch plied between the shore and the hospital ships, towing in its wake surf canoes specially constructed for the reception of the sick and invalids. The army furnished medical and other attendance for the sick, provided all clothing, bedding, medical, surgical, and hospital appliances, clothing and hospital bedding, having in reserve a large supply of medical stores and appliances; also a number of warm pea-jackets for use as the colder latitudes were reached.

When intelligence arrived at Cape Coast of the action at Amoaful, all the convalescents, and as many sick soldiers as practicable, were transferred to the Simoom at the Cape de Verde, and the General Hospital at Cape Coast and Connor's Hill were cleared of their patients, so that there was ample room for the sick and wounded as they arrived. All the more serious cases went on board the Victor Emanuel, the others being relegated to the Tamar and Himalaya. By these means floating accommodation, equivalent to the reception of some 500 sick and wounded, was obtained.

The Victor Emanuel, a wooden screw, 79 gun frigate, was fitted up in the most perfect manner for the reception of the sick with all modern appliances for the relief of human suffering when appealing to human skill. As prepared for her late service, she had a flush upper deck, with poop; a main deck, carrying 140 beds for patients; a gun or lower deck, fitted with hammocks for convalescents; and an orlop deck. On each of the decks long openings had been cut to provide for the ventilation of the spaces below. On the upper deck these openings were covered with wooden roofs or ridges with sloping sides, rising about twelve or fifteen inches, and capable of being raised or depressed by screws. On the lower decks the openings contained iron pipes, with circular holes in their lower surfaces, and were covered by iron plates. The pipes communicated with channels which opened into the tubular masts; so that all the vitiated air found its way into these channels and was discharged aloft. In certain conditions of the wind this arrangement did not work perfectly, and the action of the sails was found sometimes to produce a draught down the masts, instead of in the opposite direction. This, however, mattered little, for on the hospital deck, which was high out of the water, it was possible to keep the ports almost always open, and there was an abundant circulation of fresh air around the sick. So excellent, indeed, were the sanitary arrangements, that every patient who was in a condition to improve at all showed signs of improvement before he had been twenty-four hours on board.

Above the upper deck were placed eight tanks, each holding two tons of water. Three of them were filled with salt water, to be used for flushing the closets, two with drinking water, which was passed through Crease's patent filters before being used, and three with fresh water for washing or bathing. The action of the Crease's filters was much praised, and a glass of bright and sparkling water, well iced, was highly appreciated by those who had sickened or been wounded far in the interior, and had been carried down on litters in much suffering, and exposed both to heat and to drenching rains. The ice was furnished by one of Messrs. Siebe and West's patent machines, which was kept constantly at work. It turned out solid and transparent ice in great abundance; so that the Victor Emanuel was not only able to supply her own wants and those of all the other ships which were used for the reception of invalids, but also to send ice to the hospitals ashore. One of the very few faults found with her was that the ice-making machine might have been more conveniently placed; but its performance seems to have given universal satisfaction. The hospital deck was fitted with iron cots with canvas sides, swinging at head and foot upon iron stanchions rising from the deck. The cots were intended either to rock from side to side, so as to neutralize the rolling of the ship, or to lock to the stanchions; but it was found that the former plan did not answer in practice. The range of movement was too great, and a helpless patient was liable to fall over to one side, so as to put his cot out of trim, or even to fall out upon the deck. It was, therefore, necessary to fix the cots; but somewhat lower stanchions, and an improved method of swinging, would overcome this difficulty for the future.

There are few things on which the sick are more dependent for their comfort, and even for their recovery, than upon the quality of the food supplied to them, and in this respect the arrangements of the Victor Emanuel were perfect. The chief cook and his assistants were described by all the patients as benefactors, to whom they could not be too grateful, and who were not only masters of their business, but who spared no pains to gratify every wish of the invalids. On this account, also, the change to the Victor Emanuel from shore, or even from other ships, in many cases produced marked and immediate benefit.

In order that the nursing might be of the best quality, the Royal Victoria Hospital at Netley was, for the time, stripped of its most skilful and experienced orderlies, to the number of over 100, and their work was directed by five medical officers constantly on board.

The general result obtained was that the Victor Emanuel, although on her departure from Cape Coast she was filled with cases of the most serious description, had been enabled to deliver the greater number of her patients convalescent, and in a state to return to duty. Three officers out of seven, and seven men out of 167 died during the passage home. Of the four surviving officers three were convalescent; and the fourth, Sub-Lieutenant Sherston, of the 2nd Battalion of the Rifle Brigade, who had been in the most extreme danger, had so far improved that his ultimate recovery was fairly anticipated. Of the 160 surviving men, 129 were landed at Portsmouth to rejoin their regiments, and only 31 remained to be transferred to Netley Hospital.

Among other ingenious contrivances for the comfort of the sick, the Victor Emanuel was provided with an outside platform, on the level of the hospital deck, covered in and fenced by wire. This was called "Birdcage-walk," and was used as a place of exercise by convalescents. It was also used to receive the patients, who were hoisted up to it from the boats by a derrick on the deck above; and so admirably was this hoisting managed, notwithstanding the swell at the Gold Coast and the rolling of the ship, that the invalids were scarcely conscious of a single jerk during the process.

Of the 31 men landed at Netley Hospital, 14 are medical cases—fever, dysentery, or the like—and 16 are suffering from wounds. Of the latter only three were confined to bed, and two of these were sufficiently well to talk with animation about their adventures. Among these the storm of Easter Sunday, the only occasion on which it was necessary to close the ports of the hospital deck, held a prominent place. This storm seemed to have strained the vessel severely, and during the course of it she sprung a dangerous leak. Fortunately, the hole was nearly circular, and opened into an empty coal bunk, so that it was found and plugged without delay. But, until it was plugged, the full pumping power of the donkey engine could scarcely keep the water from gaining ground, and the circumstances were such as to enliven the monotony of the voyage by the excitement of the new danger. Of the men who are sitting up, one carried a memorial of Amoaful in the shape of a stone missile, lodged just above his right collar bone. Felt through the skin, it appeared to be a cube, somewhat smaller than a backgammon dice.

The change of climate has been rather severely felt by some; more perhaps by the convalescents than by the men who were still in the wards, and, therefore, sheltered from the external temperature.

Notwithstanding her hard service, the Victor Emanuel returned to England in a state of sweetness, cleanliness, and order, which reflected the highest credit upon her captain and officers, as well as upon her medical administration.

A Military Commandant and Adjutant were additional to the medical establishment of a Surgeon-Major and six assistants. During her stay on the Coast, 565 patients had been received on board, of which number 125 were transferred to other ships, 165 were sent as invalids to England, 2 returned to duty, 4 died, and 167 remained on her starting for England on the 27th February; 3 officers and 7 men died on the passage, and 131 were landed at Portsmouth for duty with their several corps, the remainder, as stated before, being transferred to Netley.

The Thames may be taken as an example of one of the hired transports. The cabins for the officers on board this vessel were large and comfortably fitted, and each one was provided with deck ventilators, which were a great comfort in a hot climate; but in the matter of ventilation the occupants of the troop deck, which was the hospital, were better off than the officers. To this deck were three large hatchways, and on either side of the ship a light at every six feet. The awning, too, covered the ship from stem to stern, double above the troop deck, a few inches being allowed between the two sheets of canvas for a current of air to play. The ladies' cabin was refitted for the use of the military commanding officer. Each of the other cabins contained berths for two officers, one, as usual, above the other. The Thames had no forecastle or poop on her upper deck, having, therefore, the great advantage of what may be termed a flush deck. In about the centre of the ship on the starboard side had been constructed a bread room, and also a magazine to hold the ammunition of the troops ordered to embark. The dietary scale for the troops was exhibited between decks, and it provided that each man shall be allowed daily 12 oz. of salt pork, salt beef, or preserved meat, 6 oz. of flour or its equivalent in peas, 12 oz. of biscuit on four days every week, and 1 lb. of fresh bread on the remainder, 2 oz. of preserved potatoes, a pint of porter or half a gill of spirits, 2 oz. of sugar, and ½ oz. of tea. Once a week there was an extra ration of 4 oz. of rice, and twice some raisins and extra sugar for a pudding. Each man was also allowed per week 2 oz. of salt, 6 oz. of pickles, and a quantity of vinegar, mustard, and pepper. Temperance men might have an additional allowance of tea and sugar in lieu of beer or spirits, or they might have credit for a penny per day if they preferred it. Cases of preserved sausages, similar to those on which the German Army mainly subsisted during the late campaign, were embarked for the use of the troops engaged in the expedition, no less than sixteen tons measurement of these cases being sent on board the Thames, with an immense quantity of other provisions, including one more novelty in the shape of several tons of corned beef. The Thames was 300 feet long, brig-rigged, and of 1,600 tons register.

In his rapid march from the Volta to Coomassie, Sir John Glover was obliged to leave his more seriously sick, and those unable to proceed, at the larger stations *en route*, none but effectives going with the column in his adventurous journey. Some 7,000 native auxiliaries were left behind at Juabin, Odumassie, Coningo, and Obogoo. Orders were despatched to these stations at the conclusion of hostilities to send these men and the sick and footsore to Accra. On the departure for Obogoo on the 27th January, it had been found necessary to leave 200 Houssas and Yorubas, and 150 Akims to guard the sick, wounded, ammunition, and stores. On the 28th, Sir John Glover's sick list amounted to 48 out of a force of 750 Houssas and Yorubas—6·4 per cent.

The following were the names of the medical officers who served during one or other phases of the war :—

PRINCIPAL MEDICAL OFFICER :

Deputy Surgeon-General A. D. HOME, V.C., C.B.

SURGEONS-MAJOR :

W. A. Mackinnon, C.B.	T. M. Bleckley, M.D.	A. A. Gore, M.D.
V. A. Woolfreyes, M.D.	R. W. Jackson, 100th F.	J. Kelly, 106th F.
J. E. Clutterbuck, M.D., 42nd F.	J. H. Finnemore.	J. Wiles, Rifle Brigade.
T. B. Reid, R. Art.	S. Alder, 23rd F.	E. Pennington.
D. A. C. Fraser, M.D., 103rd F.	J. G. Faught.	F. A. Turton.

SURGEONS :

W. Venour.	J. Gray, M.D.	J. F. Supple.
F. L. Low, M.B.	P. Smith, M.D.	J. H. Moore.
J. Watson.	B. Macaw, M.D.	J. B. Croker.
J. W. C. N. Murphy.	J. H. Hughes, M.D.	W. F. Bennett, M.D.
F. T. M'Carthy.	E. Ward.	T. C. W. Heather.
P. W. Stafford.	J. Maturin.	J. S. Conyers, M.B.
F. B. Wilson, M.B.	S. Robertson.	J. H. Maher, M.B.
A. Doig.	G. Archer, M.B.	J. C. J. O'Brien, M.D.
G. W. M'Nalty, M.D.	J. J. Hanrahan, M.D.	F. L. Brown.
R. W. Troup, M.B.	W. A. Catherwood, M.D.	A. A. Macrobin, M.B.
W. B. Kynsey.	E. J. Clarke.	C. B. Jennings.
J. A. Beattie, M.D.	B. W. Lowe, M.D.	D. Thornton.
A. Turner, M.D.	H. T. Brown, M.D.	W. F. Samuels.
R. H. Bolton.	E. M'Crystal, M.D.	G. A. L'Estrange.
C. A. Atkins.	J. H. Hannagan.	O. S. Eagar.
C. J. Weir, M.B.	S. Moore, M.B.	D. Parke.
T. Oughton.	G. J. Gibson, M.D.	B. D. Reunell.
J. Fleming, M.D.	J. Williamson, M.B.	F. Faris, M.B.
A. Minto, M.B.	W. H. Steele, M.D.	C. B. Stuart, M.B.

AFRICAN MEDICAL SERVICE.

SURGEONS-MAJOR :

Merrick Lloyd Burrows, M.D.
C. B. Mosse.

R. Waters, M.D.
Aug. Frederick Elliot, M.D.

Samuel Rowe, M.D.
Allan Nesbitt Fox.

SURGEONS:

E. G Ley, M.D.

J. A. B. Horton.
T. W. Wright.

V. G. Gouldsbury, M.D.

ARMY HOSPITAL CORPS.

CAPTAIN OF ORDERLIES:
Joseph Collins;

LIEUTENANTS OF ORDERLIES:
William Henry Brown.   John Francis Dillon.

Of the foregoing medical officers fifteen were at the fall of Coomassie. Upon the departure of Deputy-Surgeon General Home, to whose administrative skill and untiring devotion to duty so much of the success of the Ashanti war was due, Dr. Woolfreyes and afterwards Dr. Mackinnon succeeded to the post of principal medical officer.

CHAPTER III.

CLIMATE.

THE influence of the land upon the trade winds and intervening calms, as we have already said, is very powerful upon the seaboard of the Gold Coast and the side of the Atlantic along which it lies, the peculiar configuration of the coast of Guinea tending as it does along the very axis or line of division of the northern and southern land systems, causing a different set of phenomena to arise. During that part of the year when the sun is in the southern hemisphere the trades and calms follow their usual or normal course, as the former is then exercising its maximum force on the sea with its low absorptive and radiating powers; but when, during the northern summer, it raises the temperature of the land of the Guinea Coast, a new phase arises from the heated atmosphere over the land drawing the wind towards it, when instead of the S.E. or N.E. winds, a S. or S.W. sea breeze occurs with great regularity, commencing daily about 10 A.M., and ceasing shortly after sunset—a breeze felt most refreshing by the European residents, and one of the few enjoyments of this Coast line. May, June, July, August, September, and October are the rainy months. In November fell the light showers, coming with the southerly winds, termed the little or second rains. The only difference in the arrival of the annual torrents is an interval of some twenty days sooner or later. As is well known, to the northward of the equator the rainy season always commences at each place when the sun passes the zenith of the latter in his course towards the north, during the month previous to which the change of weather usually commences. It not unfrequently happens that along the seaboard there are irregular rains, while at the same time these last are falling daily up country, when they always commence a month earlier. These rain clouds pouring their torrents to the earth could be seen inland, the rumbling of the distant thunder indicating at the same time the far-away disturbance of the elements, while it was perfectly fine and bright at Cape Coast and along the shore as far as the eye could reach. The approach of rain here was at once indicated by the sharply cut outline of Elmina and all distant objects, which on such occasions appeared much closer: the damp feeling of the air was also an unmistakable indication.

As the S.W. sea breeze became stronger in February it not unfrequently brought with it, sometimes rain, sometimes a light thunderstorm; the heavy tempests called by the Portuguese "tornadoes," accompanied by deluges of rain, thunder and lightning, became more frequent in March and April—the first indications of the commencement of the Gold Coast monsoon. During the height of the rains (May to July) little or no land winds are felt, but as the westerly and south-westerly winds are then blowing very strongly, a very great swell rolls in on the shore, thus rendering embarkation and disembarkation difficult, and sometimes even dangerous. In August the rains on the Gold Coast begin to break, becoming smaller and smaller in amount until September. December and January are the driest months of the year, and the ones during which active military operations may be carried on with the least danger to health. During the dry season months the land-wind blows at night with great regularity. It is loaded with moisture, excessively chilly and deleterious to health, and as is the common practice, should always be shut off from those reclining in repose. The range of the thermometer is not very great as a rule, but it has fallen as low as 66°, and risen as high as 95° in the shade in the air; the average heat throughout the year being 82° Fahr. The early morning temperature between 5 A.M. and 7 A.M. rarely rose above 75 or 76 degrees. This was the most agreeable period of the day, as the air was still cool and refreshing, and the leaves as yet sparkled with dew, if possible rendering more beautiful the luxuriant tropical foliage. The temperature of evaporation fell at this early hour as low as 71°. The difference in the readings between the wet and dry bulb rarely exceeded 2° at 9 A.M., 3° or 4° at midday, indicating an atmosphere highly charged with moisture at all times. This can be easily understood, as the N.E. or dry Harmattan wind is scarcely felt on the Gold Coast, where there is no attempt at a winter season, as there is in the more northern Coast line, where the nights are really cool, the air extremely dry, and the water too cold, if anything, for bathing in. While the range of temperature during twenty-four hours rarely exceeded 10° along the seaboard, up country it reached a maximum of 24°, the mercury in the thermometer having fallen as low as 71° at the Prah and 69° beyond, where at night there was a decided sensation of cold felt in January—very trying to the poorly clad natives. In the forest, protected by the tall cotton trees from the sun, the mercury seldom rose to more than 82°; when the open and cultivated plantations were reached it expanded to 92-96° in the shade, due in part to solar radiation. I never observed the black bulb to register more than 156°, falling as low as 110° when the sky was much obscured by cloud. Tornadoes were always preceded by a calm, dead heat, most oppressive to all. After the storm, which lasted some fifteen or twenty minutes in greatest violence, had exhausted itself, and been followed by deluges of rain, the air became cool and refreshing for the time. This agreeable change did not, however, remain permanent, unfortunately. The rainfall on the Gold Coast is stated to amount to 120 inches annually. Years vary, however, much in this respect. When the annual downpours are light in one year they are usually much heavier the next. During 1873 the rains were abnormally heavy and late, and the season consequently more unhealthy. The commencement and break of the African monsoon are considered the most unhealthy periods of the year, probably owing to the sudden lowering of temperature after some months continuous heat, and the greater intensity of the terrestrial emanations, when a break in the clouds allows the sun to act upon the, until then, not actively decaying *débris*. When the marshes are covered and inundated at the height of the monsoon they seem to be, comparatively speaking, innocuous. The following abstract of the meteorological observations taken in September, October, November, and December, 1873, shows these several conditions more accurately than any verbal descriptions :—

IN THE SHADE IN AIR.

	9 A.M.		3 P.M.		In 24 hours.			Mean Temperature	Mean Barometrical Readings.	No. of Rainy Days.
	Dry Bulb.	Wet Bulb.	Dry Bulb.	Wet Bulb.	Maximum	Minimum	Range of Temp.			
Sept...	77	75	80	76	84	74	10	79	29·89	18
Oct. ...	77	74	79	77	79	75	6	78	29·52	7
Nov. ...	79	78	83	81	86	75	10	80	29·02	5
Dec. ...	79	78	83	80	85	75	10	79	29·02	4

September—Frequent calms, hot mornings, clouded, faint sea breeze towards end of month; much rain up country.

October—Cool mornings, fine weather commencing, slight showers, lightning flashing in N.E. at sunset; afternoon rains up country.

November—Few light showers, weather becoming drier, mornings cool, strong refreshing sea breeze.

December—Fine weather, hot sun, strong sea breeze.

6 A.M.—TEMPERATURES IN OCTOBER, OPEN PIAZZA FACING THE SEA.

	Deg.		Deg.		Deg.		Deg.		Deg.
1st.	76	7th.	75	13th.	76	19th.	77	25th.	78
2nd.	76	8th.	76	14th.	76	20th.	77	26th.	78
3rd.	76	9th.	76	15th.	75	21st.	76	27th.	78
4th.	75	10th.	76	16th.	77	22nd.	77	28th.	78
5th.	75	11th.	76	17th.	75	23rd.	76	29th.	78
6th.	76	12th.	75	18th.	78	24th.	76	30th.	78

The air was still, the sea breeze not having as yet begun to blow. In the yard behind, the thermometer sunk ten inches beneath the surface marked the following temperatures at 9 A.M. and 3 P.M. :

Date.	9 A.M. Deg.	3 P.M. Deg.	Date.	9 A.M. Deg.	3 P.M. Deg.
1st October	79	83	9th October	82	86
2nd ,,	79	82	10th ,,	82	85
3rd ,,	79	80	11th ,,	82	84
4th ,,	78	81	12th ,,	81	84
5th ,,	79	83	13th ,,	81	86
6th ,,	78	84	14th ,,	82	86
7th ,,	79	85	15th ,,	82	86
8th ,,	82	86	16th ,,	84	86

During the latter half of the month the thermometer was similarly placed, but left undisturbed for twenty-four hours. The readings at 6 A.M. were as below:

Date.	Black bulb, in sun, 24 hours	Mean in shade in air.	In ground, 10 inches.	Remarks.
17th October	150	82	85	Muggy, disagreeable day, threatening rain.
18th ,,	143	76	84	Appearance of rain in morning; bright afternoon.
19th ,,	152	83	85	Dull and heavy; rained at sunset; thunder and lightning at night.
20th ,,	137	81	85	Cloudy, damp, showers at sea; afternoon fine.
21st ,,	149	79	82	Sea breeze at 10 A.M.; lightning in N.E.
22nd ,,	150	80	84	Fine morning; heavy shower from S. at 5 P.M.; calm, damp evening.
23rd ,,	151	80	83	Fine morning; light breeze; cool evening.
24th ,,	149	82	84	Fine morning; sea breeze; vivid lightning in N.E. at sunset.
25th ,,	150	81	85	Damp, clouded early morning; fine at 9 A.M.; agreeable sea breeze; lightning at night.
26th ,,	150	82	85	Lunar halo previous night: thin watery sky at 6 A.M.; fine afternoon: gentle sea breeze.
27th ,,	150	82	85	Raw, damp morning; mist on hills; warm night indoors; lightning in N.E. at sunset.
28th ,,	150	81	84	Fine but close morning; bright, hot afternoon; sea breeze.
29th ,,	143	82	86	Damp, clouded, but cool morning; rained heavily 15 miles inland.
30th ,,	150	81	87	Close, warm, light sea breeze; lightning at night.

From these few observations with the thermometer placed beneath the surface, it will be seen that the temperature ten inches in the ground was, when the thermometer was left undisturbed, uniformly higher than the mean temperature of the air in the shade, and the minimum temperature also; in other words, the ground was warmer than the air in the shade, just as the buildings were at night, when they gave out the heat absorbed during the daytime, much to the discomfort of those sleeping between four walls. In consequence of this, I have often got up at night anything but in a cool and agreeable condition. Under such circumstances a land wind, laden with moisture, and blowing over the body, would cause what might be a fatal chill. According to a naval officer, "In July, 1873, there were eighteen days consecutively of very heavy rain; the thermometer in the shade never rose above 84°, and fell generally about 4 A.M. to 78°; it generally felt very chilly about that hour; one woke up shivering, and had to draw over a blanket to get warm again." In the very early morning, just before sunrise, the hill tops near the shore were chilly, damp, and raw, a drizzling mist obscuring all distant objects. At all times they were cooler than the intervening lowlands, where the sea breeze was not felt. As sunset approached, the mists could be seen settling in the hollows, which felt close and warm on descending into them; the difference was immediately perceptible. These general climatic characteristics of the Coast line were to be observed more or less in the semi-cleared country ten to fifteen miles inland, up to which distance the sea breeze was felt. In the more inland elevated crooms it was only faintly perceptible about mid-day. The forest paths were cool and shady, owing to the tall cotton trees, which, towering far over head, intercepted the direct solar rays, felt at once on entering the small village clearings *en route:* the contrast was anything but pleasant. Even here, however, the temperature was rarely higher than 72° in the shade at 6 A.M., 86° to 87° at 2 P.M.; it felt warm, but not disagreeably so, with a well-thatched roof over head and light clothing. At 3 P.M. on the 17th November, 1873, at Mansue, elevated 482 feet above sea level, and surrounded by a dense forest, the mercury stood in an officer's bamboo hut, well thatched with palm leaves, at 87°, the wet bulb 80°, a difference of 7°. The reading of the Aneroid was 29° 55'. A rain storm lowered the mercury in the wet and dry bulbs to 74° and 75°, indicating at the same moment an atmosphere almost saturated with moisture. The black bulb in the sun marked 156° when the latter was shining brightly; when clouded, as it was as a rule up country, it sank to 110°–129°; although there was no sun, the heat reflected back from the clouds acted almost as effectively on the mercury in vacuo. It rained nearly every afternoon at Dunquah, Mansue, Sutah, and beyond, commencing with the rumbling of distant thunder, and ending up with vivid flashes of lightning and terrific clashes of Heaven's artillery. At times the play of the electric fluid was really beautiful: we have often stood gazing at it with admiration and awe! These thunderstorms generally rolled away towards the westward. It was chilly, raw, and damp at night, the mist commencing to drift towards the south the moment the sun hid his golden visage beneath the tree-tops; in a few seconds our coats would be saturated as we sat round the blazing logs. These heavy mists hugged the ground until 7 A.M., when they were slowly dispelled and condensed upon the surrounding tree-tops. The amount of cloud, as already noticed, had an important influence upon temperature and the capability of sustaining for a prolonged period the effects of solar exposure. With a cloudy sky, helmets and umbrellas might be nearly always dispensed with; on such occasions I have frequently marched with nothing but a light West Indian fez, a most comfortable cap to recline in or replace the helmet when the shade was reached. A good raincloud was, of course, a far better protection than the thin grey misty one, which barely screened the sun from view.

The greatest heat on the Gold Coast was felt when the reflecting surfaces of buildings were numerous: these added much to the temperature of the air, which in their vicinity was stuffy and hot. In the height of the dry season the nights were comparatively cool: a peep at the firmament revealed myriads of twinkling stars. The days were bright and not unpleasant, owing to the effects of the sea breeze, which, commencing daily about 10 A.M., blew in increasing force until sunset; this, with the effect of the land breeze at night, was decidedly to reduce the temperature to one much below that felt in the woods, where the general absence of wind made the residence there little comfortable. For instance, at Prashne the heat was described as being far more oppressive than at Cape Coast, owing to the entire absence of motion in the air, the thermometer standing at 89° in the huts and 96° in the tents. In a double bell tent at Connor's Hill, 150 feet above sea level, with a strong sea breeze blowing, I found the thermometer only mark 86° at 1 P.M. upon a bright day. The same observation was made at the River Camp when occupied in 1863–64, when, in addition, the amount of watery vapour held in suspension by the air added much to the oppressiveness by preventing all evaporation of the insensible perspiration. Sometimes we had stifling hot nights after heavy downpours, and rolling mists rising along shore and obscuring all distant objects; even Elmina, only eight miles off, could not be seen; at other times the fine old Castle stood out in bold relief, especially upon the near approach of rain. About 8 A.M. the sun became very warm, the heat being felt in greatest intensity until 10 A.M., when the sea breeze moderated the temperature. As a rule, the increasing perpendicularity of the sun's rays did little to affect the relative humidity of the atmosphere, which for the four months—September, October, November, and December (saturation being 100)—averaged, at 9 A.M., 89°; at 3 P.M., 85°; the decrease with increased temperature averaging only a difference of 4°. This excessive degree of humidity appeared to be due to the constant high temperature of the air, increasing its capacity for holding water in solution, the retentive nature of the sub-soil of red argillaceous clay preventing the excess of rain sinking into the ground, the vast plateau of forest, and the amount of vapour constantly raised from the neighbouring Atlantic, and blown inland by the prevailing westerly and south-westerly winds, the daily rains, and evaporation from the numerous swamps.

The climate of the interior was said to be a better one than that of the Coast line. This might be true of the country some two hundred miles inland at the confines of the great paludal forest, but it was certainly not true of the intervening space. The climate of Fomanah, two and a-half miles north of the Adansie Hills, and about one hundred and twenty from Cape Coast, lying upon a small table land elevation, high above the level of the sea, was said to be cool, the nights colder and less foggy, and the breeze in greater force than at any of the stations on the march up. In the forest paths the air was laden with, in many parts (especially where the earth was disturbed), the odour of malaria and decaying vegetation. The odour from the *potta pottas*, or mud swamps, was most unpleasant, as was also that emanating from the dead bodies lying in the immediate vicinity of the narrow roadways. The stench of Coomassie did not disappear from the nostrils of the men on their return march until they had again regained the banks of the Prah. So obscured were the hill tops on passing over the Adansie range that a distant view was not possible. At Essiaman, the erection of high palisades was said to have increased much the feeling of heat by preventing all natural efforts at ventilation.

At the rendezvous, 180 miles distant from Cape Coast Castle, where the steamers remained with the white troops on board between the 18th and 30th December, 1873, the days were breezeless, excessively warm, and the cabins and between decks indescribably hot and close, and the air on deck after sundown chilly and damp. These two last rendered the deck an unpleasant and dangerous sleeping place, the stifling cabin being preferable of the two. Several cases of erysipelas broke out on board the Sarmatian among the men of the 42nd, and a few cases of insolation occurred among the 23rd, probably owing to the closeness of the atmosphere between decks. This I can easily imagine. This same dampness at night was observed up country. To hang a flannel shirt at night upon a cross beam of a hut was to have the ends dripping the morning following. I have more than once wrung the water out of mine on rising. This was obviated by folding the shirts under the pillows before going to rest, and airing them afterwards in the morning sun before putting them on. By lighting wood fires in the huts much of this unpleasantness was avoided, and the dew drifting through the slits of the bamboos rendered comparatively harmless. These wood fires were excellent institutions, and should on all occasions be made use of, not only in the centre of circles of men, but also between the groups, in order that the heat might be beneficial upon all sides. To avoid malaria the bed should be some three feet from the ground; to avoid the smoke, only some few inches. Very few of the Ashantee bedsteads were more than ten to twelve inches from the earth. We always found the smouldering logs between two of these, one of which was at either end of the little shelter shanties of their camps. The following were the meteorological conditions in the harbour while the foregoing were observed up country and on shore. The readings were taken down while on board the Victor Emanuel from the hygrometer hung in the shade on deck:—

Date.	9 A.M.		3 P.M.		Wind.	Cloud.	Weather.
	Dry.	Wet.	Dry.	Wet.			
Jan. 5th	78	76	81	76	W. to N.W.	8 to 2	Slight haze on shore; sea breeze in afternoon.
6th	75	70	82	75	W.	1	Cool morning; haze along shore.
7th	74	71	80	78	N.E. to S.W.	1	Cool morning; hazy.
8th	75	72	80	76	N.W. to W.	0 to 1	Fine, but close; hazy; sea breeze in afternoon.
9th	74	71	80	77	Do.	0 to 2	Close, calm morning; sea breeze in afternoon.
10th	77	75	81	78	N.W. to W.	2	Close, warm morning; faint breeze; oppressive afternoon.
11th	77	75	81	78	Do.	3 to 2	Fine cool morning; hazy afternoon.
12th	77	75	81	78	W.	0 to 2	Close, oppressive day; hazy afternoon; light sea breeze; muggy.
13th	77	75	81	77	W.	0 to 8	Fine, but damp morning; close, cloudy afternoon.
14th	77	75	81	77	N.W. to S.	5 to 4	Chilly, damp; rained at night; N.W. Harmattan wind.
15th	78	77	82	78	N.W. to 0.	3 to 6	Chilly, damp; close, damp afternoon; N.W. Harmattan wind (tornado); sun set in a red glare.

On the 7th January, at Prashuc, the Harmattan had unmistakably set in. It blew freshly from the N.W. on some days. On the 7th the temperature was only 75° in the shade, and the nights cold. It was found to exercise a drying effect on the bush, thus allowing of its being burnt.

On board the Victor Emanuel the second or hospital deck was by far the coolest, probably owing to its distance from the sun, and the ample ventilation. To sum up, then, the climate of the Gold Coast was characterized by—

A persistent and little changeable daily heat, followed by damp, chilly nights.

An excessive humidity of atmosphere.

An air loaded with malaria and other noxious exhalations, the former chiefly in the interior, the latter on the Coast line and in towns.

These conditions having a most debilitating effect, and causing much prostration within a short time, making the least exertion an effort. An officer, Major Brackenbury, described the climate as being "exhausting, depressing, enervating; it rendered every exertion a burden, and sapped the power of the mind and body." "No one," wrote one of the Special Correspondents, "who has not experienced it can form any idea of the debilitating nature of the climate. For two or three months it may be withstood; after that, if one escapes fever, he is seized with utter prostration, in which it is an effort to walk ten yards; he is completely done up after half an hour's walking." The same accurate observer, Mr. Henty, further wrote: "Some prefer the interior to Cape Coast. For myself, I would rather live in Cape Coast with its fresh breezes,

fruits, and comforts for a year, than exist up country for six months."
On the 20th June, 1873, there had not been a single Marine on the sick
list; by the end of the month the Druid had 35 seamen and marines on
the sick list. In July the Houssas had 32 in hospital out of 210 of all
ranks; on the 26th of the same month, 87 of 100 Marines, landed in
the previous June, had left for England, thirty-one days after landing.
On the 11th October, the sick list at Elmina averaged 6·75 per cent.; at
Cape Coast 11·51 per cent among the men of the 2nd West India Regiment. Out of 64 officers which had landed between the 2nd and 16th
October, 29 had suffered from sickness by the 8th of November, or 45
per cent. of strength. On the 15th the per centages of sick were—
Officers, 21·5; European non-commissioned officers, 18·75; West India Regiment, 12; Marines serving on shore, 18. Sixteen of the
twenty-nine officers attacked with illness had recovered and resumed
their duty, staying ten days on the sick list on an average. Seven were
invalided, two died, and one was killed. Many of the Marines who fought
at Elmina in June were ducked with the surf on landing, and detained on a
sand bank for two hours under a downpour of rain; some of them slept
all night in their wet clothes. Thirty-one days afterwards the non-
effective list was 17 per cent. A Sergeant of the Rifle Brigade wrote on
the 27th January that tropical Africa was "an awful climate for Europeans." Alluding to his regiment he said, "Two hundred men have been
admitted into hospital already; seventy have been sent back to the
Coast, and several are very ill. My section, which disembarked twenty
strong on the 1st, have now only fourteen remaining, six having been
sent back." Starting 278 strong on the 27th December, 1873, the
Naval Brigade returned to Cape Coast on the 20th of the following
February, after being *fifty-five* days up country (halts and marches included), only 119 strong; including officers (42·8 per cent. of the original strength had thus become ineffective, chiefly from fever). Forty had
been left at Prashue on the advance into Ashantee on the 5th January,
ten days after landing—a seventh of the battalion ineffective for purposes
of offence in this short period of time from the effect of climate. On
the 8th January, at Prashue, out of 427 Europeans only 13 were on the
sick list. On the 23rd, at Moinsey, 40 out of 250 of the Naval Brigade,
and 57 out of 650 of the Rifle Brigade, were already laid up from climatic diseases three weeks after landing. On the 25th January the
hospital states at Fomanah showed that out of 1,800 Europeans 218
had become ineffective. Out of 1,550 European non-commissioned officers and men only 1,375 were at Amoaful on the 31st January, 200, or
12 per cent. having succumbed to sickness in the space of a month. How
powerful must have been the effect may be surmised from the following
remark, viz.:—"The men arrived from the bush exhausted and de-

pressed to the last degree." During the ten days of comparative inaction a soldier gave the following graphic description of his daily life:— "Roused at 5 A.M.; we get our quinine and half a pint of cocoa by 5.30; wash, &c., between that and 6 A.M.; at 6 A.M. fell in on parade and work about the camp till 7.30 A.M. The work consists in the cutting and clearing away of the rank vegetation (and there is plenty of it, and half rotten), and improving the sanitary condition of the place generally. At 7.45 A.M. we get breakfast; from 8 to 9.30 we had to ourselves for washing, &c., down at the river; at 9.30 A.M. the lie down goes, and then we have to go inside the huts until 4 P.M.; at 1 o'clock we have dinner; at 4 P.M. we have tea, and wash, and at 5 P.M. we clean the camp up again until 6.30, when it is nearly dark, and we can go to bed as soon as we like after that, for we have no light, and it is not much use sitting about after dark. The proper bedtime is 8.30 P.M. So ends a day's soldiering in the bush in Africa."

The absence of wind added much to the sense of discomfort on the march. This was especially noticed on the first march out beyond Elmina, when, in addition, the reflection from the bright sand increased much the temperature of the lower stratum of the air, and made it less agreeable to breathe, and also less suitable for the respiratory process owing to its greater rarefication. In the first reconnaissance towards Abracrampa, in October, 1873, when the Marines started at 8 A.M. for a fifteen miles forced march in a blazing sun, the men suffered much from the intense heat; many of them fell out violently sick and giddy, not more than half of them reaching Assayboo, ten miles from the point of disembarkation. Of those who marched in with the head of the column, many were utterly exhausted. The chief symptoms observed were flushed face, lustreless eye, more or less pyrexia, and incoherency of speech. Up to 8 A.M. such symptoms would not have occurred, for between sunrise and that hour, or 9 A.M., the heat away from the sandy beach was not unbearable in active motion. During the various marches at this time halts in the sun were found most trying, the heat feeling less intense whilst moving. Livingstone's great experience in African travelling is confirmatory of this. In one of his last letters the great traveller wrote objecting to making journeys on horseback on account of his having felt the sun more while sitting immovable. In such a position there would be naturally no perspiration to reduce the temperature of the body by evaporation, and remove at the same time the effete materials rapidly accumulating in the circulatory fluid.

The officers stationed beyond Dunquah during the earlier military operations (at which time the ever-recurring afternoon rains saturated the atmosphere), suffered more than others from fever. A friend, who had to look up some natives to the eastward of the road to get to his destination, had to pass through a swamp two miles long: his hammock (supported on the bearer's heads, which were only just above the water), was half immersed, a fact which will give an idea of the state of the bush at that time. The carriers felt the rain and chills as much as others. I have seen them running like frightened deer from a shower. The constant exposure of the skin to a great heat appeared to have made it very sensitive to cold and variations of temperature. Beyond the Adansie Hills they were said to have been seen shivering in the early morning: proper clothing would have obviated this.

On the 3rd February, when bivouacking on the banks of the Dah without their *tentes d'abri*, after a long and tiresome march, the troops were for the first time drenched with rain, the majority to the skin; commencing in the afternoon, it rained during the whole night; fires and sleep were alike impossible. An officer mentioned to me, that by placing his hammock upon two forked sticks, and laying over the frame-work cover a couple of waterproof sheets, he was enabled to escape the ill effects of a wetting and chill on this occasion. The first thunderstorm had occurred at Ahkankuassie on the 28th January; it swept over the north end, leaving the south end of the town quite dry. The carriers and sick of the Naval Brigade were drenched to the skin by it. Again, at Coomassie, a thunderstorm burst over the town, drenching many in the leaky huts, the wet and dispirited occupants having afterwards to wade through the swollen swamps and rivulets on their homeward march, the men of the 42nd being actually obliged to strip to cross the Dah. In the earlier phases of the war, similar untoward misfortunes occurred to the Marines, Sailors, and 2nd West— as, for instance, when making a reconnaissance beyond Abracrampa, in the previous October. The chills which resulted from these several wettings had, undoubtedly, a prejudicial effect upon the health of the men, already impaired by the unnecessary delays *en route*. This was evidenced by the more frequent occurrence of bowel and dysenteric affections which followed. Although comfortably housed and sheltered on the march up, the delay led to a more prolonged exposure to the malarial poison which was consequently inhaled in a greater amount than it would otherwise have been. During these several marches, then, the most obvious exciting causes of fever appeared to be exposure to atmospheric vicissitudes, cold, moisture, excessive heat, and specific emanations from the earth. Although the marches were short, for reasons which will be afterwards touched upon, fatigue might, perhaps, be added to the foregoing.

As no deaths from disease occurred beyond the Prah, but much sickness, especially on the return march after leaving Acrofumu on the 9th February, and as "speedy improvement in the physical and mental condition of the invalids was produced by the quiet, orderly, and skilful arrangements carried out in the hospital ships," we cannot but conclude that the majority suffered from little more than a climatic or seasoning fever, aggravated by the inseparable surroundings and circumstances of war. After leaving Prashue on the return to the Coast, when officers and men were again well housed, cared for, and fed upon the abundant supplies and medical comforts which had accumulated in their absence at the various halting stations, the numbers going sick diminished rapidly, and the men rejoining the ranks increased in number in a proportionate degree, a few hours' rest in a hammock picking up many who were unable to proceed farther from sheer weakness. This experience was only the counterpart of Livingstone's on the eastern coast, while travelling along the Zambesi. The same prostration was observed to follow attacks of fever: when this last was checked, the strength was quickly restored. As a sedentary life was then said to predispose to the diseases of the climate, so did the ten days' delay on the march up, proved by the fact, among others, of the earlier admissions in January being almost entirely confined to the men of the 23rd, who had re-embarked, and were consequently suffering much from the disappointment of being not able to get to the front. Although only a day or two on shore, the wing of this regiment suffered more in proportion than the other corps who had gone on to the front. It would appear that the climate and experiences of 1873 differed little from those of 1863, for a young sub-altern of the Gold Coast Corps, writing from the Protectorate to a friend in the latter year, says—" The war is made most trying to our force; we can do nothing but move from place to place, trying to get up to them, enduring all kinds of privations and hardships, long and forced marches under a broiling and nearly vertical sun; not a breath of air stirring; often no water and no food, because these rascally Fantees won't carry their loads, that is, baskets of provisions, although specially engaged and paid high wages. The Ashantees are at Boccobie and Bisiassi, about two hours from this. My quarters are a mud hut, 3 yards by $2\frac{1}{4}$, a mud flooring for my bed. Of about twenty-five officers in the field with Cochrane's force, only six or seven are on the duty roster. The paths are numerous, from three to five feet wide. In marching along in Indian file in the early morning, the dew from the surrounding bush wets one from the shoulders to the feet. Sometimes the paths are gullied by the rains, and one has to stick one's legs over the gullies which are too narrow or too deep to walk in. This is very trying, and soon tires." These excursions appear to have been made early in 1863 in the eastern districts, from which the Ashantees retired unmolested, to the number of some 12,000, abandoning their camp at Swadroo Akim. They had suffered greatly from small-pox and dysentery during their occupation of the country.

Eighty miles east of Cape Coast the physical configuration of the country completely changed. The vast forest plateau was replaced by open plains, covered in parts by a low scrub, and backed thirty miles inland by the Acropong range of hills, those highlands where the members of the Basle Mission resided in health and vigour. Accra, the capital of this district, was an open town, surrounded by undulating savannas, abounding in game of all sorts, a country where horses lived and cattle did not die, and where the climate was decidedly better and more healthy, judging by results. Life there was certainly more enjoyable, because better food was obtainable, physical exercise in the open air unrestricted, and an agreeable change to the hills always at hand—a change of infinite value to health in Africa.

The climate of these Acropong Hills, tested by results, must have been far better than that of Cape Coast. A spring of pure water gushed forth from the primitive rock, uncontaminated by swamps or the excretions of the inhabitants. This was only fifteen miles from Accra, to which it might be as easily conducted in pipes as was the water from the mountains of Sierra Leone to the lowlands. Accra has had always the reputation of being a healthy situation, and although the roadstead was an open one, it was in every respect suitable for a European settlement, far preferable to Cape Coast.

Since writing the foregoing remarks it has been decided to make Christensberg Castle the seat of Government, and to have a sanitarium at Alburi, on the Accra Hills, twenty miles distant, and from which the view is magnificent. These hills are 1,400 feet above sea level. A bridge was also being constructed across the Sweet River, so as to connect Elmina with Cape Coast.

CHAPTER IV.

COMPOSITION OF THE FORCE.

BETWEEN the ages of 22 and 35 years men seem to be at their best in Western Africa. During this interval they can undergo most hardship, and rally quickest from attacks of the diseases incidental to the climate. Some, far long past their prime, may occasionally undergo great hardship, and get through much hard work. They are the exceptions, for individuals so advanced in life are far more liable to succumb when suffering from the more serious forms of fever, especially if at all dissipated. This is my experience and impression. In his despatch to the Secretary for War, Sir Garnet Wolseley wrote:—" Every officer should be carefully selected for the service, as peculiarly fitted for the work, both physically and mentally. To take any non-commissioned officer or private, unless of the best constitution, would be merely to increase the difficulties of the operations."

The value of the different classes of troops employed in any expedition will vary with their age, physique, and race principally. Even in our native corps, very great differences are observable. This is seen from the following table:—

1860-71.—RATIO PER 1,000.

	West Indians in West Indies.		West Indian Troops in West Africa.		Ceylon Rifles in Ceylon.		Asiatic Troops in Hong-Kong.		Asiatic Troops in Straits Settlements.	
	Admitted.	Died.	Admitted.	Died.	Admitted.	Died.	Admitted.	Died.	Admitted.	Died.
Total	918·1	22·84	1254·1	33·50	623·5	9·48	1066·1	18·30	1786·3	17·54
PRINCIPAL DISEASES.										
Fevers	147·5	2·30	318·0	9·48	101·1	1·52	401·6	2·02	603·5	3·19
Constitutional Affections	227·3	10·06	256·6	6·32	61·8	1·89	52·7	2·24	157·0	1·60
Respiratory	54·3	2·30	158·8	3·70	50·8	3·03	45·6	1·87	27·1	1·60
Digestive	71·7	1·47	22·6	5·00	48·5	1·14	224·1	7·47	384·4	11·15
Debility	2·1	—	2·5	—	4·2	—	10·8	—	27·1	—
PAROXYSMAL FEVERS.										

West Indians in West Indies.		Ceylon Rifles in Ceylon.		Asiatic Troops in Hong-Kong.	
Admitted.	Died.	Admitted.	Died.	Admitted.	Died.
95·5	1·25	170·7	·76	478·9	2·24

It will be seen from these very instructive figures that the West Indian soldiers became much more sickly on being transferred to the Coast of Africa, as did the Asiatic troops when sent from Madras to Hong-Kong, or the Straits Settlements—the Malay of the Ceylon Rifles being on the whole the healthiest. The prevalence of constitutional affections in the Negro is strikingly shown, as well as the increase in febrile diseases and diseases of the digestive system on the change of station in the Negro and Sepoy. If the latter had been sent to the Gold Coast he would probably have suffered more than the men of the West Indian regiments who served there.

The second batch of Marines were not at all picked men, several being mere lads. The best of the corps were absent at the Dartmoor manœuvres when the others were sent at a moment's notice to Cape Coast Castle. Previous to the despatch of the infantry regiments the men were carefully inspected, and all the very young retained in England—an absolute necessity when we know so well that boys are useless in war, as they cannot endure the hardships and exertions incidental to military operations in the field. Although young men of 21 or 22 years of age can occasionally undergo a great amount of temporary fatigue, it is very questionable whether a soldier is worth very much until he has reached 24 or 25. Before that he scarcely gets the set-up or looks the *parfait homme de guerre*, or has become sufficiently the mechanical military machine. In her account of a bivouac in South Africa, Harriet Ward puts these facts very strikingly forward. She says—" One by one the tents had risen; arms were now piled; *the younger soldiers, tired with their first march, lounged on the ground in clusters*, till roused by the *older and more experienced men*, who despatched them to gather wood and water"—a little piece of military experience which may be always learned under similar circumstances.

As far as can be judged from a few isolated recorded instances and observations, the admissions on the sick list were more numerous among certain sections of the European than among similar parties of the regular and irregular native levies.

Party of 2nd West, 200 strong, 235 casualties in 154 days, or 2789·2 per 1,000 per annum.
Naval Brigade, 278 strong, 159 casualties in 55 days, or 3794 per 1,000 per annum.
Section of Rifle Brigade, 20 strong, 6 casualties in 27 days, or 4055 per 1,000 per annum.
1st West, 552 strong, yielded 46 per cent. of sickness.
2nd West, Wood's, Russell's, Rait's Corps, 1,605 strong, 64 per cent. of sickness.
Three European Regiments, 1,578 strong, 71 per cent. of sickness.
Naval Brigade, 260 strong, 95 per cent. of sickness.

In a War Office return published, it was stated that the European or white troops, numbering in all 2,507 strong, yielded 511 casualties from disease in 55 days,

A ratio of 1347·2 per 1,000 per annum,

more than that given by West Indian soldiers serving in Western Africa between the years 1860–71, during which period the ratio was

1254·1 per 1,000.

The latter portion of the above return is interesting, as showing that the Europeans and natives, who had been, on the whole, least exposed, and who had done least work, had the least per centage of sickness. Of *fifteen* officers of the 2nd West India Regiment who sailed from Demarara in June, 1873, for the Gold Coast, where they arrived on the 12th of the following month, only *four* returned with the regiment to Barbadoes, 7th May, 1874. Of the rest, *two* had died and nine had been invalided home. Twenty non-commissioned officers and men died from exposure in the field. Between the 27th February, 1874, and 22nd May following, six officers of the 1st West India Regiment, then stationed on the Gold Coast, were stated to have died, and seven to have been invalided home. One European sergeant died and four were invalided. On the 24th March Colonel Maxwell wrote to England that the sickness had increased to such an extent among the troops up country that he was obliged to replace them by Houssas, who, of the irregular native forces, appeared to be the least sickly. Sir John Glover reached Odumassic on the 28th January, after an eighteen days' rapid and difficult march from the Volta, partly over a mountainous country, with 350 Houssas and 400 Yorubas—an allied tribe. His sick list only amounted to 48, a ratio of 1,298 per 1,000 per annum. It is difficult to say positively in what ratio one class of troops excel the others for hard work and exposure, for each class appears to have its special advantages, and are evidently supplemental the one to the other. The natives for a prolonged period, if clothed, housed, fed, and disciplined as irregulars, will undoubtedly stand a malarial climate and a tropical sun better than white troops, as they are not subject to the more severe forms of malarial diseases or yellow fever, which last affection would put a European force in a very short time *hors de combat* if it broke out amongst them. Neither do the former class of troops *die* in the *same proportion* when attacked with paludal fever as the Europeans. They are also less costly and more easily fed—two very important *desiderata*. Trained, well disciplined, and properly led, they would always follow their officers and stand by them; but they appear to want that *elan* and contempt of danger which will make the average European soldier face a position under a fire which would cause the natives to stand still.

These facts were strikingly exemplified during the progress of hostilities. At Essiaman the Houssas showed great excitement until got under control. This batch was composed of very young troops. Russell's Regiment, was composed of six companies:—1. Houssas; 2. Sierra Leone Men; 3. Mumfords; 4. Winnebahs; 5. Opobos; 6. Annamaboes. Wood's of four companies:—1. Cape Coast Volunteers; 2. Elminas; 3. Kossoos; 4. Bonny Men. The first of these regiments had been at first unsteady under fire, but afterwards quite the reverse. The Opobos, at Ordahsu, dropped flat on the road, and immediately commenced a wasteful and ill-directed fire at the bush, the same process being repeated at every few paces, until the European troops came up to lead the column. A similar state of things was more than once observed elsewhere, showing the necessity for white allies, if success was to be calculated upon.

As fighting units the Fantee levies were, as a rule, most unreliable, especially prone to panic, and so very dangerous to officers who commanded them in action. Entirely wanting in dash, they were only with great difficulty prevented from decamping upon the least excuse. A few companies had some faint idea of the manual exercise, and of forming fours, firing and loading their pieces, beyond which they scarcely advanced during the continuance of the war. The Winnebahs were of fine physique, as were the Assins and some other tribes. With prolonged training and discipline they might make fair native soldiers, as evidenced by former experience in the Gold Coast Corps, but as extemporized irregulars they must be ever worthless. To individual officers the Fantee servant was, as a rule, faithful and honest, and on some very trying occasions behaved extremely well. In fact these people presented all the features and characteristics of the least noble and more degraded of these two great African families, the pure breed of the aboriginal and typical African, characterized by a low cast, prognathous face, retreating forehead, a defective *morale*, destructive power, and a love for a mere sensual and animal existence. Elevated by education and discipline, as was the case with the Cape Coast Volunteers and Sir John Glover's companies of native Christians, they were evidently capable of doing much good service. The Cape Coast Volunteers did very well, and showed a patriotic spirit and eagerness for the fray while in the bush. Several members of this corps served in it at a great pecuniary sacrifice and much inconvenience. Previous to their departure from Cape Coast they had been drilled regularly on Connor's Hill by the Sergeant-Major of the 2nd West India Regiment, to which corps they were attached, at their own request, throughout the remainder of the war. They were also drilled and paraded very frequently while at Mansue. The Assins were, on the whole, good scouts, and the Kossoos, or Mendy Men, drawn from the Plantain Islands, at the mouth of the Sherborough, and from the confines of Sierra Leone, showed much dash and contempt of the enemy, as they did on a former occasion when our allies in the Quiah Expedition of 1861—discarding rifles, they rushed with much spirit into the bush, frightening their foes with their horrid yells. To these were added, afterwards, the Opobos and Bonny Men, the latter partially disciplined and accustomed to the use of the rifle by Captain Hopkins, our Consul in the Bights. They were described as steady, well-conducted working men, wearing a head-dress of monkey skin, which made them look grotesque and fierce. As the war progressed, the *morale* of these native regiments improved much; their assaults and charges were delivered with far more pluck, and they were more eager to take part in the various skirmishes, rushing forward instead of halting as before. An officer of the Rifle Brigade gave an amusing sketch in Colborn of the advance of the Kossoos and Bonny Men at Amoaful:— "Their advance up the height to their front was a most amusing sight. They danced about and flourished their cutlasses with savage delight." Previous to this their chief had strutted up and down in front of the line, crowing like a cock, in derision of the Ashantees, one of whom, shot in a tree, was set upon and cut to pieces scarcely had he touched the ground. In addition to their fighting duties these men were employed a good deal upon fatigue work, such as erecting huts, clearing roads, &c., in the advance; they also carried with them ten days' provisions, in addition to their clothing, weapons, and accoutrements. They were well looked after by the officers who commanded the different companies into which they were divided (a most important point to be recollected in all future wars undertaken under similar circumstances), received their food regularly, were made as comfortable as possible, and consequently got on much better than the carriers who, unorganized, and little looked to until towards the close of the operations, came to frequent misfortune.

The Houssas and men of the West Indian regiments were the more regular coloured troops, and also the best drilled. The former, Mahomedans, were quiet and orderly in barracks, very fond of games of chance and of their *dames d'amour*, suffered little from sickness, and soon picked up the irregular drill and discipline required of them. Under fire, however, they were sometimes wild and excitable, as formerly noticed, wasting their ammunition, which, previous to the commencement of a fight, they removed from their pouches and placed in the fez, the rim of which, when turned up, retained it in *situ*. Much ammunition was in this way lost. The men of the West Indian regiments were trained more in accordance with our pre-conceived notions of military discipline; they were steady in action, and followed their officers, and liked those who treated them with firmness, kindness, and consideration. Still they were constant grumblers, noisy and talkative on the march, disliked African service and surroundings, and looked forward to a return to the West Indies much as the European thought of a homeward voyage. "This country no good for we," was a frequent expression. Although clothed, fed, and treated in every respect as white troops, their social ideas were entirely those of the Negro. Upon their African *confreres* they, however, looked with supreme contempt. As compared with the Houssas they were, as a corps, expensive—not in themselves, for they would get on upon a very simple diet, but owing to their being officered and supplied as regular, not irregular, regiments. While the Houssa received one shilling and three pence a day, from which he provided his own subsistence and not very elaborate kit, the West Indian soldier had to be supplied with his rations after European fashion, necessitating a large and expensive administration, was subject to a variety of complex regulations, and obliged to wear full dress uniform, which might have well been dispensed with, with the effect of increasing his inefficiency. The semi-semiatic negro, Houssa, or Yoruba slept upon a mat, lived chiefly upon vegetables, had strong sensual appetites, gratified without being incontinent, carried his belongings on his head, and was, comparatively speaking, free from *impedimenta*. The West Indian soldier had become so accustomed to have all his wants supplied, that he grumbled immediately if his usual requirements were not at once forthcoming. The Fanti Police were chiefly employed as runners, getting over distances at about the rate of five miles an hour: they also garrisoned towns and small posts. The party of the corps at Dunquah behaved very well. Nothing showed so much the discipline and steadiness of the white soldiers of a good regiment than the small expenditure of ammunition by the 42nd at Amoaful, noticed in General Orders subsequently. The best fighting force for such a climate would appear to be Europeans in reserve or support of disciplined and irregular native auxiliaries, who should prepare for and cover their advance, and save them from all unnecessary exposure in the bush. For ordinary Coast warfare, disciplined and irregular native regiments, well officered and led by Europeans.

CHAPTER V.

DRESS, EQUIPMENT, AND WEIGHTS CARRIED.

These varied with the corps. The Fanti auxiliaries carried little during the active operations, and wore less. A rifle, or flint musket, knife, waist-belt, not unlike the old *bandolier*, carrying together ammunition and fibre, used as wadding. A goat-skin round the loins, and a red velvet ribbon encircling the neck, to show their nationality, constituted their outfit. Some had, in addition, a white or blue cloth to rap round them at night: a bundle of plantains, carried on the head, provided for internal wants. In 1863, 64 these people carried packages made up in 60 lb. each; in 1873, 74 the maximum weight was 57 lb. They were capable of carrying for themselves a weight equal to 100 lb., but would rarely allow employers to load them with more than 70 lb. The Awoonahs complained of the weight of the kegs of salt meat, which weighed over 70 lb. The men of the irregular regiments wore strong white canvas frocks, difficult to tear, but very soon soiled. This was their only attempt at a uniform, the head-gear and nether garment being of all shapes and colours. Their arms and accoutrements consisted of a rifle, cutlass, black pouch, and waist-belt, sixty rounds of ammunition, a canvas haversack, and ten days' provisions: no shoes or leggings. The Houssas went also barefoot, except when in full dress, when they wore white stockings and shoes. They wore on ordinary occasions a blue baft breeches, loose, and stopping short at the knee, and a shirt of a similar material, over which was pulled a blue serge Zouave waistcoat, embroidered with red braid: a red fez completed their uniform. They carried a breech-loading rifle, bayonet, pouch, waist-belt and pouch-belt; from the former, on the march, was suspended knives, daggers, brass cooking-pots, and other articles of *vertu*. The bedding and kit, rolled up in a mat, was carried on the head. Their appearance, when thus singularly accoutred, was most amusing. The West Indian soldiers went to the wars in a red fez, white duck smock-frock, grey flannel shirt, blue serge Zouave breeches, brown stockings, shoes, and white gaiters, the handsome full dress being discarded for the time being. They carried on the march a great coat, waterproof sheet, blanket, tin water bottle, haversack and three days' provisions, belts, pouches, and sixty rounds of ammunition, breech-loader, and bayonet. The regulation uniform of the Cape Coast Volunteers was a black serge frock, bound with scarlet, black breeches, stockings, shoes or elastic boots, and helmets. In practice they wore very much as they liked. The Fanti Police had as a uniform a blue baft frock and breeches, the latter coming only to the knee. The Kroomen acted chiefly as carriers, for which purpose they were eminently fitted.

During the earlier operations of the war south of the Prah the Marines carried a haversack, with provisions, a water bottle, rifle, accoutrements, and 70 rounds of ammunition, wore a wicker-work helmet, well padded with wadding, and protected by a white linen cover and puggaree: the sides and back of this helmet came well over the temples, eyes, and nape of the neck. A ventilating rim encircled the head, and a small ventilator at the top allowed the egress of the heated air. Although somewhat heavy, these helmets were excellent sun repellents. The clothing consisted of the ordinary blue Navy serge patrol jacket and trousers, socks, and Blucher boots.

The men of the European regiments who advanced to the Prah on the 1st January were quite differently equipped. Each of them had a puggaree of karkic brown, a grey helmet, lighter than the one worn by the Marines, a blue veil to filter malaria in its transit to the lungs, and keep off mosquitoes, two grey tweed Norfolk jackets, one pair of grey tweed trousers, and a pair of dark ones for bush work; two flannel shirts, white and soft, and which in the washing shrunk a good deal; wooden Piedmontese-pattern canteen or water bottle, clasp knife, and lanyard; two towels, two pairs of socks, a handkerchief, pair of brown canvas leggings, two pairs of boots, nightcap, haversack, canteen, great coat, blanket, and a canvas bag, and *tente d'abri* between every three men. On the march each soldier wore and carried

        Helmet, puggaree, and blue veil,
        Norfolk jacket, trousers, leggings, boots, socks,
        Flannel shirt, cholera belt, handkerchief,
        Haversack, clasp knife, pocket filter,
        Bayonet and short rifle,

found of more advantage in the bush, and of less weight. The surplus kit of each man was placed in his squad bag; three of these and a *tente d'abri* were rolled up in a waterproof sheet, weighing, with the sticks, 57 ℔., and carried by an attendant native. One pair of boots sufficed for the seven weeks' campaign, only a few surplus ones being carried with each regiment. Blankets were not carried beyond the Prah. Of the foregoing the belts and straps were alone complained of by the men, because, as one of them wrote, "preventing the free action of the limbs for easy walking in any country," an impediment stated to have been "felt the more the warmer it was," a complaint easy to understand when made in the tropics, where the least imprisonment of the limbs, or pressure on the chest, or excessive weight, prevents active movements being carried on with any degree of comfort. To move freely and with ease a European should only wear his helmet, flannel shirt, sash, breeches, and socks, and have all his *impedimenta* carried by a faithful attendant of tried valour. Stick in hand, and revolver in belt, he can trudge on at ease. A private of the Rifle Brigade who was under treatment in the King's Military Infirmary, Dublin, complained of the weight of ammunition he had been obliged to carry in Ashantee, which he felt especially when symptoms of dysentery and pain occurred. On taking the waist-belt off, these were somewhat relieved. The grey tweed suit, of light texture, worn by the officers and men of the European regiments, and afterwards by the 1st West, appeared to answer its purpose, the only objection to the colour being that it became soiled so soon; when clean it had the advantage of all light colours, viz., that of being non-absorptive of the heat rays; very similar in texture to blue serge, it was equally well adapted for the climate. Suits of the latter material were mostly worn by officers who had been accustomed to serve in West Africa; also by the sailors and Marines. This serge washed well, and did not soil soon; of the two, the lighter colour looked the best. Porosity and lightness are the chief points in regard to the texture of clothing in a West African climate. It must be not too thin, except when worn over a flannel shirt, as the cold sea or land breezes are apt to strike upon and chill the perspiring cutaneous surface when not sufficiently protected, and cause a perceptible sensation of cold, a fertile cause of rheumatism, fever, and dysentery. I always wore on the march a marine helmet, substituting in the shade of the forest or while resting, a red fez, which made also an excellent night cap, a light-textured blue serge patrol jacket, breeches of the same material, cotton drawers, coming to the knee, a soft flannel shirt, thrown open at the neck, red sash, thick worsted socks, and laced boots, the socks being pulled over the lower end of the breeches; carrying, in addition, a handkerchief, pocket filter, small revolver, twenty rounds of ammunition, and a silk umbrella. The latter is always most useful, as it assists in protecting the head from the rays of a powerful tropical sun, and in a heavy shower keeps the upper half of the body at least, dry and unchilled.

ACTUAL WEIGHT OF THE ABOVE.

	lb.	oz.
Helmet, well padded, puggaree, and white cap cover	1	8
Umbrella, green silk	0	12
Thin blue serge patrol jacket	1	0
Thin blue serge breeches	1	0
Soft flannel shirt	1	0

	lb.	oz.
Loose thin cotton drawers, coming to the knee, red cotton sash and handkerchief	0	8
Thick worsted socks	0	4
Boots, laced, strong	2	8
Revolver and strap	1	0
20 rounds of ammunition	0	8
Waist-belt	0	8
Pocket filter and tin cup	0	4
TOTAL	10	12

My experience is that no greater weight can be carried with comfort in a climate, the temperature of which averages from 80° to 90° Fahrenheit in the shade, and 156° in the sun, and which is at the same time highly charged with moisture. But if you really want comfort you must hand over your coat, revolver, ammunition, and umbrella to an attendant, and march stick in hand in a flannel shirt, sash, and breeches. In this costume the weights are reduced to 7½ lb., which is felt to be, in practice, a lighter and far more agreeable load to carry. Hence, to walk with pleasure in African forest paths, the traveller must do so without a coat, and only in his soft and warm flannel shirt, weighing about a pound, open at the neck and turned up at the wrists, which, with a helmet, broad sash to protect the abdomen, thick socks, and fairly strong laced boots, with good soles and soft uppers, is the dress *par excellence*. The comfort of such a free and easy uniform is indescribable. When resting, or during a shower, or in chilly weather, the serge jacket should be put on immediately, the helmet removed, and a light fez or Glengeary substituted—the first to prevent chill, and the latter to relieve the brow from unnecessary weight. In a word, the neck must be free, and the movements of the chest and limbs unconstrained. It will be found, then, that in proportion as you load the body will be the rate of progression and distance got over.

In a very hot sun an umbrella becomes almost a necessity, even when wearing a helmet. Umbrellas were found most useful by the European non-commissioned officers while superintending the preliminary preparatory works. As already said, with a large and light umbrella, a shower is, comparatively speaking, harmless, the legs being, at most, drenched. It, however, protects better from a heavy downpour than drifting rain. In addition to the foregoing, an officer's servant should carry on the march a canvas haversack and cloth waterproof cloak, a tin water bottle of cold tea, or slightly acidulated and sweetened lemon juice.

In Sir John Glover's eighteen consecutive days' march from the Volta to Obogoo, in Ashantee, about 160 direct miles over, in greater part, a rugged and mountainous country, difficult to traverse, his fighting men crossed the Prah on the twelfth day, carried on their heads, in addition to their own arms, ammunition and food, 400 cases of Snider ammunition, and some 1,900 packages of rockets, spare arms, pork, bread, rice, gin, and rum, without which last stimulants it was stated that they would have never reached their destination. His carriers carried on their heads the seven-pounder guns: this was a remarkable and almost unique instance of hard work in a tropical climate.

The following was my reserve kit—about the minimum a European officer can do with, except upon an emergency or forced march:—

	lb.	oz.
2 white cotton towels, 1 rough towel	2	0
Sponge bag, sponge, 2 tooth brushes, 1 nail brush	0	8
Hair brushes and comb	0	8
4 pieces of soap	0	8
8 candles	1	0
2 boxes of matches, 1 box of pins, 1 box of pens, 2 quires of paper and envelopes, 2 pencils	0	4
A soldier's blacking and polish brush	0	4
2 tins blacking	1	0
Small looking glass, candlestick, clasp knife, scissors	0	4
1 pair of laced boots, 1 pair of slippers	2	8
Soldier's tin canteen, packed with spare boot laces, darning needles, 2 reels of thread, needles, a few balls of blue for washing white clothing, &c.	1	8
1 tin plate, 1 soup plate, 2 knives, 2 forks, 1 tea and 1 table spoon, enamel cup and saucer, wine tumbler	1	0
Pocket charcoal filter, case and cord	0	8
2 pairs of merino and 2 pairs of thick worsted socks	0	8
4 handkerchiefs, 4 pairs of thin, loose, cotton drawers, coming to the knee	1	0
2 thick cotton vests	1	0
2 spare soft flannel shirts	1	8
2 thin cotton night shirts	1	0
Thin flannel jacket and pajamas	1	0
Spare white helmet cover, puggaree, and cap	0	8
Spare serge or blue flannel patrol jacket and breeches	2	0
Note book and everlasting ink bottle	0	8
Two pairs small cotton sheets, 2 pillow covers	5	8
A rug, or pair of light blankets	4	0
Soft hair pillow	2	8
Waterproof sheet, with four eyelet holes	2	8
Regulation black waterproof cloak	4	0
Odds and ends	1	0
Black canvas leather-bound portmanteau, 27 inches long, 9 inches high, 13 inches broad. Cost, 25/-	10	0
Total	50	0

Six to eight hammock bearers usually accompanied each officer when travelling on the Gold Coast, from two to four being required for relays. One would carry the portmanteau; the rug or blanket and waterproof cloak being wrapped up in the waterproof sheet on the top, the pillow being left in the hammock, which, at night, slung upon two forked sticks, would make by no means an uncomfortable resting place, when no other was obtainable. With a waterproof sheet properly adjusted over the frame of the awning, it was impervious to rain.

Within doors on the Gold Coast, sufficiently thick white cotton vests, arms cut off above the elbow, and thin loose cotton drawers coming to the knee, not woven in one piece, but specially cut and made, and fastening with a button in front; cotton socks, undressed soft leather or canvas shoes, a print calico shirt, light flannel or tweed Norfolk jacket and trousers, with a broad cotton sash, was the best costume. For out of doors a sufficiently thick, but soft flannel shirt, cotton drawers, grey serge Norfolk jacket, with broad plaits and belt, small stand-up collar, hooking in front, sleeves buttoning in at the wrist, knickerbockers or trousers to match, merino socks, comfortable laced boots, with broad soles and heels, helmet and puggaree, was more suitable. Collars are a mistake, and are scarcely necessary when a beard is worn. The jacket should not weigh more than $1\frac{1}{4}$ lb.; the breeches 1 lb. The mess jacket and vest should be devoid of all padding, and should be made of the thinnest cloth, and the uniform pants of a light-textured Oxford mixture. Leggings are an unnecessary incumbrance: long boots, coming to the knee, are far better of the two. These long boots require to be constantly and carefully cleaned. After each march they should be wiped dry, and well greased, otherwise they become too hard to get on or off afterwards. For myself I have always preferred the lace boot, with hooks coming half way down, as easiest to get off and on; thick socks, pulled over the lower end of the breeches, answering all the purposes of gaiters. The chief points to recollect are these: that the chest and neck must be free, and the texture of the clothing sufficiently warm and porous to guard against the chills arising from the cold damp winds of the Coast: nothing can ever supersede flannel for this purpose. When cotton is worn, the chill under such circumstances is immediately perceptible, especially on the heights, where the wind is naturally felt in its greatest force.

Belts impede the free motion of the thorax and abdomen, more especially in the tropics: with them a free and full inspiration and expiration is next to impossible; the proper oxidation of the blood becomes imperfectly performed, and a rapid accumulation of effete materials takes place in the circulatory fluid: early exhaustion during a march, and a pre-disposition to sun attacks, is the result. A European, to fight and march in such a climate, should be attended by an esquire, as was the knight of old, to carry all but his short rifle, ammunition, a few biscuits, and his water bottle; even his coat should be discarded. Only those who have done a hard day's march, with *impedimenta*, in Western Africa, can form any idea of the discomfort, or the feeling of relief, ease, and freedom when circumstances admit of these articles being transferred to a willing slave.

Our West Indian regiments are far too heavily clothed and accoutred; at least one-half the articles which they carry might be dispensed with. With natives the more we approach the actual reality of their former life and instincts in this respect, the more effective do we make them when trained soldiers. The French are far in advance of us on these points. The Zouave clothing of their Tirailleurs Senegalais is much lighter than that worn by our Zouave Corps, without losing any of its distinctive character. The objections to the dress of our West Indian regiments are these:—

(*a*) Excessive number of articles.
(*b*) Unnecessary weight.
(*c*) Unsuitability of material.

The West Indian soldier's dress should be confined to the following articles of uniform: a thin white serge and loose patrol jacket, or a scarlet one if preferred, without a collar, but with regimental buttons and shoulder straps; blue serge Zouave breeches, with a yellow stripe, but of a material far lighter than now provided; long brown stockings, white gaiters, and shoes of soft, untanned leather, as formerly used by the Dutch African troops; a grey flannel shirt, not nearly so thick or cumbersome as the one he is now compelled to wear; a red fez, regimental tassel, and white turban. The fez alone is a scarcely sufficient protection against the sun's rays for men whose artificial barrack life keeps them so much indoors. Headache was not unfrequently complained of by men of the 2nd West India Regiment after long marches in the sun during the late operations on the Gold Coast; so was the thick white serge jacket when worn. Off duty shoes and stockings might be dispensed with. On the march in the bush they were often not used: it was by no means uncommon to see a private of one of these regiments trudging along with his shoes slung to his rifle. Except in full dress, shoes were never worn by men of the Houssa Corps. A broad red cotton cummerbund should be worn instead of a cholera belt, and a strap and buckle might replace braces for retaining the breeches above the hips. The Zouave jacket and waistcoat of the French African Tirailleur is in one piece, and much lighter in texture than the one worn by our black troops. The dress, such as I have described, would, without being unbecoming, be far more useful than the present one, which, in addition to other evils, is unnecessarily expensive. Owing to the nature of their training and duties, the West Indian troops were scarcely better adapted to carry weights on their heads than their white comrades. This was evidenced by their coming into Prashue from Assin Yancoomassie quite as much prostrated as the latter, when they attempted a similar unaccustomed feat. The hair should be always worn short in the tropics, because conducing to comfort and cleanliness.

CHAPTER VI.

FOOD SUPPLY.

It can never be forgotten that as all the force manifested by animated beings is originally furnished to them as food, an army must march upon its belly. An adequate quantity of food is required not only to supply the daily wants of the system, but as a reserve to draw upon during emergencies, and at those moments when it becomes temporarily poor in quality or deficient in quantity. In this form the hydrocarbons furnish the bulk of the acting force, and are the fuel of the body *par excellence;* the nitrogenized elements evolving the manifestations of energy rather than providing the material convertible into force. In the normal condition of man the production of energy is altogether regulated by the daily amount of food taken and assimilated.

The portion of the Gold Coast where the military operations of 1873, 74 were carried on was singularly barren of those important commissariat supplies so essential to an army's existence. Fish at certain seasons were abundant; thousands of herrings being caught on the banks some fifteen miles distant, during the months of September and October. From fifteen to thirty, according to the take, could be bought for 3*d.*, the lowest coin circulating at Cape Coast. Coarser fish, such as sharks and rays, were consumed largely by the natives. The richer and more delicate varieties, which frequented the mouths of the more northern rivers and creeks, were apparently wanting, as they were never to be seen in the market. In the larger inland streams, such as the Sweet River, Okoe, &c., prawns were caught in numbers in conical cane baskets. When boiled and curried with rice they were very palatable. Larger and smaller land snails were in much request by the Fantees and allied tribes, who made them into a soup with pounded and boiled plantains. A few wild hogs and antelopes lived in the forest, which appeared on the march almost devoid of animal life. Fowl, goats, sheep, small eggs, kankie, or fermented meal; Indian corn, limes, oranges, sweet potatoes, yams, bread, rice in small quantities, peppers, smoked fish, and a few other African dainties could be purchased in the market. None of these articles were, however, very abundant. Beef was imported from Sierra Leone, and turkeys from Accra. With a little trouble, salad, tomatoes, cucumbers, radishes, and shalots might be grown from seed on the hills, if well watered, and shaded from the sun by matting. As a supply of fresh anti-scorbutic vegetables, of a kind to which the European palate was accustomed, was all important, this trouble should become a necessity. The wretched meat styled mutton cost one shilling a pound. In consequence of the poverty of the local supplies, most of the residents relied upon the steamers for a periodical replenishment of their stores with Madeira potatoes, and onions, and preserved provisions, without which they could have scarcely lived in any degree of comfort. An English sheep, or piece of beef preserved in ice, were rare and much sought after dainties. The difference in flavour between the flesh of these last and that obtainable on the Gold Coast was remarkable, and distinctly perceptible to the palate, the richness and bouquet of the one contrasting with the poverty and leanness of the other. The officers' mess was chiefly supplied from the steamers and from Accra, the latter station eighty miles distant. Were it not for these sources of supply they could have scarcely kept up a mess at all. As the Ashantees had destroyed all the neighbouring farms, the natives were in a wretched plight for food. Just before my arrival in September, a cargo of rice had been sent out by the Government to stay their dire necessity; fowls and corn were also being imported from Lagos.

During the preliminary operations of the war the native forces and Marines were chiefly supplied with salt rations, varied by a little fresh beef, sent periodically from Sierra Leone, and supplemented by soups, cocoa, tea, sugar, and raisins, from the stores of the squadron. Shortly afterwards large supplies of Australian tinned meats and soups were sent by Government to the Colonial authorities, from whose Commissary they were drawn by requisition and repayment. Upon food of this nature the earlier work of the campaign was performed, at that period of the year which former experience had led Lord Kimberley to direct that operations should not be undertaken, "which would involve the exposure of officers and men to climate in the interior at any considerable distance from their resources." It was upon food of little variety, cooked in the most primitive fashion, deficient in fresh vegetables, which, scarce at all times in the vicinity of the Fort, were then scarcely obtainable, and consequently with little to stimulate the flagging appetite of the men, or to render the little they had sufficiently palatable and nutritive in a climate where good, fresh, abundant, and easily assimilated food was undoubtedly the "staff of life," and the great *desideratum*, that the arduous work at this time was performed. That so many lived through it was due alone to the care and attention bestowed upon them immediately they fell ill. Fanti land was one of those countries where the native population relied almost exclusively upon a vegetable diet, deficient in those nitrogenous food principles necessary to form a strong and vigorous population. As in all similar cases, the people were inactive, indolent, defective in intellectual endowments, and the easy prey to epidemic diseases when they occurred. Indian corn made into an acid, fermented mess, called kankie; plantains, smoked fish, and a large land bulamus or snail was their chief food. Their mode of cooking and dining was characteristic and primitive. The plantains culled from the neighbouring bush, were at first peeled, next pounded in a wooden mortar, and afterwards boiled. The mess was then turned into a large pot of snail soup, round which our savage auxiliaries squatted, each thrusting in a hand and devouring his portion as fast as he could swallow it, until the prominent abdomen and indolent expression indicated satiety. A *siesta* was the *dessert* to this luxurious repast. The Ashantees while in the Protectorate lived in a very similar manner. Towards the end their slaves dug up the roots of the wild yam, adding earth from the ant hills to increase the bulk, so badly off were they for food. Rice was chiefly used by the imported irregulars.

The following scale of ration was allowed to native levies in the field, the same scale being afterwards applied to men of the West Indian regiments when the paucity of carriers compelled a reduction of the food supply borne on their heads to a minimum. The men were given a money allowance to make up for the deficiency:—

> Rice 1½ lb., or biscuit 1 lb.
> Salt meat ½ lb., or equivalent of
> Preserved meat.

Pork was not issued to Houssas or Mahomedans: men of the Carrier Corps were allowed 1¼ lb. of rice in addition to their pay. The non-appreciation of the regulation ration by men of the West Indian regiments was shown by the fact of there having been a regular trade at Elmina and Cape Coast between them and the natives, to whom the ration was sold, and some other food purchased for the money received.

The ration sanctioned by the Right Honourable The Secretary of State for War, for issue to the regular forces employed in the West African Expedition, while in the field, free of all stoppage, was as below:—

BREAD	{ Soft bread, 1½ lb. Or Biscuit, 1¼ lb. Or Flour, 1 lb.
MEAT	{ Salt Pork, 1½ lb. Or Beef, 1½ lb. Or Fresh Meat, 1¼ lb. Or Preserved Meat, 1 lb.

WEST AFRICAN CAMPAIGNS. 81

VEGETABLES { Rice, 2 oz.
Or Peas, 2 oz.
Or Preserved Vegetables, 4 oz.
Or Fresh Vegetables, 1 ℔.

TEA AND CONDIMENTS { Tea, 3¼ oz., Sugar, 3 oz.
Salt, ½ oz., Pepper, $\tfrac{3}{16}$ oz.

Half an ounce of cocoa was afterwards substituted for ¼ oz. of tea, in order to allow of the men having an early cup of cocoa previous to their commencing their morning march. The estimated value of the European ration at Prashue was 2s. 5¾d.; of the native ration 9d. The nutritive value of the following ingredients of the above scale, viz., 19 oz. of fresh beef (5 oz. deducted from 24 oz. for bone), 24 oz. of bread, 2 oz. of rice, 3 oz. of sugar, ½ oz. of cocoa, and ½ oz. of tea, would be:—

Albuminates	5·96 ounces.
Fats	2·20 ,,
Carbo-hydrates	16·83 ,,
Salts	0·74 ,,
Water	24·23 ,,
TOTAL	49·96 ,,

Or 25·73 ounces of water-free food.

Slightly in excess of Moleschott's standard diet for a male European of average height and weight, in moderate work, but less than the average water-free food required for an adult man in very laborious work, such as a soldier in the field.

Ashanti ration	25·73 ounces.	
Moleschott	22·866 ,,	
Soldier in the field	26·700 ,,	minimum (Parkes.)

The Ashanti ration contained less albuminates, fats, and saline matter than the latter; it exceeded Moleschott in carbo-hydrates, albuminates, and was in this last respect on an equality with the minimum required for a soldier on active service. It was more of a respiratory than flesh-forming ration. The 1½ ℔. of rice given to the Native Carrier Corps contained:—

Albuminates	1·20 ounces.
Fats	0·19 ,,
Carbo-hydrates	19·96 ,,
Salts	0·12 ,,
Water	2·40 ,,
TOTAL	23·87 ,,

G

21·17 ounces of water-free food, upon which, supplemented by plantains when obtainable, and a little smoked fish, they did much hard work. The amount of rice alone was scarcely enough for their capacious appetites, bulk being with them essential, probably owing to the easy digestibility of boiled rice (one hour according to Beaumont), which fact may also explain the feeling of emptiness so soon felt after an early meal of rice and milk had been partaken of, or the latter and oatmeal porridge. While on the subject of war rations, it appears to me that the field rations of the English soldier in the reign of Edward VI., viz., 2 lb. of meat, 1 lb. of bread, and 20 oz. of light French wine, containing in active principles, not calculating the claret, and making the usual allowance for bone—

Albuminates	5·18 ounces.
Fats	2·42 ,,
Carbo-hydrates	7·87 ,,
Salts	0·61 ,,
Water	25·90 ,,
Total	41·98 ,,

was an excellent one, for the wine made up to a great extent for the deficiency in carbo-hydrates, and added important elements—the antiscorbutic and the mild alcoholic stimulant. One pound of fresh vegetables and a few condiments would have added all that could be desired.

Taking the military operations as a whole, the issue of salt, fresh, and tinned rations was pretty evenly balanced in quantity. Bullocks, obtained by great exertions, were driven to the front in sufficient numbers to allow of the white troops having fresh meat at least twice a week. In the first phase of the war, during the most unhealthy season, the drying up of the rains, in September, October, and November, this luxury was not obtainable, preserved Australian beef or mutton, or salt pork or beef having been alone issued. Of Australian tinned meats men soon tired: they palled upon the appetite, the stomach refused to receive them, and at the most they were only advisable as a change once or twice a week. They were of course preferable to salt pork or old salted beef, for the obvious reason, that when properly cooked they were more digestible, less likely to cause thirst or remove the potash salts of the blood, and so lead to scurvy. Yet under certain circumstances they were stated to have conduced to the production of the latter disease among the men of the 23rd on board the Tamar, who not liking the food, did not consume their ration, and consequently starved themselves. Somewhat in the same way that men, in their desire to accumulate their savings in the Navy, instead of absorbing them into their system in the shape of food, have suffered similarly. When preserved

Australian meats are used, cooking becomes, if possible, of more importance than before, for, by the addition of a few savoury articles, it may be served up in a far more palatable form. I have seen this food at one station sent up to the table by a good native cook with an excellent and appetizing *bouquet* and flavour; while at another, some miles further on, it was turned into the dish, a mass of stringy fibre, devoid alike of taste and odour. In the former case yam, nicely boiled, and afterwards mashed with some butter and fried in small cakes, was an admirable addition. Salt rations came naturally to the Marines and sailors who were accustomed to their constant use; they consequently got on better and did not suffer so much from the change of diet as the soldier, who thinks nothing is equal to fresh beef or mutton. The Australian meat was equally disliked by the men of the West Indian regiments, who preferred pork as an article of diet.

In the middle of the last century, Donald Munro recommended that cattle, butchers, and bakers should accompany every army in the field, in order that the men should have fresh meat and bread daily. He appears to me to have hit off the great desideratum to their health and efficiency. Nothing in the end can compensate for these two ingredients of a soldier's ration. Over driven or badly fed cattle are tough, and occasionally engender disease, when the flesh is eaten while they are suffering from the effects of over fatigue; exemplified in the Austro-Italian campaign of 1799, when epidemic typhus broke out amongst the badly housed and over-marched men, subsisting upon cattle scarcely better than themselves; but in bush expeditions there is no reason why this should take place. Cattle should be brought together in sufficient numbers to be within easy reach at the onset of war, in order that the necessity for sending after them here, there, and everywhere during its continuance may be avoided. Before the march of the troops to the Prah, an attempt had been made to do this, oxen having been collected at the Salt Pond, but, however, in wholly insufficient numbers. In the last campaign against the Dufflas, it was found more economical to drive cattle with the troops than to send up preserved meats from Calcutta, as the former carried themselves and required no transport. The Sepoys were supplied from time to time with sheep and goats in addition to their ration of grain. The general idea carried out in the Gold Coast was not dissimilar to the precautions undertaken by Monk, when he entered the mountains of Scotland in 1654—to the English at the time almost as great a *terra incognita* as Ashanti was to us in later days. As he advanced into the Highlands, he secured all posts susceptible of defence, in which he left small garrisons; establishing at Leith, St. Johnstown, and Inverness, large magazines of fodder and biscuit, from which he drew the supplies for his small posts. He thus had all the requisite

G 2

stores at all times within his reach. Making his soldiers take provisions for *six days*, and burdened with only their light baggage, he was enabled to penetrate into retreats hitherto considered inaccessible by the Highlanders. His marches were short, and he almost always reached by midday the place at which he intended to encamp. With but little variation in details, history repeated itself in our bush campaign of but yesterday. Cold meat followed him always in abundance, and was a favourite article of diet among officers and men. In the Duflla expedition, a depôt was formed at Harmatti, and stocked with five months' provisions. Supplies for eight days always accompanied the troops advancing; officers and men carried two days' rations each, and fifteen days' rations for the whole force was kept a day or two in the rear. In Peninsular days, according to General Mercer, it was generally believed that the more flesh a horse carried on entering a campaign, the more he had to lose, and the longer he would be able to bear privation, and also that an opportunity should never be lost of feeding man and horse. The first we never attend to: we are content to increase the ration in the field, but not before.

Much of the rice sent up country in the Gold Coast in 25 lb. boxes lined with tinfoil, fermented and spoiled from the great damp and moist heat of the latter rains. The desicated potatoes appeared to keep better; they had a peculiar taste, but were not unpalatable when nicely cooked, and made into small cakes, lightly fried in butter or the fat of the preserved meats. The tins of the latter, when cleaned out, were found useful for many purposes, such as cooking, boiling small quantities of water, &c. The sugar and tea were sent to the front in small square wooden boxes, lined with tin, and hermetically sealed: the quality of both was excellent. Towards the close of the operations preserved sausage and cheese were also made use of. The biscuit was dark-coloured, hard, and little palatable to those accustomed to fresh wheaten bread. On all future occasions it should be not only of a finer quality, but be packed in hermetically sealed tins of moderate size, by which means it would retain its freshness and crispness; packed in bags it soon dries, becomes broken, and crumbles into dust. Dr Home mentioned to me that in the Crimea they found it a very good plan to steep the biscuit over night, and fry it afterwards in butter or fat on the following morning. On a few occasions the Australian beef was made into soup either to start upon in the early morning, or as a restorative after a long march, when more solid food was not cared for or tolerated by the stomach. The men of the West Indian regiments appeared to prefer coffee to tea: to the use of the former they had been more accustomed. It has now become quite evident that if rapid marches are to be made by soldiers, and that if the service in which they are engaged is to be short and to the point, much of the *impedimenta* formerly sent with them must be sacrificed, and the *number* and *variety* of articles reduced to a minimum, not only in order to attain the former purpose, but to avoid confusion. Cattle present this great advantage that they *carry themselves*, and that much of the offal may be made into nutritious soups, stews, &c., and that with a diet of fresh meat scorbutic symptoms are less common. Next in portability come Liebig's essence, which with a few additions can be made to fulfil all the purposes of a complete diet. The extract kept well on the Gold Coast, and on more than one occasion I found it, after a long march, when made into a warm drink, restorative to a degree scarcely to be believed. Mixed with port wine and preserved milk, or made into a soup with pea flour, it became highly nutritious. A few ounce jars of Liebig's essence, packages of pea flour, and tablets of compressed vegetables, are so easily carried in a hammock, they should never be left behind. The three most portable and easily carried articles of diet, are extract of beef, Symington's pea soup packages, and cakes of compressed French legumes, a dozen rations of which might be carried in a space of a few inches square.

Soup in the tropics is always sought after and liked: it is never refused after a long march, because it seems the only kind of food which can be partaken of immediately, and if available *at once* does away with the natural wish for a spirit ration to restore the flagging powers. It is also a capital digestive for hard biscuit, always so much less appetizing than bread, which last was fortunately available for the men as far as Amoaful, portable ovens having been carried up from Cape Coast in pieces, and quickly put together and got to work at all the stations, when this most necessary ingredient of a soldier's ration met him on his return march. The greater part was fermented with palm wine, much of the yeast powder sent out having lost its power owing to the dampness and heat of the climate. When fermented with palm wine, bread is occasionally slightly acid. This would not appear to make it inimical to health. The kankie used by the natives has a similar characteristic. The baking arrangements were under the superintendence of Control master-bakers, who looked after the subordinate native staff hired at Sierra Leone and elsewhere. The bread was described as having been excellent on the whole. The native women of Cape Coast made very good and palatable bread. The site of a field bakery is of some importance. In selecting it, it must be remembered that it should be in the vicinity of good water, where clay is available, and not in a hollow or damp situation.

Having had experience of all kinds and most varieties of preserved food while serving in Africa, I would say the following are the most palatable and best adapted to the climate:—

Liebig's essence, Symington's packages of pea flour, tablets or small squares of dried French legumes, tins of French haricot verts. These, with some vinegar, mustard, olive oil, and egg powder when obtainable, makes an excellent salad.

Mashed potatoes and meat in tins—the former preponderating—called by Morton, "Irish stew," patés, sardines, Bologna sausages in skins, German sausages, in long round tins, French sausages, in square tins.

Potted beef, ham and bacon, tinned curried fowl, slightly and recently salted beef.

Mutton broth, hare soup, fluid essence of beef. This, with the addition of some water, fresh or pickled onions, potato cut into small pieces, pepper and salt, makes an excellent soup.

Maccaroni, boiled if possible in milk, and afterwards fried with a little cheese, an onion, and a few thin slices of pork or butter, makes a highly nutritious and palatable mess.

Dried ling, boiled, and served with eggs, butter, or made into cakes, with mashed potatoes and an onion—called "twice laid."

Tins of Danish butter, Swiss preserved milk, coffee and milk, cocoa and milk.

Boiled rice, fried slightly with some tomato sauce, hard boiled eggs, an onion, a few slices of pork, and a boiled fowl cut into pieces, is a favourite dish on the Coast.

Jams there are always in request.

A light pudding or dumpling should follow every meal. There is always a craving for this agreeable finish up.

When tinned meats are only available on the march, fresh bread should, if at all possible, be provided, as many varieties of preserved provisions go well with bread, badly with biscuit. To have even one fresh article of food is an advantage: from flour, with a little suet, can also be made those highly nutritious dumplings, so much in vogue in parts of Germany. With a little sugar and butter they possess the additional advantage of being a favourite article of diet with soldiers.

It should never be forgotten that any of the foregoing lose *half their nutritive value* by being presented to the palate in a rude or unadorned state. Man is distinguished from the lower creatures in that he is a "cooking animal," by which means he assists his digestion, supplies his food in a warm state to his stomach, and renders it more pleasant to the palate. Nothing is so essential to health as artistic cooking. Anyone who has had the misfortune to sit down before a lean tropical boiled fowl, served up in a primitive fashion, and the same nicely covered with a little bread sauce and surrounded by a few slices of toast and bacon, will appreciate the difference, and never forget it. *Apropos* of fowl, it may be remarked in passing, that they should be used, when obtainable, as a change during the continuance of a more or less constant red meat diet. It is the attention to such minutiæ as these which makes all the difference with an army in the long run. If troops march upon their bellies, they must have plenty of fresh anti-scorbutic food, and a *brigade of cooks* with all their paraphernalia, to make it digestible and palatable. The army best fed, most suitably clothed and accoutred, will have the greatest staying power, traverse the longest distances with least difficulty, encounter obstacles, and bear the vicissitudes of war with the most equanimity, lose least by sickness, approach the enemy with the best countenance and *bon courage*, and ultimately conquer even superior numbers. Where these conditions are reversed with regard to the enemy they will melt away without almost being attacked. The late operations on the Gold Coast proved this, as did all previous wars, little or great.

During a campaign in the bush, where officers have to subsist upon their rations, this can be best accomplished by clubbing together and forming small messes. Three is probably the best number. More variety is obtainable in this way, and the ideas of the members as to the hours of breakfasting and dining are more likely to agree. Any attempt at large messes is a mistake in the field, where officers are not, as at home, tied down to a mess parade. Different meals at different hours disarrange cooking, harass the cook, and "spoil the broth."

Under the present supply system, the various articles forming the soldiers' diet in war are forwarded to the front, as they were on the Gold Coast, in different packages, a system which it appears to me leads to much unnecessary trouble and confusion, and in practice to the occasional *contretemps* of one portion of the ration being available while perhaps the other may be miles away. It would be far better when preserved food is issued to pack up the several ingredients in *one box*, as was done with the medical comforts.

A 28 ℔. package might contain the following, viz.:—

Rations for six men, or one man for six days, or three men for two days.

Biscuit 4 ℔. tin, flour 3 ℔. tin, preserved meat 4 ℔. tin, slightly salted beef 3 ℔. tin.

Rice 4 oz., peas 4 oz., preserved potatoes or vegetables 8 oz., salt 3 oz., pepper $\frac{1}{8}$ oz., small Dutch cheese 2 lb., tea 4 oz., sugar 18 oz., cocoa 3 oz.

Essence of meat six $\frac{1}{4}$ jars, to add to vegetables made into soup.

Weight 19 ℔. 5 oz.; box and tins 8 ℔. 9 oz. Total, 28 ℔.

Two of these could be carried upon an African negro's head.

CHAPTER VII.

NON-ALCOHOLIC BEVERAGES.

OF these cocoa is certainly for an early morning meal (which should be prepared before sunrise by cooks previously told off for the purpose, in order to avoid delay and allow of an early start), by far the best. It is pleasant to drink when properly made and sweetened, more bread is eaten with it, and owing to the starch intermixed to suspend the oleaginous matter in the form of an emulsion, it presents the additional advantage of *bulk*. Cocoa is in reality food rather than drink, containing as it does a large proportion of available fat, flesh-formers (about 20 per cent.) and very much phosphate of potash combined in the soluble form, and so easily passing into the circulation. Cocoa is hence one of the richest flesh-formers we have. Tea contains little, if any, of these, the phosphate of potash, as pointed out by Wanklin, not being combined in the form of a soluble salt, but as phosphoric acid and potash separately. The phosphoric acid, being insoluble, in this condition does not pass into the blood. Infusion of tea-leaves is, on the other hand, little more than an agreeable and refreshing nervous stimulant, unsuitable as an early morning drink on an empty stomach, owing to the rapid way in which a sense of emptiness comes on: in a few minutes the viscus feels as great a want as before. Both contain the important chemical constituents, viz., theobromine and theine, which constitute their stimulant and refreshing element. Throughout the world it will be found that the instinct of man has led him to seek some substance which contains one of these principles, which owe their value to the specific influence they exert on the nervous system, stimulating it, and checking want of tissue. According to the analysis of Dr. Muter, the best homœopathic cocoa contains—

Starch and Sugar added	53·00
Cocoa-butter	20·13
Albumen and other component parts of Cocoa	26·85
	100·00

The following table shows in a rough way the largely preponderating food value of cocoa over either tea or coffee:—

	Fat.	Flesh formers.	Active principle.
Cocoa	47·0	15·50	1·35 per cent.
Coffee	11·5	10·00	0·75 ,,
Tea	0·60	2·60	1·80 ,,

From personal experience I am inclined to think that too much tea-drinking spoils the appetite for more solid food. On one occasion, after a tiresome day's march through the bush near Acrofroom, on arriving at the latter place, I drank five or six cups of tea one after the other, with the effect of taking away all sense of fatigue, but doing away at the same time with all immediate desire for dinner served up shortly afterwards. Many people cannot take tea in the early morning in the tropics: it makes them sick at once. This I have observed! Several friends have also mentioned to me that they could never drink cold tea out shooting in India, as it made them sick in the stomach immediately. In a long seven hours' chilly night march with the 2nd West India Regiment between Dunquah and Mansue, I observed that cold tea had with some of the officers a similar effect.

Recent experiments made to ascertain the physiological action of *theine*, have shown that when injected into the circulation in large quantities ($\frac{1}{10}$th of a grain over the back of a frog), it causes at first a gradual loss of all motive power and all evidences of reflex action, the animal being reduced to a state of complete prostration. The number of respirations being at first increased and subsequently diminished; the temperature rising and afterwards falling slightly below the normal line; injection of the cutaneous and mucous surfaces being produced with enlargement of the small vessels, and engorgement of blood in the capillaries, with stasis of blood in the interior, from which effects the frog only slowly recovered. An increase of the dose to $\frac{1}{12}$th of a grain was sufficient to cause death. Between $5\frac{1}{4}$ and $5\frac{1}{2}$ grains was the minimum fatal dose of the drug in a rabbit weighing from 3 lb. to 4 lb. Tea used in large quantities, frequently and constantly repeated *de die in diem*, has led to the following series of very serious symptoms, which, according to an Australian physician, have become endemic in that colony, and to which he gives the term tea-poisoning, viz:—"Great mental excitement, præcordial distress, acute pain and spasms in the region of the heart, sensation of weakness, an anxiety and feeling of approaching death, irregular, feeble, and intermitting pulse, irregular and oppressive respiration, and approaching asphyxia. It was also noticed by the late Dr. Gregory that a disposition to hæmorrhœa petechialis (land scurvy) appeared as a consequence of deficient nourishment, and other most unquestionably debilitating causes among persons of all ages who lived in close situations, enjoying but little exercise in the open air, *whose chief diet was tea*, and who were exposed to much fatigue, long watching, and great mental anxiety; and more recently, Dr. Dobell, in his handbook on 'Diet and Disease,' in the section on 'afternoon tea' and late dinners, points out that the custom, unless cautiously arranged, is apt to lead to dyspepsia." He insists that "the rule should be that the tea should precede the dinner by three hours, and not come sooner after lunch than three hours, assuming the lunch to have been a good meal; and if any tea or coffee is taken after dinner, it ought to be immediately after, so as to constitute part of the same meal, and to partake in the same process of digestion."

The late Dr. Percival, in Volume I. of the *Dublin Hospital Reports*, p. 219, wrote—" The familiar use of infusion of tea as an article of diet, has rather withdrawn than attracted scientific inquiry to the peculiar effects induced, by its use or abuse, on the animal economy. A case illustrating the mode in which green tea, *when taken in excess*, may operate as a poison, occurred to me about twelve years ago (1805). A gentleman, intending to walk some distance along the coast of Devonshire, set out in the morning of a hot summer's day, having previously breakfasted on strong green tea, a beverage to which he was not unaccustomed. Having walked twelve miles, he refreshed himself with a repetition of the same meal. Resuming his journey, he walked nine miles further without hurry or fatigue. The heat of the day indisposed him to dine, as usual, on animal food, and he therefore called a third time for green tea, and drank copiously of a strong infusion, eating at the same time only bread or biscuit. He retired early to bed, resolving to use a similar diet on the following day. Soon after he lay down he began to feel some unusual and distressing sensations about the præcordia, as if he were continually on the verge of fainting; he passed two hours in a round of troubled slumber, waking at short intervals. His respiration became irregular and oppressed, and his heart some times palpitated, and at other times seemed motionless. At length he awoke suddenly and entirely as from a struggle of incubus. He now experienced acute pain, as from spasm in the region of the heart, and in spite of all his efforts, he felt as if he were continually falling into delirium. His pulse was feeble, irregular, and intermittent, and slight fits of apparent asphyxia recurred every five or six minutes. Rousing his servant, he took two grains of opium in pill, and a small quantity of cold brandy and water, which gave him some temporary relief; but after an hour's slumber, almost as distressing as before, he awoke in great agitation, gasping for breath, and bedewed with a chilly moisture. Another opium pill was procured, and a strong glass of hot brandy and water, from which he soon derived the wished for relief, and at length fell into a sound and natural sleep, from which he awoke at the usual hour in the morning in perfect health:" the bane and the antidote seeming eventually to cancel each other's noxious qualities. Other similar cases are quoted.

According to Dr. Fergusson, Certifying Surgeon under the Factory Acts at Bolton-le-Moors, the substitution and frequent use of tea as an article of diet, instead of milk, among the factory children in their earlier youth, has led to a serious degeneration of physique.

On the other hand, the advantages of tea on the whole are its great portability, that the infusion has a purifying effect upon water, which *must be boiled* to make it, and that on the march *in the sun* it is unquestionably a good drink to work upon and relieve thirst, provided it is taken in small quantities. A warm infusion is also more palatable than a cold one, anomalous as it may appear. The best plan is to make it just before starting. I always made my servant carry a hospital tin water bottle of it; the little cup on the top I found very useful, and the quantity of liquid it contained ample for each dose: a water bottle of tea sufficed for the purpose of quenching thirst during a march of fifteen miles from Cape Coast Castle to Acroful, starting at 6.30 A.M., and arriving at 1 P.M. When tea is extensively used during a campaign ¾ oz. is the lowest quantity in my experience which should be issued, with half an oz. of cocoa for the early breakfast. The total would be about equivalent to 1 oz. of dry tea, which was the ration of this substance issued during Sir Garnet Wolseley's Red River Expedition. It would be also well that medical officers, before recommending issues of these substances, were to make a practical experiment themselves, in order to see the bulk of ¼, ½, or ¾ oz. On all occasions when possible, scientific or theoretical teaching should be tested by actual practice. Coffee was scarcely used during the active operations. Half-way coffee-shops, established midway between the terminal points of some of the longer marches, as between Sutah and Assin Yancoomassie, were found useful, and appreciated by the men. This beverage is next best to cocoa for a morning cup, and is in much request in Western Africa, where the shrub thrives well. It is regularly issued to men of the West India regiment during peace time, who prefer it to tea, and who did not at all relish the change to the latter. A considerable portion of their tea ration remained untouched. I found a mixture of coffee and milk put up in bottles a very excellent beverage. In consequence of the fact recently pointed out by M. Doyen, viz., that only 20 per cent. of the alimentary matter of coffee becomes dissolved by coction, and that 40 per cent. remains undissolved, he suggests that to save all, the roasted berries should be ground into an impalpable powder, slightly moistened and combined with twice its weight of sugar, pressed into tablets like chocolate, dried and wrapped in tinfoil. When required for use, the latter removed and the tablet thrown into boiling water. Tablets of condensed tea have lately made their appearance, each little square making four very good cups of the infusion, and Professor Cameron, of Dublin, has succeeded in making tablets of tea, milk, and sugar combined.

These tablets would answer admirably for a field ration, owing to their portability and small bulk. Essences of these several substances are not nearly so pleasant to drink as the warm liquids made from the cocoa, coffee-berry, or tea leaf. Like most preserved, or more or less artificially produced decoctions, they are deficient in *bouquet*, and seem to pall on the appetite. Cocoa essence contains, according to Muter—

Cocoa-butter	19·22
Albumen and other component parts of Cocoa	80·78
	100·00

A favourite drink on the march with some officers was water slightly acidulated with lime juice, and sweetened with sugar. It was grateful to the palate, refreshing, and anti-scorbutic, and usually easily obtainable. At the halt at the village of Amquassie, after the burning of Essiaman near Elmina, and a prolonged march in the sun, some delicious cocoanut milk was stated to have been most refreshing and harmless, as was always palm wine in the early morning, before it had commenced to ferment. When the boats of the Decoy brought to the shore a case of claret and condensed water, the mixture of the two was eagerly swallowed by the detachment of Marines who had been marching all day in the sun, after which and a short halt they became "new men." Before the embarkation at Elmina at three A.M. on the 13th October, the meal of cocoa which was issued was highly spoken of by the recipients. There were many instances during the operations on the Gold Coast, as, for example, the marches to Assayboo and Abracrampa, in October, 1873, where soup and biscuit before starting, and a little preserved meat at the termination of the respective journeys, was found to be most refreshing. A Sergeant of the Rifle Brigade, writing from Acrofumu, some sixty or seventy miles north of the Prah, says in one of his interesting letters, "We get no cocoa up here, for the simple reason that none has got so far; but we get tea instead. Before leaving England I could not bear the smell of cocoa, but now I can drink it as well as anyone: it is far better than tea in the morning to march on."

After a long march, Liebig's essence made into a warm drink was certainly very refreshing, A cupful of beef-tea makes a man feel stronger when tired, and apparently endows him with energy, but it is in reality little more than a loan, for its protein or nitrogenized components evoke little actual force when oxidized in the body. It does nothing more than enable him to borrow from himself, and if its use is carried too far it may end in a mischievous and injurious result, manifestations of energy being evoked which are not evidences of power, but exhausting discharges of force. A late Governor of Sierra Leone drank, while on the Coast, nothing but milk and water—a beverage which might be experimented upon with future advantage.

The canteens established at some of the stations south of the Prah by a few enterprising civilians were found most useful, many articles not issued by the Control Department being obtainable at them. The prices were of course very high, but even with this disadvantage these small stores were acceptable. Under proper regulations, especially in regard to the sale of spirits, sutler adventurers might be encouraged in similar campaigns with advantage to all.

CHAPTER VIII.

SPIRIT RATION.

THE value of alcohol as an integral portion of a diet has been the subject-matter of much scientific inquiry. According to our distinguished Professor of Hygiene, Dr. Parkes, the use of alcohol causes—

A scarcely perceptible lessening of temperature when taken with food.

A more distinct lessening of temperature when given during fasting and rest.

A primary acceleration of the pulse, and subsequent fall below the normal standard when the first effects have passed off.

A relaxation and dilatation of the cutaneous capillaries.

No very marked effect upon the respirations.

A stimulating, but not strengthening, effect on the heart.

Finally, that one and a-half fluid ounces of absolute alcohol, equal to three ounces of brandy, is the maximum amount admissible in twenty-four hours to produce a useful effect, and that this quantity does not seem injurious to health. According to the late Dr. Anstie, 600 grains is the maximum quantity taken without ill effects to the system.

While Lallemand and some other experimenters maintain that every drop of alcohol taken into the system passes away unchanged, Thudicum claims that it is largely consumed within the body. The recent experiments of Dupré, Anstie, and Schmidt establish, apparently beyond doubt, that alcohol is oxidized in the body. If this be the case, and the oxidation or combustion of blood is one of the sources of animal motive power, as taught by many physiologists—alcohol being one of the most readily combustible of the hydrocarbons, which combustion means heat or force—must be a force-bearing food of a readily available character, although it may be incapable of forming tissues. In moderate doses it undoubtedly relieves various nervous symptoms, and enables a certain quantity of food to be assimilated which would be otherwise unavailable, and may be thus classified among those other stimulants which are among the group of foods becoming narcotic, and exercising a paralyzing influence upon the nervous tissue in larger doses. Hence the danger. There is also reason to believe that the administration of alcohol prevents the burning off of fats and sugars, whether derived from the food or the consequent waste of tissues. In other words, it retards metamorphosis of tissue, and thus leads to the accumulation of the first-named of those substances in the body. As is well known, the functions of food are twofold—it repairs the animal machine, and it evolves force. Admitting that alcohol is oxidized in the body, the advantages of employing it in diseases where there is great waste of tissue and no appetite, and in similar conditions brought about by exhaustion of any kind, must be apparent to all.

In actual practice, stimulants are given as if there were no limits to their use; the important fact being apparently overlooked, that the system has to bring about the conversion into force; that its powers to do so are limited, and beyond a certain point it cannot go. Every unnecessary expenditure of force is waste, therefore waste should never be deliberately induced. The navvy's idea that a pint of good ale gets him through the last hour of his toil all the better, may not be an ill-founded one, for the better ales contain a large amount of carbo-hydrates, so that there is not only the alcohol, but also the other force-bearing material in a readily oxidizable form furnished to the organism in his favourite draught—the exhausted reserve store being afterwards repaid by the liberal supper. The navvy has here found out empirically the easiest and most economical method of raising the force requisite for the discharge of the last hours of toil. One hundred and thirty-five years ago the British soldier looked upon his three quarts of small beer, one to each meal, as by no means a large quantum. We come then to see that the administration of stimulants, alcoholic or nitrogenised, should always be in proportion to the reserve fund and the pressure of the emergency. According to Dr. Carpenter, one of the ablest advocates of the physiological advantages of total abstinence, it must be admitted "that occasions *may* arise when it is of the utmost importance that a certain amount of exertion (bodily or mental) should be temporarily made, to which the over-taxed and perhaps exhausted powers of the individual may be inadequate; and that no assistance can so effectually supply the deficient energy as that which is afforded by alcoholic liquors sparingly administered . . . There may be occasions in which individuals, whose vital energies have been previously depressed by over-exertion, deficiency of food, &c., may be temporarily sustained under exposure to inclement weather, or to morbific agencies, by the judicious use of alcoholic liquors in small quantities, when other substances are not to be obtained." He quotes the well-known example of the case of the mutiny of the Bounty, in which it could not be reasonably questioned, that the occasional administration of a tea-spoonful of rum was of the most essential service to the starving, chilled, and ocean-tossed crew of Captain Bligh's open boat, by whom hot tea, coffee, or cocoa were not obtainable, or any substantial food.

What are in practice the effects of a dose of alcohol when shelter has been reached, wet clothes removed, and a warm fire available? The cutaneous vessels so long contracted by cold or chill, under the influence of a small dose of spirits, more quickly dilate; the blood, no longer pent up in the interior of the body, circulates more freely on the surface, and carries the warmth of the fire back to the internal viscera, the extreme pressure upon which is in the meantime revived, and with it the danger of congestion. If, however, the spirit is taken while the capillaries are still exposed to cold, it only warms the outside at the expense of the inside, for the more rapidly cooled blood returning to the vitals, quickly causes a depressing chill to succeed the first feelings of comfort, and thus it is why alcohol is so fatal to life when taken while extreme cold continues. At the same time that the cutaneous vessels dilate, the activity of the sudoriporous glands is increased, the surface becomes covered with moisture, by the rapid evaporation of which in warm weather heat is abstracted, and this is why a "brandy and soda" on such occasions is called for to cool the body. Referring to the fatal railway accident near Norwich, a physician who was present alluded to the craving for brandy and extra clothing which all the unhappy sufferers who were injured manifested in their cold, collapsed state, indicated by the feeble, fluttering pulse, and the cold and corpse-like feel of the skin, and also to the *undoubted fact* that brandy administered to them in this collapsed state was a great comfort and support, and helped to restore warmth and cardiac steadiness.

The detailed record of Captain Webb's swimming feat across the Channel appears to prove conclusively the value of alcohol; and at the same time shows the relative value of various stimulants, alcoholic and non-alcoholic, in a crucial manner. Captain Webb dived into the water at 12.56 P.M., doing afterwards twenty-two strokes a minute.

- 2.35 P.M., or 1h. 39m. after starting, required the bottom of a flask twice full of ale.
- 3.40 P.M. or in 1h. 5m. more, required another tin tot of ale; doing mile and a-half the hour.
- 5 P.M., or in 1h. 20m. more, required two tin tots of ale and a little beef tea.
- 5.45 P.M., or in 45m. more, required a little beer and beef tea, taxing powers of rowers to follow him.
- 7 P.M., or in 1h. 15m. more, required some beer.
- 8.30 P.M., or in 1h. 30m., called for some warm coffee; enjoyed; feels very fresh.
- 9.25 P.M., or in 55m., calls for some brandy.
- 11.30 P.M., or in 1h. 55m., had some hot coffee : doing a steady stroke.
- 12.50 A.M., or in 1h. 20m., asked for a little beef tea and a drop of brandy.
- 1.25 A.M., or in 35m., calls for some hot coffee; swimming freely.
- 3 A.M., or in 1h. 35m. more, requires coffee; getting weaker.
- 4.30 A.M., or in 1h. 30m., orders hot coffee and hot bricks.

5.30 A.M., or in one hour more, beef tea.
7.30 A.M., had little refreshment; toiling hard; very much fagged.
8.30 A.M., or in another hour, took some brandy.
10.41 A.M., on his feet.
10.43 A.M., on beach, after 22 hours and 45 minutes' hard swimming, during which he required a dose of stimulant fifteen times, or, on an average, every hour and thirty-one minutes, without the administration of which he would certainly never have reached his destination. On landing Captain Webb did not feel at all cold, but fearfully tired and exhausted, and very sleepy, so much so as to require frequent rousing; temperature 98°, pulse rather slower than usual. After five hours' sleep awoke, hot and feverish; temperature 101° Fahr.; face flushed, skin hot and dry. After some hours' further sleep awoke all right, with the exception of a troublesome stiffness of the arms and legs.

Here, then, are several situations where the use of alcohol in moderate doses has been shown in practice to have been of much benefit by many writers in the current literature of the day, whose opinions it would be folly to ignore. M. Lendet, a writer in a recent number of the *Clinique Médicale* of Rouen, has stated, as the result of his extensive experience, that even the constant and considerable use of alcoholic stimulants, almost unvarying in quantity, with *sufficient and good food*, only appeared to give rise to trifling disturbance of the gastro-intestinal mucous membrane among his upper-class patients, the deleterious action of the toxic agent being put off to a much longer time in such cases than among the lower classes, who took quite as much, and at more or less protracted intervals committed enormous excesses upon *insufficient and indifferent food*. It was only among such patients that he observed a rapid cachexia to be produced, and the more acute and important inflammatory hepatic affections to be seen. In his "Maintenance of Health," Dr. Fothergill, the latest writer on the subject, summarizes the relative advantages and disadvantages of the non-alcoholic and alcoholic beverages as below:—

1. Alcohol is a respiratory food.
2. Abstainers consume more food than non-abstainers.
3. A stimulant enables the system to use some of its reserve force.
4. In small doses alcohol aids digestion; in large doses hinders it.
5. Alcohol is not necessary to sustained muscular activity.
6. But it is not a poison under all circumstances, as maintained by some.
7. It is often a useful agent for meeting an emergency.
8. When the brain is wearied alcohol may be taken at bedtime with benefit.
9. Tea, coffee, and cocoa are true stimulants, but not intoxicants.
10. As stimulants they are much used by abstainers from alcohol.
11. More objectionable stimulants are also used by abstainers.

Or, as Dr. Sutherland puts it, "Wine is a good friend, but a bad enemy." It is the abuse and not the use of alcohol which is injurious. Dr. Chambers writes in his recently published work, "Its moderate use will not shorten, but cheer and lengthen life." Most objectors to the use of a spirit ration in warlike expeditions refer to this abuse of alcohol, and to the unassailable fact that this has been the cause of much military crime and disease, not only in camp but in quarters, and to the result of the sad experience, that men who had been accustomed to drink to excess were the first to fail when strength and endurance were required, and the least likely to rally from disease or the effects of exposure, injuries, or wounds. The history of the Royal African Corps, already referred to, is perhaps one of the most pertinent examples.

The use of tea as a substitute for spirits was first regularly introduced into the service in the Royal Navy by Sir John Phillimore, in 1825, on board a frigate which he commanded, in order to check the scandalous excesses arising through drunkenness; and subsequently into the Army, in the form of an evening meal, by Sir Richard Airey, when commanding the 34th Regiment, in Canada. Since then, and even before, there have been, and were, many isolated instances, proving beyond question that the most severe exertion in the tropics might be undergone without the use of spirits. But in the great majority of the instances recorded there appears to have been no lack of food.

One or two instances will suffice. In the early part of the year 1847 the 84th Regiment marched by wings from Madras to Secunderabad, a distance of between four and five hundred miles. They were forty-seven days on the road, and during this period the men were practically teetotallers. Previously to leaving Madras, subscriptions were made among the men, and a coffee establishment was organized. Every morning when the tents were struck a pint of hot coffee and a biscuit was ready for each soldier instead of the daily morning dram which soldiers on the march in India then almost universally took. Half-way on the day's march the regiment halted, and another pint of coffee *was ready* for any man who wished to take it. The regimental canteen, when opened for a short time, was not frequented, and the most judicious precautions were taken to prevent the men obtaining arrack at the villages *en route*, seconded by the admirable conduct of the majority of the men, who were fully persuaded of the noxious influence of ardent spirits during exercise in the sun. The results were shortly these. Although the road was proverbial for cholera and dysentery, and passed through several unhealthy and marshy districts, the men were free from sickness to an extent previously unprecedented. They had no cholera and no fever, and only two men were lost by dysentery, both of whom were old chronic cases taken out of hospital at Madras. The men marched infinitely better, with less fatigue, and with fewer stragglers; and it was noticed by every one, that they were unusually cheerful and contented. During the whole march the regiment had not a single prisoner from drunkenness. The concurrent opinion of the practical witnesses examined by the Admiralty Committee, to inquire how far the discipline of the Navy might be improved by the reduction or withdrawal of the spirit ration, was, that the disadvantages of the ration in regard to discipline was not counterbalanced by any benefit regarding the health of the men, or to their power of sustaining heat, cold, or labour. Instances were given where the men themselves preferred a non-alcoholic beverage, as, for example, when the Quail cutter was wrecked in the Bay of Biscay, in 1836, and for ten days (during which the weather was so bad that the man at the helm was obliged to be lashed, the sea at times making a clean breach over her), although grog was offered to the men on deck every hour they refused it, preferring warm tea; not that they disliked the grog, but that the warm tea proved in their case the most invigorating beverage. One of the witnesses stated that the only case in which he thought it likely that the allowance of spirits was positively beneficial, was that of men exposed in boats to the malaria of swampy districts, as on the Coast of Africa; and even then he thought that hot coffee, could it be procured, would be just as efficacious.

This is confirmed by the greater experience of Livingstone, who wrote twenty years since—before he had arrived at that age when alcohol is said to be its cream—" I have acted on the principle of total abstinence from all alcoholic liquors during more than twenty years. My individual opinion is, that the most severe labours or privations may be undergone without alcoholic stimulant." The great traveller should have added that he drank largely of milk, one of the most nutritious and easily assimilated of diets. I can confirm his experience, for I have met with more than one total abstainer from alcoholic drinks in West Africa who appeared to enjoy as good health and vigour as the nature of the climate would allow of. It is only fair to say, that they were men of strong constitutions, who lived upon a highly nutritious diet, composed in great part of concentrated soups, and who always had at hand some sweetened lime juice or other agreeable drink to quench their thirst. Then there is the fact that the Basle Missionaries marched as captives to Coomassie from beyond the Volta, traversing during twenty days (while subject to every privation) some 200 miles of swamp, mountain, and forest, and living there for five years subsequently, it is to be presumed, with little chance of obtaining that potent native charm—trade rum. All these facts taken together prove the correctness of the view that spirit may be dispensed with, without disproving the benefits which occasionally accrue from the administration of wine or some other form of diluted alcohol, not indiscriminately, but under proper supervision.

In West Africa especially, and when going on shore inot her tropical climates to procure wood and water, or perform other laborious duties, it was always the custom in the Navy to issue Peruvian bark or quinine in a gill of wine, or one-eighth of a gill of rum mixed with a fourth of a gill of water. Many instances are on record of the beneficial influence of this practice, according to various authorities. Among the crews of the vessels visiting the highly malarial waters of Aspinwall, the use of "wine bitters" was found to be most useful as a preventive of fever, and the daily issue of a glass of rum (taken, as a rule, undiluted), to the sailors of the West Coast steamers and trading vessels, seemed to make them more contented, and certainly did not appear to do them any harm whatever.

The following negative evidence would also appear conclusive that in a not dissimilar climate a large amount of sickness may prevail, and not be in any way aggravated by intemperance. In the table is shown the list of casualties between the month of February, 1850, date of the arrival of the 59th Regiment in China, and the 31st January, 1851, where the crimes for drunkenness are placed in juxtaposition with the admissions into hospital:—

Month.	Strength on 1st Month.	Average No. of Sick in Hospital.	Deaths.	No. of Drunken Crimes.
February	613	26	5	21
March	617	39	1	32
April	615	49	2	19
May	606	59	8	12
June	698	83	8	9
July	570	119	28	6
August	526	133	44	5
September	515	116	10	7
October	500	125	13	10
November	494	139	3	11
December	480	132	14	19
January, 1851	438	93	1	3

Every man was in hospital nearly six times, every officer nearly three times during the year under review.

In an after campaign in that country, Dr. Rutherford, the Sanitary Officer, recommended that a canteen should be established, and measures taken to supply the men with wholesome liquors, in order that they might in this way be prevented from using the "Samshoo," a fiery native spirit distilled from rice. The value of moderate doses of alcohol seems to have been fully appreciated, and as quinine wine, porter, and rum was issued more or less frequently, and no adverse comment made afterwards, we must conclude that the use of these several stimulants was beneficial.

During the Abyssinian Expedition a ration of rum was allowed daily, and was, in the opinion of the principal medical officer, conducive to health. Bowel complaints were less frequent when it was given than when the men were unavoidably deprived of it. Quite recently a medical officer of rank, who was present during the various operations of the first Sikh War, informed me that during the long and arduous marches previous to the battle of Moodkee, six glasses of spirits were issued daily to the men by order of Lord Gough, and that without it they would never have got through the immense exertion they underwent. In those days the ranks were largely recruited from stalwart Irishmen. Their countryman and gallant commander knew their failing, and how to adapt it to his purpose. Exactly in the same way, it was only by the profuse issue of gin and rum that Sir John Glover was enabled to get his men, while heavily weighted, to perform their twenty-mile marches over the mountains between the Volta and the Prah. The late Dr. Gregory relates an anecdote, showing how a generous diet and moderate amount of stimulant may act as a prophylactic against ague. His father was studying with twenty-four other English students at Leyden, in Holland. Of the twenty-four one only was a water drinker: the others partook of a pint of claret daily. The water drinker was alone seized with paroxysmal fever. The idea of a purely non-alcoholic or tea diet for soldiers in the field was brought into prominence in later years by Sir Garnet Wolseley's Red River Expedition, when tea was used to a large extent, the result being a very low rate of sickness and mortality. Commenting upon this, the principal medical officer, Dr. Young, reported: "I do not think one instance sufficient as a precedent for all future expeditions, *as the climate and weather of this one was exceptional.*" It may be added, that there was no deficiency of good food or non-alcoholic beverages. During the many bush expeditions undertaken against the various predatory tribes in Western Africa, it was always the custom to issue a gill of rum to officers and men while in the bush, usually at the termination of the march, the officers, in addition, providing themselves with sparkling wine and brandy. It was used during three months' bush fighting in Quiah, on the confines of Sierra Leone. Most officers carried a small flask of brandy, in order to use a little with water on coming to a halt. After a more than ordinarily long march on one occasion, a pint of Moselle was taken with an absolute sense of relief. A very similar practice was carried out in the military operations conducted by Major Cochrane's columns, which started from Winnebah to Swadro Akim, in 1862, in pursuit of the Ashantees. The result was certainly in favour of the practice, and that no ill results could be traced to its use, but much occasional benefit. A brother medical officer, who was present in the bush at that time, informed me that they were frequently without food, and that only for their pint of Moselle, or ration of rum, when they came in at night, they would never have got on at all. The privates of the Gold Coast Corps rationed themselves during these operations, and were well supplied with the trade spirit by their native wives, who brought it up from the Coast. When joined by the first detachment of the 2nd West they were allowed a free ration. Previous to the starting of the first detachment of Marines to the Gold Coast, in May, 1873, I recommended that large supplies of these alcoholic restoratives should be forwarded to Africa, being well aware of their value from previous practical experience. On arriving on the Gold Coast a few months afterwards, I found that a gill of rum had become a part of the authorized field ration, and that it was always issued until its prohibition in October, when it was ordered that it would be only allowed to the troops when the issue was recommended by a medical officer. Rum was frequently used during the preliminary phases of the war, and on subsequent occasions when it could be obtained, with the general result that its issue was of great benefit when given at the proper time and in proper quantities, because enabling the men to rally after the exhaustion of a long march; promoting digestion and enabling them to relish the monotonous and sometimes tough food; inducing tranquil sleep, and obviating the effects of the damp and chilly climate; and because it had the additional moral and physical advantage of comforting them, and putting them into good humour and spirits. Before the arrival of the European troops, in December, 1873, I recommended to the Quartermaster-General that a plentiful supply of port wine, preserved milk, essence of beef, and rum, should be available at all the stations, but that on no account whatever should spirit be issued during a march, but that afterwards it might be occasionally necessary and useful. Every officer with whom I conversed during the earlier or preparatory stage of the war, and since its termination, confirmed the correctness of these views, which they acted upon whenever practicable. In January, 1874, we find the Correspondent of the *Standard* writing from Prahsue—"Doctors were almost unanimous in their opinion that in this damp, unwholesome air, a small allowance of rum was beneficial."

"The doctors who knew the climate, and all old residents here, have a strong opinion of the utility of a small glass of rum or brandy at night, and there was scarce an officer in camp who did not manage to bring up a bottle of brandy, and who did not sparingly treat himself to a nightly half-glass." In the previous November, when following up the retreating Ashantees in the neighbourhood of Mansue, our small party, under the command of the late Captain Huyshe, were obliged to bivouac after a tiresome day's march on the banks of a small swampy stream in the midst of the dense forest, with the vapours of malaria rising up all round. Our solitary bottle of champagne and brandy proved most useful, the party being unanimous in favour of the immediate disposal of the contents. On our return a ration of rum was issued to the men with great benefit, tired, dirty, and wet as they were. At this time it rained nearly every evening in torrents. After a long night march of seven hours with the 2nd West, between Dunquah and Mansue, early in November, the officers were regaled with a mixture of Liebig, port wine, and condensed milk at its termination, and the men with their "tot" of rum, to the benefit of all. An officer who was among those who bivouacked on the banks of the Dah during a night of continuous rain, told me that he and a few friends of the 23rd would scarcely have survived were it not for a bottle of most excellent brandy, previously obtained from the Staff, the contents of which were quickly swallowed by himself and his chilled companions. Another, that were it not for repeated small doses of brandy after being attacked with dysentery at Fomanah, he would never have reached the Coast alive. An officer also mentioned to me that were it not for a pint of champagne which he got on the return march, after a long day's work, he was certain he would have had fever. I asked a brother officer, of very temperate habits, how he liked his ration of rum? After a pause, he replied, "My dear fellow, it went down like milk." The Senior Medical Officer at Mansue stated to me also, that those men of the Engineers who took rum escaped fever, while the non-spirit drinkers were all attacked. During the Expedition just concluded against the Congo pirates, a ration of rum was issued to the sailors and Marines on their return to the ships at night. It was stated to have been conducive to health, comfort, and good spirits.

With such facts and opinions as these, and many others of a similar nature before us, all tending in the same direction, it would appear unwise to deny the use of alcohol, when given in *moderate doses and under proper restrictions*, during the active operation of war in a damp, enervating, tropical, or malarious climate. I have mentioned them in order to show that there appears to be some benefit in the administration of alcohol, not by any means for the purpose of advocating its indiscriminate use. My personal experience in West Africa is fully confirmatory of that of other practical surgeons. It must be remembered that the march to Coomassie was made almost entirely upon a non-alcoholic diet, yet the admissions, in spite of every precaution against disease, averaged a ratio of 65·30 per cent. The percentage of fevers from 30 to 57; of diarrhœa and dysentery, 6 to 34 among the white troops.

My experience as to the use of alcohol in tropical Africa is as follows:—

1. When a glass of brandy and water is taken upon an empty stomach

during the warm hours of the day within doors, it gives rise to an immediate agreeable sensation, followed by increased action of the skin, indicated by slight diaphoresis; the pulse rises by several beats; symptoms followed quickly by a disinclination to proceed with any mental or manual occupation, and a decided inclination for the recumbent position and repose. If, however, the individual is performing some active, physical exertion, such as a game of billiards, or has just entered a room perspiring profusely after a fatiguing walk, the brandy and soda does not appear to have its secondary depressing or somnolent effects, unless the dose of alcohol is excessive or frequently repeated.

2. If taken with food at breakfast, in moderate quantity, and in the shape of a light and sparkling beer, it does not appear to have any specific effects, especially if the morning has been one of active exercise, and the individual not of the "bilious temperament." Even when of this peculiar disposition, the beer only does harm after some days, when it appears to work itself off in an attack of slight diarrhœa.

3. When taken with food, either in the form of *vin ordinaire*, beer, or some other diluted alcohol, at the *dejeuner* of the French, or lunching hour of the British residents, it seems to increase the subsequent inclination for repose *pari passu*, with the amount of spirit and food ingested. After returning from a fatiguing walk in the evening in time to change and dress for dinner, a glass of sherry and bitters, brandy and water, or sparkling Moselle, is rather reviving than otherwise.

4. At a late dinner, a glass or two of beer, or a few glasses of sherry or claret, appears to increase the appetite for food, and have a very comforting effect, far more so than when a meal is taken without such agreeable additions. When, however, taken in more than moderation, especially in the forms of "brandies and sodas," and sparkling wines, in addition to claret, sherry, or beer, the usual accompaniments of a big dinner, the subsequent sleep is heavy instead of refreshing, only lasting for a few hours, when the imprudent individual awakes with a parched mouth and much thirst, feels wretchedly uncomfortable, and in a half febrile condition, with a warm and moist skin, to relieve which he rises and swallows a quantity of water. Such an excess is followed next morning by headache, emesis, or nausea, pain in the side, foul tongue, moist state of the skin, a urine loaded with sediment on cooling, diarrhœa, and disinclination for work, symptoms lasting for one, two, or three days, if not followed by febricula, for which state the best remedy is an almost entire abstinence from alcohol until the symptoms disappear. Such results as the above do not follow the moderate use of alcoholic drinks with meals.

5. Those who live generously in West Africa, avoid unnecessary exposure to sun and rain, and at the same time are most active in their

mental and physical occupations, get on the best; while the intemperate, on the other hand, more especially if exposed much to the sun, are most liable to the ardent fevers of the dry season, and congestive remittents of the rains, which in such persons are intractable, and often incurable. When not attacked with fever, the intemperate not infrequently suffer from recurring paroxysms of febricula, in the older nomenclature graphically expressed in the happy term "*ebriositis;*" in other words, a short febrile affection, falling short of alcoholism, and characterized by a flushed countenance, foul tongue, more or less tremor, hot, moist skin, excessive irritability of stomach, constipation, &c., symptoms totally unfitting the sufferer for some days for the performance of his duties, and best treated by saline effervescing draughts, bitters, abstinence from alcohol, nutritious soups, purgatives.

6. When the accustomed dose of alcohol at dinner time is dispensed with, a want of a something is immediately felt, a craving which may be satisfied by a cup of coffee or some other non-alcoholic stimulant; but that the meal appears more satisfying, the sense of comfort greater, and the subsequent digestive powers more complete when the usual modicum of sherry, beer, or claret has been partaken with it—a fact I have frequently verified.

7. For the first fortnight, or longer, total abstainers feel the loss of their accustomed stimulant most: so does a soldier. Hence the query: Is it wise to commence a purely non-alcoholic diet immediately on the commencement of a march, or upon the onset of hostilities?

8. Alcoholic liquids render more palatable, and aid in the digestion of salted and preserved meats.

9. Warm soup and Liebig's essence may in some instances replace with advantage alcoholic liquids.

10. The necessity for alcoholic beverages is least felt when the diet is digestible, sufficiently varied, presented in the most agreeable form to the palate, and where fresh animal and vegetable food and soft bread are abundant; also, when flavoured effervescing drinks, sweetened lime juice, or similar pleasant liquids are *immediately available* at the moment when thirst requires to be satisfied.

11. When no other drink is available in the early morning, an egg beaten up in a cup of warm milk, with the addition of a teaspoonful of brandy or rum, may be substituted occasionally with advantage.

12. The good effects of alcohol are best seen in the treatment of exhausting malarial affections, from which the patient would in many instances not rally without it; and more especially in the oftentimes exhausting and prolonged convalescence which occasionally follows upon the cessation of the acute symptoms. Under such circumstances, frequently repeated doses of alcoholic stimulants can be taken with

advantage, and it is then that such beverages appear to act as food, and provide force for the exhausted powers of the system.

13. While marching exposed to the sun the use of alcohol is decidedly injurious and unnecessary, except when men are so utterly exhausted that no other means are available to spur on the failing powers. On the march in the sun alcohol serves rather to increase than do away with the sense of thirst, and to render further progress more difficult and tiresome; but that after the termination of a long and exhausting march, when men have reached rest and shelter, a dose of diluted alcohol is refreshing and exhilarating, an effect especially observable during damp and chilly weather, at which season, even during a march, a small quantity may be sometimes swallowed without any ill effect being observable. If any form of alcohol is taken during a march in the sun, a glass of light and sparkling beer is the most harmless.

14. Of alcoholic beverages, claret in the form of claret cup, or simply diluted with water, is the least hurtful and most agreeable, and from its well-known anti-scorbutic qualities, the most healthful drink for the climate of Western Africa. Heated, with a little sugar, nutmeg, and a few cloves, it makes an excellent warm drink for damp or rainy evenings.

15. In febrile affections good sparkling Moselle, brandy, and beer are of most advantage: during convalescence, Madeira, stout, port wine. Whiskey is very unsuitable for the climate, and "cocktails" and other sweet mixtures are so much rank poison.

16. The foregoing are, according to my experience, the advantages and disadvantages of alcohol when used either as a diet, stimulant, or medicine on the Coast. That it can be dispensed with in Africa by men of hardy frame and indomitable perseverance under great exertion has been proved by more than one great traveller; but that it does any harm, when taken in moderation at proper times and places, I do not believe.

CHAPTER IX.

MEDICAL RESTORATIVES.

DURING the Gold Coast Expedition these entered largely into the medical arrangements for its successful termination. During the earlier operations of the war small quantities of brandy, port wine, essence of beef, preserved milk, sugar, tea, and arrowroot, were put up in small square deal boxes, with a hinged cover, padlock and key, weighing in all about 25 lb. A proportion of these, varying with its strength, and in charge of the medical officer, accompanied each column. On the march they were found most useful. Afterwards large stores of Moselle, Champagne, brandy, soups, jams, and many other luxuries, accumulated in rear of the European troops at the various stations and station hospitals. They were obtained upon the requisition of a medical officer. Perhaps of these sparkling wine was the most easily tolerated and reviving. The rapid metamorphosis and waste of tissue is sometimes very great in the more severe and prolonged forms of African fever, very similar to the loss of flesh, debility, and anæmia following an attack of typhoid at home. Under such circumstances medical comforts become the stay of life. I can never forget how I enjoyed some good Dublin stout kindly given to me by a brother officer, when hobbling about, weak and thin, after recovering from my first attack of Coast remittent, or the intense sense of relief, when tired and weary, after the contents of a pint bottle of Moselle had been eagerly swallowed.

CHAPTER X.

TOBACCO.

When the white troops arrived at Prashue, tobacco was issued to the men by the Control Department. Not being a professed smoker, I can say little of its practical value, except that most of those who indulged in a pipe seemed to enjoy it. The correspondent of the *Standard*, a devotee of the weed, " thought that it should be issued regularly during all similar campaigns, being, in his opinion, as a practical judge of many years, as good a defence against fever as quinine." "I should stick to tobacco, and relinquish quinine without hesitation," wrote Mr Henty. He goes on to say, " its use adds to a soldier's power of endurance, enables him to bear cold, fatigue, and wet with comparative impunity; it is, in fact, at once a necessity and luxury, and should form part of the issue in the field." It certainly appears to me to be harmless in practice, to have a soothing effect, and be a pleasant solace. According to a very high authority on the subject, Dr Richardson, "In an adult man, who is *tolerant* of tobacco, moderate smoking, say to the extent of *three clean pipes* of the milder forms of pure tobacco in twenty-four hours, does no great harm. It somewhat stops waste and soothes. The ground on which tobacco holds so firm a footing is, that of nearly every luxury it is the least injurious. It is innocuous as compared with alcohol; it does infinitely less harm than opium; it is in no sense worse than tea; and by the side of high living altogether contrasts most favourably. A thorough smoker is never a glutton. It brings quiet to the overworn body and restless mind in the poor savage from whom it was derived, killing wearisome, lingering time. The overworked man discovers in it a *quietus* for his exhaustion, which having once tasted, he rarely forgets, but asks for again and again. Tobacco will hold its place with this credit to itself, that bad as it is, it prevents the introduction of agents that would be infinitely worse."

Tobacco is largely used by the Negroes in West Africa, who regard the dried leaf in almost as much favour as their common stimulant, white rum.

According to Gamble, Chaplain to General Monk, when the latter arrived at Coldstream, on the 8th December, in his march towards London, he found the place so destitute, that he was obliged to *stay his hunger* by " falling to his good cheer, chewing his tobacco, which he used to commend so much." There is therefore a very old military authority for its value on the march.

CHAPTERS XI. AND XII.

WATER.

THE rainfall on the Gold Coast amounts to some 120 inches per annum on an average of years; but here, unlike other portions of the seaboard, the rains are distributed more equally throughout the whole period of the year, being occasionally light and variable. At Cape Coast Castle the yielding power of the roofs, containing a superficies of 7,194 square feet, amounted to 448337·6 gallons per annum, for the reception of which were tanks capable of holding 111,000 gallons of water. Owing to leakage and other imperfection in the pipes, much of the precious fluid was necessarily lost, and thus one of the purest sources of water supply was greatly curtailed in amount, and by inattention to the cisterns allowed to become in part impure. The tanks at Elmina, kept in admirable order and repair by the Dutch, were capable of containing 157,620 imperial gallons. With care and proper supervision, the supply obtainable from the clouds should have been ample for the usually small garrisons of these Castles, well-water when necessary being used for ablutionary purposes. Attached to all the better class European houses were tanks, kept carefully locked up, and from which the liquid contents were measured out morning and evening, a ration of pure water being much sought after.

In the Court-yard of Cape Coast Castle were seven tanks, six in the lower or eastern yard, and one (the Guard Room), in the upper or western enclosure. The former of these required to be continually supplemented by the addition of water, rolled in casks from the krotakraba wells, situated about a mile inland, at the foot of Barnes' Hill. Upon Connor's Hill, 150 feet above sea level, was an iron tank filled from the roof of the officers' quarters and kitchen; and at Fort William, an isolated hill, was another large tank, surrounded by the basement walls of the Fort: these two last were manifestly above any sources of town impurity. Attached to some of the private houses, occupied as officers' quarters, were open tanks sunk in the yard, and cased with brickwork, lined with cement, and having a bottom of asphalte. One of these, in the yard in rear of my quarters, had a capacity of 67,618 cubic feet, but owing to defects in the roof, rarely contained more than a foot of water.

The natives depended for their water supply upon a variety of sources—pools, surface wells, and rivulets. A number of these wells, varying in depth from two to ten or twelve feet, were interspersed throughout the town and its immediate neighbourhood, in many instances receiving the surface *debris* and impurities of this noisome place, and at the time one of the filthiest of native towns. The water was thus much discoloured with red, blue or white clay, *debris* of plants and animals, and fine sand, much of which sediment subsided in twenty-four hours, leaving a more or less clear supernatant liquid. When discoloured with decaying vegetable matter, the greenish or olive tint and peculiar smell and taste remained permanent. Along the borders of the small rivulet which trickled through the centre of the town, were a number of wells, largely used by the natives; water was also collected in open reservoirs, surrounded by raised mud walls. At the crossing to Connor's Hill, a Norton's tube had been sunk; the water obtained was abundant, but so brackish and impure that it could not be used. Further north in the valley, at the foot of Barnes' Hill, and upon the outskirts of the town, were the krotakraba wells, some of them scarcely more than surface excavations, others deeper and kept pure by being covered by a wooden frame-work and trap-door. In the intervals between those in use were several others, the sides of which had fallen in, and the hollows of which had become receptacles for various kinds of filth, fæcal matter, and the soap suds and washings of the natives, who cleaned themselves on the bank. Several other wells were in the vicinity of grave yards and along the sea shore. The Sweet River, rising some two or three miles north-east of Fort Napoleon, and meandering to the sea, which it reached after a course of eight miles, a mile east of Elmina, was the only source of fresh running water in the more immediate vicinity of Cape Coast. Further up country were several similar streams.

The tanks in the lower or eastern yard of the Castle were built beneath the pavement and old grave yard of the Castle, great arched receptacles of brick and cement; others were in the foundations of the sea battery. The water was conveyed to these tanks from the roofs of the officers' quarters through iron piping, and was chiefly used by the non-commissioned officers and men of the native corps for drinking, ablutionary, and culinary purposes. The Guard-room tank in the upper yard received its supply of water from its own roof and that of the transverse line of buildings, or Palaver Hall. This tank was sunk below the level of the yard, and considerably below the level of the highest point of the "Tabara Rock," or mass of dark gneiss, upon which the foundations of the Fort were laid. This water was kept exclusively for the use of European officers and non-commissioned officers, being passed previous to use through one of Crease's admirable filters. As the roofs of the Castle buildings were exposed during high winds to the spray of the sea, the fluid collected from them would at times be slightly impregnated with saline ingredients, especially sodium chloride. Exactly opposite, in the sea wall of the Spur Battery, but on a lower level than the tank, was a slit or opening, through which trickled a minute stream of pure water, increasing *pari passu* with the overflow of the tank, and apparently connected with it. The water was clear and agreeable to the taste, and collected by the natives when obtainable in sufficient quantities. It seemed to be in some way or other connected with the Guard-room tank, which last was said to be never empty, even in the driest weather; if true, pointing to the presence of a spring, a not by any means improbable supposition. I think the idea is corroborated by the following measurements, which show the height of the water during certain days of the months of March, April, May, and June, 1873, and from which it will be seen that while the water in the other tanks was very low at times, the level of that beneath the Guard-room was never below five and a-half feet:—

Tank.	March.	April.	May.	June.	July.
No. 1	2 ft. 9 in.	5 ft. 5 in.	4 ft. 3 in.	6 ft. 10 in.	5 ft. 0 in.
No. 2	2 ,, 5 ,,	2 ,, 2 ,,	5 ,, 0 ,,	2 ,, 2 ,,	6 ,, 0 ,,
Guard-room	5 ,, 9 ,,	5 ,, 6 ,,	5 ,, 7 ,,	5 ,, 6 ,,	6 ,, 1 ,,

It rained so heavily and continuously in July that many of the houses in the place fell to the ground. Unlike other towns in West Africa, the buildings at Cape Coast were quadrangular in shape, and evidently erected with flat roofs and small parapets, for the purpose of collecting the rain as it poured from the sky. The soil upon which this last was received was a reddish brown argil, covered with many beautiful varieties of quartz, glittering scales of mica, and fine sand. The cuttings revealed blue or white clays, layers of fine or coarser saline sands. The primary rock was granite or dark gneiss, with masses of different conglomerates. In parts, especially up country and in the valleys, was much dark and rich vegetable loam. The water naturally partook of much of the characters of the surface upon which it was received. The soil of the valleys was mostly a reddish earth, largely composed of the constituents of disintegrated granite and quartz, nine-tenths silica and alumina hydrates.

The following, for all practical purposes, constituted the principal varieties of water:—

(*a*) *Tank waters.*—On the whole pure and wholesome, and whose only sources of impurity were the washings from the roofs, aerial gases carried down with the rain, and slight traces of chlorides from the spray of the sea in stormy weather. These waters were, as a rule, tasteless, odourless, and agreeable. When received in receptacles on the heights above all sources of town impurity, and some short distance inland, as the tanks on Fort William and Connor's Hill, the water contained the faintest possible traces of lime salts and chlorides when examined in September, less than a grain to the gallon of the latter salt, no ammonia or organic matter, and not more than three degrees of hardness. The water of those nearer the sea, intermixed with well-waters, contained more chlorides, five or six grains to the gallon, traces of organic matter, and a greater degree of hardness—about four or five degrees. The amount of lime salts remained unaltered. When the chlorine was derived indirectly from the sea, the water was, even without filtration, drinkable. Such water would only become impure when the receiving surfaces were not attended to, or the supply allowed to become too low, or leakage into the tanks permitted.

(b) *Well waters*.—The very best of these, such as the better guarded krotakrabas, had a perceptible taste, a faint alkaline reaction, and milky haziness, and a few floating impurities; a trace of lime salts, much chloride—several grains to the gallon; the worst abounded in floating *debris*, living organisms, had a decided brackish taste and odour, either depositing a light brown sediment or much silica and aluminous matter, previously held in suspension; contained little lime, only a trace; very large quantities of chlorides, derived from saline sands, and also probably from sewage; much organic matter, and an excessive degree of hardness, mostly due to objectionable salts. Such last described specimens of well-water were manifestly unpotable. When only coloured with clay and fine sands held in suspension, as many of the up-country and inland wells were, such as those at Inquabim, &c., and in which the chlorides were only possibly derived from the soil and not sewage, the water was perfectly potable after filtration, which process rendered the previously milky-coloured fluid almost perfectly clear.

(c) *River waters*.—Represented by the Sweet River, Okee, and other inland streams. These were as a rule discoloured with suspended clay, giving them an earthy or disagreeable vegetable taste and odour. Some had a greenish tinge, others deposited much sedimentitious matter on standing (clay, sand, vegetable *debris*); in some instances they were only partially discolorized and purified by passage through a charcoal filter. Showed faint traces of lime salts, little more of chlorine, but much organic matter, chiefly of vegetable origin, which was indicated by the rapid discoloration and browning of the permanganate solution, and the purple deposit or black powder (reduced metal) yielded, when a small portion was heated with a few drops of the terchloride of gold. When such waters contained the flushings of the swamps, as they did after heavy rain, they were evidently highly malarious. The river waters were soft, and only yielded two or three degrees of hardness. The water of the Prah was muddy, but cleared after a while when placed in a vessel, as the sediment fell to the bottom.

(d) *Condensed water.*—Almost pure, colourless, odourless, insipid; contained about a grain of chloride to the gallon, probably from the primings, and less than three degrees of total hardness. By the close of September a condenser had been erected on the borders of the Salt Pond, a saline lake a mile westward of Cape Coast Castle, and only separated from the sea by a bank of sand. It was in operation and capable of delivering 1,500 gallons per diem with good coal. Not more than half the quantity was required. After being condensed the water was received into several large puncheons connected with each other, and from which it was conducted into smaller casks, and conveyed in China handcarts to the Fort, where it was distributed in rations to the garrison.

In the bush we used our waterproof sheets as collectors of the rainfall, a simple means of obtaining a good supply of a very pure and soft water.

Specimens of these various waters were in my piazza for a fortnight exposed to the air with the following results:—

Fort William tank water remained perfectly clear, odourless, and agreeable.

Sweet River water became much decomposed, had a disagreeable, earthy smell, and nauseous taste, and was loaded with white shreds.

Water of the Krotokraba wells had a faint milky colour, slight earthy taste and smell; a small quantity of a brownish-white deposit was seen upon the bottom of the vessel.

Water from Norton's tube well at Connor's Hill crossing—supernatant liquid clear, brackish; slight odour, reddish-brown deposit at the bottom of the glass, diffusing itself through the liquid upon the least agitation.

The amount of sedimentitious matter increased much in all the streams and rivers after heavy rain. Tube wells were sunk at Acroful, Dunquah, and elsewhere. Water was easily obtainable in the hollows, intermixed in some cases with sand, which choked one or two of the pumps in a short time. When cleared out, kept clean, and protected from the influx of surface impurities, the well water up country was, after filtration, by no means unpalatable. The wells sunk to the west of the road at Inquabim yielded a water quite milky in appearance, from fine white clay, after filtration marking 10° of hardness. At Coomassie, after getting through the red surface clay, the well sinker came upon the blue or white clay, below which was found good water.

During the earlier phases of hostilities an attempt was made to carry condensed water inland in 56 gallon casks on China handcarts, drawn by fourteen men. The attempt proved a failure, owing to the excessive weight. On the next occasion, viz., the second march to Assayboo in October, condensed and filtered tank water for the use of the seamen was carried by men-of-war's Kroomen in nine gallon breakers slung on bamboo poles. During the operations round Elmina, water was landed in boats from the Decoy in similar receptacles, none being obtainable along the seashore where the troops were marching. The men of the West India Regiment always carried the old pattern tin canteen, not by any means a good kind of water bottle, as the bottom soon rusted out, and perfect silence was impossible with them on the march, owing to the noise which they made when knocking against the bayonet. The wooden Piedmontese water bottles were in every respect much neater and better, and the water contained in them cooler. They formed part of the equipment of the European troops on their march up in January.

For the purification of water, three principal methods were resorted to: (a) Crease's charcoal filters; (b) basket filters; (c) pocket charcoal filters. Of the filters in use, Crease's were by far the best, for they had the great advantage of allowing water to pass through in large quantities, a *sine qua non* of effectiveness when bodies of troops have to be provided for. Water quite muddy and full of impurities passed through them perfectly clear. Not only were the larger and grosser impurities intercepted, but much of the organic matter, soluble impurities, and gases—compressed animal charcoal, of which the filtering ingredient was composed, having the property of removing much organic matter. This action of compressed animal charcoal continues unimpaired from three to six months, or more. All granular substances that are themselves not soluble in water, have this power of retaining matters dissolved or suspended in it, such as sand, gravel, loam, clay-soil, charcoals, and fibrous organic substances, as wool, cotton, hair, and sponge. Of these, animal charcoal or bone black is incomparably the best, because to a great extent rendering innocuous the deleterious portions of organic matter by oxidizing them, and because as a filtering medium it fulfils the following requirements as a water purifying apparatus:—

It is capable of acting upon the impurities held in solution, as well as upon those held in mechanical suspension. It is composed of materials incapable of communicating any taint to the water passing through it.

Its action remains unaltered for a considerable time, and it is attended with the least possible trouble for remedying its defects by cleansing, renewal, &c., and because it effectually separates the low forms of animal and vegetable life, which indicate that the waters in which they grow are rife with dead organic matter. These filters were got up as far as Sutah. The basket filters did very well at those stations where Crease's filters could not be got up to. A number of them were placed in a row, and by this means a considerable quantity of a pure fluid obtained. These filtering arrangements should always be in charge of some one person, who should be responsible that they were constantly supplied with water; they should be also placed in a shed, and carefully protected from vicissitudes of weather, and all sedimentitious matter should be allowed to subside from the water before it was passed into the filtering medium. This tendency of suspended matters in water to be precipitated should, under all circumstances, be taken advantage of, in order that the gross impurities may not choke up the pores and crevices of the charcoal. The rapidity of the flow is in proportion to the density of the charcoal; in other words, its purifying power. A rapid stream points to a too great porosity of the charcoal and defective filtration.

I always found my small pocket filter, contained in a tin case, suspended by a green cord, to act admirably. By putting three or four of these filters in a large vessel, well raised, and conducting the India-rubber tubing into a bottle, the latter would be filled in a very short space of time. A tumbler became full in eight minutes from a single filter. A good plan was to set the little filters going over night. On rising in the morning an ample supply of filtered water would be found available. The improvements in this form of pocket filter indicated are—a slight alteration in shape, so that the tin case might, when the charcoal was withdrawn, act as a cup when required; and a metal outlet, which would allow of the charcoal being made occasionally red hot. After use these little filters should always be blown through, dried in the sun, and if necessary brushed, to remove surface impurities, which impede their proper action. These little charcoal filters were chiefly useful in removing sedimentitious and floating impurities, a portion of the organic matter, and saline ingredients; they acted also as deodorizers and decolorizers. One which I had in use for four months retained to the last its properties of rendering impure and much coloured water, clear and agreeable to the eye, as evidenced by the following experiments, which also give an idea of their value for the purpose for which they were intended:—

SPECIMEN OF IMPURE LIFFEY WATER BEFORE FILTRATION, TAKEN
5TH OCTOBER, 1874.

Physical characters . . .	Tasteless, odourless, contained much suspended matter.
Microscopic examination of sediment	Shreds of green vegetable matter, rounded ochreous bodies, numerous living organisms, infusoria.
Lime salts.	Very slight turbidity.

Chlorine and chlorides	7·7 grains of chloride of sodium, equivalent to 4·11 grains of chlorine to the gallon.
Organic matter	11·12 grains.
Total hardness	14·70 ,,
Permanent hardness . . .	4·20 ,,
Total solids	35·00 ,,

SAME WATER AFTER FILTRATION THROUGH A POCKET CHARCOAL FILTER, MUCH USED ON THE GOLD COAST.

Physical characters . .	Clear, scarcely any sediment, tasteless, odourless.
Microscopic examination of the sediment	One or two vegetable shreds in the field of the microscope, and an ochreous body.
Lime salts . . .	Slight turbidity.
Chlorine and chlorides	3·27 grains of chloride of sodium, equivalent to 1·90 grains of chlorine to the gallon.
Organic matter	10·92 grains.
Total hardness	13·30 ,,
Permanent hardness . . .	8·40 ,,
Total solids	33·60 ,,

VARTRY WATER, 5TH OCTOBER, 1874.

	Unfiltered.	After being passed through a Pocket Filter, used on the Gold Coast.
Physical characters .	Clear, tasteless, odourless .	As before.
Microscopic examination of sediment	Scarcely any, one or two vegetable cells and shreds	None.
Lime salts . .	Faint traces . . .	Very faint traces.
Chlorine and chlorides	1·39 grain chloride of sodium, equivalent to ·84 grains of chlorine to the gallon.	1·39, equivalent to ·84 grains of chlorine.
Organic matter .	2·66 grains . .	3·36 grains.
Total hardness .	3·15 ,, . .	4·55 ,,
Permanent hardness	2·80 ,, . .	4·20 ,,
Total solids . .	3·50 ,, . .	7·00 ,,

The net result of these experiments appears to be this:—That a very impure water lost, when passed through a pocket charcoal filter, used for some months, about half its chlorides, a moiety of its organic matter, total hardness, total solids, and all its colouring and sedimentitious matter; and that a very pure water, on being passed through the same filter, became somewhat more impure by taking up or washing out of the charcoal some of its organic matter, total solids, and soluble salts, with which it had been previously saturated.

In addition to the use of charcoal, boiling, making infusion of tea, or the addition of small quantities of spirit, were believed to have some purifying virtues on the water. The effect of boiling alone is shown below upon a very impure water:—

IMPURE LIFFEY WATER.

	Before Boiling.	After Boiling for half an hour.
Physical characters .	Tasteless, odourless, much suspended matter.	Clear on standing, floating particles browned.
Microscopic examination	Shreds of green vegetable matter, ochreous bodies, living organisms, infusoria.	All living organisms disappeared, vegetable matter less green, two yellow bodies in field, some amorphous matter.
Total hardness . .	14·70 grains	10·85 grains.
Chlorine . . .	4·11 ,,	4·34 ,,
Chloride of sodium .	7·7 ,,	10·63 ,,
Organic matter . .	18·12 ,,	8·12 ,,

The effect of boiling was evidently to destroy the living organisms, and practically destroy much of the floating vegetable and other matter; to decrease the total hardness by precipitation of the soluble carbonates, but to increase the chlorides by the natural result of rapid evaporation. A portion of the organic matter was also rendered inert.

WATER ITINERARY TO COOMASSIE.

In September, 1873, I compiled the following brief itinerary of the water supply to Coomassie for the information of the Army Medical Department. At the close of the month our knowledge on this subject was confined to a distance of little further than Dunquah, some twenty miles distant from Cape Coast. " Some of the earlier writers and later observers have very accurately described the general nature of the water supply on their route as far as it was possible to do so from practical observation. They have shown that many small streams intersected the paths, as well as morass and pools. At Acroful, fifteen miles distant from Cape Coast, is a small rivulet, the water of which, according to Dr Fox, is a little dark, but pleasant and cool to the taste; boiled and filtered, passing through a filter quite clear. Close to Dunquah was another small stream, stated to be 'pure water.' Between Dunquah and Mansue, fourteen miles further on, sheets of clay-coloured water were to be found, the country being swampy, and the sides and bottoms of the cavities a spongy slime. (This description exactly coincided with one given to me in September by two privates of the Royal Marine Artillery, invalided from Yaucoomassie, a station midway between Dunquah and Mansue, and also by officers who had served in the former abortive expedition). Between Mansue and Abandue, fifteen and a-half direct miles, is a little running stream, the Swary, twelve or fourteen feet in width, impregnated with decomposed vegetable matter, which when disturbed rises as a turbid cloud from its bed, not unlike 'coffee grounds.' The Obree or Okee further on is described as being better, a small river running over a bed of granite and white sand, twenty-four feet broad, but of inconsiderable depth, passing another small stream, the Agoga, eighteen feet broad, shallow, and running over a compact bed, with steep embankments. Further on are passed several swampy streams, exhibiting strata of red and dark clays, surmounted by light and sandy mould, decaying wood and vegetable matter in all its stages.

"Three miles on the journey between Abanduo and Acomfody, a distance of nineteen and a-half direct miles, is reached the little river 'Kotoa' flowing over a bed of rock and sand. Two miles further the Okee, whose bed was found intersected with chains of rocks; then the Adanso and Atonsie, running into the Prah beyond Fusubye, morass or white sand predominating more than water. Next comes the Yaucomfody, a little stream, followed by the Kotassie, a stream ten or twelve feet broad, after which was met with the Ambassie, Soubin, and Aniga. A rich black loam frequently bordered these streams. This was also found occasionally in the marshy spots. Sometimes a fat unctuous marl in extensive sheets; sand, however, predominated. Here and there a few pieces of quartz and mica were found, and spots on the sand emitted odours of decomposed vegetable and aromatic shrubs. Between Acomfody and Kirkiwarrie, twelve miles, a small rivulet called the Shambany is passed, flowing into the brook Barraco, which was swampy. After this came the Prah, a fine stream or river, whose margin is overgrown with rank grass and flags, the bottom rocky, and the bed a light sand. Upon the southern bank was Prashue, the site of the encampment in 1864. Some distance beyond the river was the village of Kirkiwherrie. The Prah was fordable in the dry season, but impassable except for boats or canoes in the rains, or after heavy showers, when it also overflowed its banks. Between Kirkiwherrie and the first village, after crossing the Prah and Ansah, nine and a-half miles, was the Ading, a stream twelve feet broad by one foot in depth; next the Anoles, then the Pagga, and lastly the Propong, a rivulet twenty-one feet broad by two feet in depth. After passing Ansah, and before reaching Acrofumu, six miles further on, was the Foomusu, a fine little rivulet, whose margin was covered with beautiful shrubbery, its width being eighteen feet by two feet in depth. After crossing the Parrakoome, between Acrofumu and Dunpassie, thirteen miles, was observed first the Parakomee, a rivulet, flowing upon a bed of loose sand; next the Bohmen, a very good, sweet flavoured, upland stream, embowered in shrubbery, the bed studded with brilliant little rocks and shelving slabs of granite, iron stone and mica, mixed with clear white sand and yellow gravel. This stream is close to an abrupt hill, 1,600 feet high, the commencement of the Moinsee or Adansie range, which terminates in the neighbourhood of Accra. From here begins Ashanti proper. Some hundred yards beyond the summit of this hill is a sort of table land, greatly incrusted with slopes and ridges; at its foot on the other or northern side flows a small stream. After leaving Dunpassie behind, and before arriving at Datchiassie, the Bomin is first met with, and another small river flowing through an open and planted country. The distance between the two places is five direct miles; Datchiassie to Amoaful $8\frac{3}{4}$ direct miles: between the two are three small streams. Between Amoaful and Akkankuasie the land is swampy, but in the distance of $12\frac{1}{4}$ direct miles is passed a superior rivulet, 24-30 feet broad, another small stream, and afterwards the Basqua, passing over a surface of indurated clay, now and then alternating with iron ore and white sand. Then there is the Dah, a rather extensive river near Akkankuasie, fifty-two feet wide and two or three feet deep, with a bed of clay and white sand.

"Between Akkankuasie and Coomassie, a distance of six miles, water is not very abundant, but a swampy sheet of water stretches south and east of the capital, the use of which is said to cause dysentery among the natives. The climate here is described as more salubrious, pure, and less humid and vaporous than that of the Coast. The water on the route is stated to be, with few exceptions, limpid and sweet flavoured: the quality and quantity would naturally vary with the season. The greater number of the smaller rivulets would be of course much smaller in the dry season on this coast, which may be said to commence in November and terminate towards the close of February, when tornadoes commence, and usher in the African monsoon. To sum up:—In a computed distance of 140 direct miles between Cape Coast and the capital of Ashantee, have been described thirty-eight rivers, streams or rivulets, or about three to each march of twelve miles."

CHAPTER XIII.

MARCHES.

Some of the marches during the first or Protectorate phase of the military operations were long and tiresome, and gone through under much exposure to sun and rain, the season being then the wet and unhealthy one. On the 18th August, Lord Kimberley wrote to Colonel Harley, the then Administrator, that it would be "unsuitable that operations should be undertaken which would involve the exposure of officers and men to the climate at the present season in the interior at any considerable distance from their resources," thus endorsing the opinion previously expressed and surmised by medical officers of experience on the Coast, that the wet season was unfavourable for bush marching and warfare. The attempt had been made in the previous June, when the rains were very heavy, with the result that many of the men suffered from fever and dysentery. On the 12th of July, when the Marines were marched out from Elmina, "their weary condition was most conspicuous," a conclusive proof that previously expressed opinion was supported by facts. A fortnight afterwards only 44 out of 104, landed on the 9th of the previous June, were effective for duty.

In tropical West Africa, ten miles, with halts, may be considered a good morning's march; fifteen an excessive one; twenty may be done occasionally, with a long rest from the mid-day sun. When quite a young officer I have frequently marched twenty measured miles in northern West Africa, a brother officer and myself having to pay periodical visits to a detachment stationed at that distance from our quarters. We did the first half in the early morning, starting just before sunrise. Our road lay across a tidal swamp, and afterwards through forest and scrub. We reached our destination in about three hours, or eight A.M., just as the sun was becoming too warm to be pleasant. We started on our return at 4 P.M., and reached home about 7 P.M., feeling that we had had quite enough of it. I then had had my seasoning fever, having landed in the country about six months before. During the Quiah expedition in 1861, we had one very long march. Setting out before daybreak, or about 5 A.M., we were doing good walking in sun and shade, wading several streams, until 9 P.M., getting in wet, tired, and exhausted.

Excluding halts, we must have done twenty-five or thirty miles, and this in forage caps, for helmets were then a luxury unknown. I remember perfectly upon getting in, drinking a pint of Moselle, and sinking down on a sofa, wet clothes and all, into a heavy sleep, so thoroughly done up did I feel. Wet handkerchiefs and cold water had been in constant requisition to keep the head cool during this long and tiresome march. One of our party was knocked over by sunstroke, from the effects of which he fortunately recovered.

During the various actions and reconnaissances in October on the Gold Coast, the Marines, 2nd West, and Houssas performed some arduous marches. At the attack on the villages round Essiaman they marched, according to Major Brackenbury—

From Elmina to Essiaman	.	.	.	.	3.5 miles.
Essiaman to Amquana	.	.	.	.	4.0 ,,
Amquana to Ampene	.	.	.	.	4.5 ,,
Ampene to Elmina	.	.	.	.	9.0 ,,

Total twenty-one miles, much of it in the sun. Only two of the twenty Marines who went along shore on the return, fell out—one from sunstroke, the other from "fits." More than one officer suffered much from the exposure to the sun. The Correspondent of the *Standard*, who had seen in his day a good deal of marching, expressed an opinion at the time that fifteen miles was an immense distance "for the tropics." A fortnight after the exposure to the sun in these affairs several of the special service officers were laid up with their first or seasoning fevers, the exposure being evidently the exciting cause. On the 28th of October, the same Marines started from Cape Coast for Assayboo, ten miles distant, halting half-way for ten minutes to drink cold tea. They reached their destination a little before 8 P.M., after a five and a-half hours' march, felt by all to be a long one in the hot, heavy, tropical air. Every one felt done up, and were much revived by a cup of hot broth. The march of four miles to Abracrampa, owing to the bad roads, numerous impediments, frequent stoppages in the sun, and absence of wind, was felt far more tiresome. Starting at 7 A.M., the column took two and a-half hours to get over these four miles. The advantage of a prepared and good road was thus self-evident, also, in another way, for on this last occasion a larger proportion of men fell out than on the previous day, when they were marching on a good and comparatively speaking open road, with the sea breeze in their backs for much of the way.

On the 6th November was illustrated the folly of attempting a forced march in the sun on the Gold Coast. Three hundred Marines and Blue Jackets were landed at Cape Coast Castle at 8 A.M., in order that they might march to the relief of Abracrampa, then threatened by the Ashantees. The heat was intense, and the suffering proportionately great.

The road was soon lined by the men that fell out; several had to be sent back, and not more than one-half reached Assayboo with the head of the column at 1 A.M., five hours after starting. The greater part of the men were fearfully exhausted, stragglers coming in afterwards in great numbers: 100 of the most exhausted were left at Assayboo. After a long halt the remainder marched to Abracrampa, four miles distant, which they reached in good spirits. This great amount of suffering was attributed to the hour selected for marching, exposure of the men while heavily weighted to the intense heat, and the want of proper and frequent halts. The better influence of an early start and an adequate number of halts was conclusively shown upon the following day, when the 100 Marines and Blue Jackets, who had been so much done up in the previous day's forward march to Assayboo by the causes already described, returned to Cape Coast at a good pace in the hottest part of the day, comparatively fresh, halting for ten minutes every half an hour. On their return they would also have had the advantage of the sea breeze in their faces. But even black soldiers will not bear, when heavily weighted, this exposure to the sun. A party of the 2nd West, who marched back in the sun from Elmina to Cape Coast after Essiaman, took a long time to do it, and were much exhausted when they arrived, by no means in compact order. A party of the same regiment started for Acroful, when first occupied, in their white serge jackets, cross belts, and service kit. They marched out at 5 P.M., and did not arrive until midnight, barely two miles an hour. The men had to wade up to their knees through much water, and complained very much of the sense of constriction of the chest from the belts, weights, and jackets. I made the same journey on the 1st November in light marching order, viz., in a flannel shirt, collar thrown back, chest free and unconstrained, a sash round the waist, light serge breeches, marine wicker helmet, white cover, and puggaree, carrying no weights save a revolver, twenty rounds of ammunition, pocket filter, and a stout stick cut from the neighbouring bush, a few mouthfuls of warm tea being taken occasionally to relieve thirst. Starting at 6.30 A.M., I reached the Cassada Gardens, beyond Inquabim (a little over seven miles from Cape Coast), at 9.15 A.M., two and a-half hours' smart walking, one hundred and twenty paces to the minute. The morning was a very fine one and somewhat clouded. Fifteen minutes after arrival the hygrometer read 86° and 79°; the black bulb, exposed to the sun, 156°; the aneroid barometer 29·950; there was little breeze. I arrived not at all tired. Starting again at 11 A.M. for Acroful, after a light breakfast of tea, bread, and some potted beef, I arrived there at 1 P.M., doing the fifteen miles in *five hours'* actual marching, during which the solar temperature varied from 127° to 156°, according to the amount of cloud; and the temperature in the shade from 83° to 86°, the difference between the bulbs varying between 5° and 6°. After a short rest, a glass of lime juice and water, given me by a brother officer out of his slender store, and a tub, I sat down to our meagre, early dinner, quite refreshed.

Some time afterwards, accompanied by Major Home, I marched from Mansue to Sutah. The grass was up to our hips, obstacles of all kinds in the way, and several small swamps to be passed, for the road had at the time not been cleared, and the enemy were well in our rear. Starting at 6 A.M., we reached Sutah in four hours eight minutes, a rate of close upon three miles an hour. We felt this to be very good walking, and were very glad of a rest when we got in, the shade of a few banana leaves, and a drink of warm soup. We had several similar marches hunting up the retreating Ashantees under Amenquatia, as they cut their way through the dense jungle to the westward of the road.

Night marches are always to be avoided. I made one with the Head Quarters of the 2nd West between Yancoomassie Fanti and Mansue. We started at 12.30 A.M., and reached Mansue at 5.45 A.M., halting midway for exactly forty minutes, being thus on foot for four hours and thirty-five minutes: the distance traversed was about twelve miles. The night was a fine moonlight one, but as the morning approached the mist fell heavily, and made the atmosphere damp, chilly, and uncomfortable. Our march was slow, owing to the many obstacles in the path, there being several rivulets to wade, and the weights carried by the men, viz., blanket, great coat, waterproof sheet, and field kit. I did not at all relish the cold tea in the damp, chilly air, as it was not a very exhilarating beverage under the circumstances. We were all delighted on arrival at Mansue to get a little port wine, beef tea, and preserved milk, as a restorative. We had been constantly stumbling over obstacles in the way, wading through swamp and water, and felt very tired, and glad to get some rest when we got in and had our beds put up. Nothing compensates for a good night's rest; the want of it tells in the end.

From these and other observations, I have come to the conclusion that two and a-half miles an hour is very fair progress for a European to make in the march on the Gold Coast, three miles the maximum, two miles the minimum; and that a dawdle along, with frequent stoppages, is far more trying than a good smart walk; and that in so debilitating a climate it is a mistake for a European officer to exhaust his strength by over marching, when he has a hammock to carry him; also, that the best hours for marching are from 5 A.M. to 8 A.M., and from 4 P.M. to 7 P.M., screened by the dense forest or cloud at any time.

The light mules used by the staff were rough and slow to ride, but saved a certain amount of fatigue.

The stations fixed upon as halting places south of the Prah were from seven to twelve miles apart; the two first marches, viz., Cape Coast to

Inquabim, and the latter station to Acroful, seven miles each; Yaucoomassic, ten miles; Mansue, eleven miles; Sutah, twelve miles; Yaucoomassie Assin, twelve miles; Barraco, eleven miles; Prashue, ten miles. Between the Prah and Coomassie Sir Garnet Wolseley had established eleven fortified posts, each of which was garrisoned with between 60 and 100 men. Fomanah, which was the largest post north of the Prah, with 200. The garrisons daily patrolled half way, on either side, until the patrols met. Beyond the Prah the first march was to Essiaman, twelve miles distant; next to Acrofumu, ten miles; Mansue, ten miles; Fomanah, seven miles, reached on the 24th of January; starting again on the 29th for Akinquassic, six miles; the columns advanced on the 30th to Insarfu, two miles; 31st, Amoaful, *via* Quaman, four miles; after leaving Amoaful, six hours were taken to reach Aquamemmu, only eight miles further, owing to delays. Here orders were issued that the force would advance at daybreak, every man to carry a day's biscuit in his haversack; all baggage to be left behind in charge of weakly men, and those unable to march, officers being allowed to take with them what their servants could carry, and the men their great coats. On the 3rd of February, starting at 9.30 A.M., it required eight hours to go six miles, owing to the opposition of the enemy, and continued halts, in order to get over streams, swamps, &c. The Dah was reached by the advanced guard at 3 P.M., by the rear guard four hours later. On the following morning the troops started at 6.30 A.M., and reached Ordasu at 2 P.M., fighting most of the way, the road being sunk fully two feet in the ground below the level of the surrounding country, the distance being about a mile and a-half. By this time the force had been reduced to 118 officers and 1,044 Europeans, and 449 natives. When the baggage was got in, a move was made for Coomassie at 3.30 P.M., six miles distant, which place was reached in about three hours, or eighteen days after the last division had crossed the Prah, seventy miles in their rear. On the last occasion the men had been twelve hours on the road; only a few fever-stricken soldiers dropped out.

MARCHES.

South of the Prah.			North of the Prah.		
1. Inquabim	7	Miles.	1. Essiaman	12	Miles.
2. Acroful	7	,,	2. Acrofumu	10	,,
3. Yaucoomassie	10	,,	3. Moinsee	10	,,
4. Mansue	11	,,	4. Fomanah	7	,,
5. Sutah	12	,,	5. Akinquassie	6	,,
6. Yaucoomassie Assin	12	,,	6. Insarfu	2	,,
7. Barraco	10	,,	7. Amoaful	4	,,
8. Prashue	10	,,	8. Aquamemmu	8	,,
			9. Dah	6	,,
			10. Ordasu, Coomassie	7½	,,
TOTAL	79		TOTAL	72½	

On the 6th of January the return march to the Coast was commenced at 6 A.M., the roads and streams in the interim having become much swollen through previous heavy rain, which caused considerable obstruction. The advanced guard of the Naval Brigade reached Aquamemmu by dusk. On the morning of the 7th the white troops, who had encamped upon the banks of the Dah the night before, arrived at Aquamemmu by 11 A.M. Starting again at 3 P.M., they reached Amoaful two hours after dark. On the 8th they reached Akinquassie, eight miles; 9th, Fomanah, in nine hours; 10th, Acrofumu; 11th, Essiaman; 12th, the Prah—seven days' march, averaging ten miles per diem.

1. Dah	. .	7 miles.
2. Amoaful	. .	14 ,,
3. Akinquassie	. .	6 ,,
4. Fomanah	. .	10 ,,
5. Acrofumu	. .	17 ,,
6. Essiaman	. .	13 ,,
7. Prashue	. .	13 ,,

From Prashue the troops came down to Cape Coast in eight days, halting at each of the stations prepared for their onward march, reaching the Coast on the 16th, the last regiments on the 20th and 22nd. Some officers who were anxious to push on in hammocks, arrived at the Castle in four days from Prashue. On the 12th January the journey between Coomassie and Prashue had been made by the Basle Missionaries in their hammocks in four days. Starting from Karsi, three miles from Coomassie, at daylight on the 9th, they reached Coutassie, about twenty miles distant, at 4 P.M.; 10th, Quesa, fifteen miles; 11th, Essiaman, thirty miles, a long day's march; 12th, Prashue, thirteen miles. Their hammock journeys averaged twenty miles a day.

Sir John Glover's Auxiliary forces left Ahwouna under Lieutenant Moore, R.N., reaching the Volta in three days; Obogoo, in Ashantee (carrying heavy weights over in greater part a mountainous country and forest tracks, much impeded by obstacles), in eighteen consecutive days from the Volta. The distance traversed would be from 160 to 200 miles. His marches averaged eight or ten miles each. On the 21st December Sir John Glover crossed the Volta, near Adedomey. Starting from Blappa with all his available disciplined forces, 700 Houssas and Yorubas, and a party of Akim carriers, he reached Chebi on the 29th, the Prah on the 15th January. The surface between the Volta and Chebi was described as level and park-like compared with that between Chebi and the Prah, which was a series of steep mountains and deep ravines, difficult to ascend and descend. The columns reached Obogoo, four days distant from Coomassie, on the 17th; Odumassie, eighteen miles from the capital, on the 27th; many halts having taken place in the interval. Sir John Glover left Odumassie on the 8th; reached Coomassie on the 12th; Moinsee on the 15th; Mansue on the 20th February; two months after crossing the Volta. The great difficulties met with and surmounted by the Volta forces caused much damage to them from foot-sore. This might be naturally expected, as they marched with naked feet through paths little better than watercourses, and encumbered with boulders and smaller rocks.

"I now find," wrote Captain Butler from Eastern Akim, "that a long hard day's march through swamps is almost certain to be followed by fever." The peculiar fatigue so frequently felt and complained of by those who underwent much muscular exertion at the high African temperature, was solely attributable to the unfavourable nature of the conditions under which the exertion was made, and easily explainable on physiological grounds, one of the most important of which was the interference with the vaporous or insensible transpiration produced by the accumulation of the liquid or "sensible" perspiration on the surface of the skin, and the saturation of the garments in contact with it. Owing to the atmosphere being loaded with dampness, the due vapourization of fluid at the surface of the skin was checked, the cooling influence of the perspiration was not exerted, and the heat of the body was injuriously augmented. A greatly increased amount of refuse matter was imparted to the blood, which was not got rid of owing to the diminished activity of the respiratory functions, and consequently retarded combustive powers. Effete matter was, as a result, largely accumulated, with all its concomitant evil effects.

ON THE MARCH.

The following extracts from an interesting letter, written by a Sergeant of the 2nd Battalion Rifle Brigade, from Prashue and Ashantee, gives a Soldier's account of what he and his comrades did and saw:—

"When you read in the daily papers of the excellent road made through the bush (says the writer), do not imagine that it is anything like an English road, for if you do you will be a long way out. Suppose, now, I try and give you some idea of one day's march—the last, as it was, I think, the worst, and it was also the longest, being between twelve and thirteen miles. 'Not a very long march,' you will say. You must, however, consider all the disadvantages under which a European has to labour in this country, and you will admit that they are quite enough. For instance, coming from the ship and marching straight away at once, with rifle-belts, seventy rounds of ammunition, water-bottle, haversack, pocket-filter, and several other little things which we have to carry on the person. None of these are very heavy, but the belts and straps round you prevent that free action of the limbs necessary for easy walking in any country, and this is felt more the warmer it is.

"I must tell you that the forest is becoming thicker every day's march. Down on the coast there are no large trees, but now they are of tremendous size and height, and, no matter how high the trees are, I see the vine and creepers run to the top, and there all the trees and vine form one mass, all matted together, through which neither sunlight nor moonlight ever penetrates. All this is necessary for you to understand to know anything of a march in this bush and the difficulties each individual has. Well, yesterday morning we got up at one o'clock; fifteen minutes after parade, and every one receives one ounce of quinine; fifteen minutes after that, or half-past one o'clock, each man gets half-a-pint of cocoa and a little biscuit, and parade for the march follows at two o'clock. But in the hour we have to wash, pack up our traps, dress, and everything. Each man has one of that kind of bag that I had with me last year, in which everything you have has to be packed, including coat, water-proof sheets and tent-pegs. There is one *tent d'abri* for three men, and this tent is put round three men's bags, the two poles through the centre, and the whole is bound firmly together with a good rope, and one nigger carries the lot, which must not weigh over 56lb.; and very well satisfied the blacks are to go with us, for they get all the spare food, and only go the same distance, where, if they were not with us, they would have to carry an equal load double the distance. So, of the two, they would rather go with us than be carrying provisions and stores. Well, as I was saying, we paraded for the march at two A.M., and started a few minutes afterwards. The road lay through a very low, flat forest, where there is always water. (I don't mean that the trees were short and stumpy; quite the reverse.) Well, there is a road cut through this. The underwood is cut away some eight or nine feet wide, and all the stick and small trees are cut into lengths of about six or seven feet long, and these small trees are laid across the centre of the road for you to step on, otherwise you would be up to your knees in water, mud, or slush. In some places they are laid close together; others twelve or eighteen inches apart; so that you are walking on a kind of ladder laid on the ground; and if you don't place your foot on these round pieces of wood nice and even, the chances are that you slip into the mud, or the wood turns round and tips you on head first, your rifle one way, yourself and helmet another; all of which irritates and strains the feet and legs, and causes the blood to go coursing through your veins far above fever heat all in a moment. You must bear in mind that we are marching by moonlight, but it is very little we see of her ladyship, for it is seldom her rays penetrate to the earth in this dense jungle. Well, the last day's march was most of it through the above kind of road. Here and there we found the road pretty level and good for a few hundred yards, but I should think we had seven miles out of the twelve to walk over sticks. I think you will agree with me that ten or twelve miles is a good march over such a path, and in such a country. For my part, I should rather go twenty miles on a good English road—yes, so I would twenty-four miles.

"Don't think for a moment that I am writing this in a grumbling way. Quite the reverse. I know that those who have gone in front of us have done all that was possible in the time and under the circumstances for our benefit, and comfort we don't expect; and we are, I assure you, duly thankful to them for it.

"Now, I think, I will give some idea of a day's life in the bush among us soldiers, now we are on the halt. Rouse at five A.M., and we get our quinine and half-pint of cocoa by 5.30; wash, &c., between that and six A.M. At six A.M. fall in on parade, and work about the camp till 7.30 A.M. The work consists in the cutting and clearing away of the rank vegetation (and there is plenty of it, and half rotten), and improving the sanitary condition of the place generally. At 7.45 A.M. we get breakfast; from eight to 9.30 we had to ourselves, for washing, &c. I wish you could have seen us this morning down at the river. There were about 300 men, all as busy as bees, in the water, first washing ourselves, then our clothes. I can tell you it is a sight not to be seen every day, and once seen not to be forgotten in a hurry. I washed my tweed suit of clothes this morning, which I have worn ever since it was served out. Yesterday I washed my white trousers, and to-morrow I must give a shirt, drawers, and pair of trousers a turn, and then I shall have everything clean. This river where we wash is about 600 yards from the camp, and we have to go down there to wash our faces and hands. It is a little clear stream, with nice sandy bottom, and this white sand answers the purposes of soap for all our things, except the white flannel shirts. The real bed of this stream, just where we use it, is rock, and on the rock at the side we wash and scrub our things. The sand must be brought down with the water and deposited in every hole between the stones on its way. A little further down the stream becomes a mere swamp, the water disappearing to rise again to the surface and become a river, it is to be hoped, miles away in another part of the forest. Well, you see at 9.30 A.M. the lie-down goes, and then we have all to go inside the huts, and there remain until four P.M. At one o'clock we have dinner; the remainder of the time, from 9.30 A.M. till four P.M., we can sleep, write, or anything else that we might have to do. You may thank these stringent orders for this long letter, for if I had been allowed to go rambling about the jungle all day I should never have written half this. Let us see. I got as far as four P.M. Well, at that hour we have tea and wash, and at five P.M. we clean the camp again until 6.30, when it is nearly dark, and we can go to bed as soon as we like after that, for we have no lights, and it is not much use sitting about in the dark. The proper bedtime is 8.30. So ends a day's soldiering in the bush in Africa. And now a word or two about the natives of this country. First, they all smoke pipes of European make—women and all. They are as black as a sloe, with curly heads; as a rule, very ugly—with their nose spread all over their face. They wear no clothes except a bit of cloth round their loins, often not sufficient to cover their nakedness, which does not seem to trouble them in the least. The women are much the same as the men, the only difference being that they wear a larger covering round them, and they have a lump behind. The child, as soon as born, is tied tight to the mother's back, where it is always carried, and that accounts for their flat noses. The women seldom cover up their breasts, or the upper part of their body, and when walking along with the child behind, and the child wants the breast, they bring the youngster's head under the arm and put the breast to its mouth, and so they travel on mile after mile, the mother often with fifty pounds of a load on her head, besides the child; in fact, the women carry an equal load to the men, and the child in addition. I never heard one of these little things cry, but the ride must be anything but comfortable.

"I am as well as ever I was; in fact, I never was in such good health since I came from India. This sort of life seems to agree with me better than the humdrum garrison life in England. If the fever keeps away, I would rather be out here than in England."

"Qua Nimma, Jan. 24.

"We have had a lot of sickness in the regiment, but I have had none as yet. We have had to send back 80 or 90 to Cape Coast Castle. We marched from Yaucoomassie on the 19th, and have been marching ever since. Some of them were very long marches—17 miles or thereabouts. Crossed the Prah last Tuesday. That was the first time we got into the enemy's country. The wood is not so thick on this side as on the other side of the Prah, but, of course, it is nothing but wood everywhere. There are no huts made for us on this side the Prah. We have to make a sort of one for ourselves. We have passed several villages, but did not destroy them. There was a skeleton in one of them lying close to the road. There is more fruit in this country, but the Fantees charge very dear for everything they sell, and they want money for everything they do; but, of course, they do not get it. We give them a fair price and take the article, whether they like it or not; and we are more up to them now than when we first landed. We marched over the Moinsey hills this morning, but have not marched far. We passed through one large village; the Ashantees made a trench round it. I expect they ran away as soon as the first shot was fired. It is called Quesa. We are in one of their towns now, stopping in their houses. They are not far away, and I hear they are only three miles in front. We have not been in action yet, because we have blacks to go on in front and search the bush, so, of course, they soon get out of our reach. There was an Envoy yesterday from King Coffee. I saw them escorted into camp—two white men (I believe they call themselves German missionaries), one white woman, and a little boy. They say the King has kept them prisoners for some time, and now he has sent them to see what they can do. This is a curious place: the houses are built in a kind of square, with a court in the centre and open—I mean with no covering; then there are walls built and thatched, having the front or side facing the court open. I should think the square outside the hut is about 10ft. each way; the floors are about 3ft. from the ground, and made with red clay. Plenty of fruit trees growing; I only saw one tree with fruit any good, and they were oranges, but, of course, the Ashantees would have taken everything away that was any good. There is plenty to be got at if we were allowed to go and fetch them; but it is too hot, and they are afraid we should get a sunstroke. Only our battalion and the Naval Brigade are here; the rest are coming up country. If they do not make haste, we shall be in Coomassie, as we are only about 25 miles from it. I should like to get rid of some of my ammunition; it is too much to carry. I would sooner let the Ashantees have it, or rather the bullets. There is a plain not far from here. I wish they would march us up there and put us to work, and we would soon let King Coffee know what we came here for. We can't do anything in the bush. They are just as good as we are there; but they do not know it. Why, if they had stood and fought us at the Moinsey hills it would have been hard fighting; they would have killed a good many. I do not think much of them now, except they fortify Coomassie, and if they do we can soon put some shells and rockets into it. Well, I think I must finish. The post goes out shortly, and I want a sleep, as I feel rather tired after marching over these great hills. I thought I would send you a few lines to let you know I am living and well, and that is more than half the battalion can say. I sent you a letter on—I forget the day—from Yaucoomassie, Assin. I hope you got it all right. I shall soon be back—we expect it will be in March."

The writer of the foregoing letter from the seat of war wrote again as follows:—

"The Town of Fomanah, Ashantee Country, Jan. 27.

"We left Assin Yaucoomassie on the 19th inst., and marched to a place called Barraco. There is nothing particular to relate of this march, except that on leaving the former place we had no sugar for our cocoa or tea. Neither had we at the latter place. Here we got salt rations—not the best food for a march in a hot country like this, where the water is so bad. Our thirst the following day was something dreadful, and to drink water in this country when you are so thirsty is almost sudden death—that is, unfiltered water; but, I suppose, these little things can't be helped, for altogether I consider we have done very well, for it is very difficult to provide what is desirable in sufficient quantities. A nigger carries, say, a box of rice up the country, for which he receives 1s. and 1 lb. of rice for each day's work, so that by the time he carries it a few days he eats half the box of 45 lb. It does not matter what he carries, he gets the same amount of money and rice, and there are a few thousands of these carriers, besides woodcutters, roadmakers, and others. So you can tell it takes something to keep all the lot of us.

"On the 20th inst. we marched to Prashue, on the banks of the River Prah, the Fantee side, or left bank. Here we caught up with the other half of the battalion, and we have remained together ever since.

"Prashue is a large encampment, where all the provisions are stored for our use during our stay on this side of that river, and they are forwarded on from station to station all day and every day. The West Indian and native troops are stationed every four or five miles all the way up this side of the Prah, for the purpose of guarding the road and stores and keeping the carriers on the move.

"We crossed the River Prah on the 21st inst., just two months after leaving Queenstown. It is a large river, from 80 to 100 paces across. The Engineers have thrown a pontoon bridge over it, just fit for foot passengers, light animals, or small guns. The river is deep now, and the banks high and steep, and I believe the water rises 20 or 30 feet higher in the rainy season. I don't see much difference in the forest on this side. The first day's march after crossing the river was to a place called Essiaman, about 14 miles distant; the road was as before—the old native path widened. The swamps, with slight rises here and there, were just the same, and one or two small streams. We got cocoa half way this day to help us on the road, which was very acceptable.

"What do you think now of all the stuff that was published about the time Sir Garnet Wolseley came out here? They had about as much knowledge of the features of this part of the country as they have of the bottom of the sea, for before we landed we were taught to expect to come on to a large open plain soon after crossing the Prah, but, instead of that, we have traversed between 40 and 50 miles, and the jungle is as dense it was on the other side, with no sign of an end to it. Then, again, the railway was to have been made through the jungle, which, according to some writers, did not extend more than 30 or 40 miles from the Coast. But, from what I have seen of this country, and from what I know of railway making, I should say it would take thousands of English navvies years to make 30 or 40 miles of railway from Cape Coast Castle inwards, and I reckon 1,000 English navvies would do as much of that kind of work as 10,000 of these natives in any given time. If bricks were used they would have to be made, and if stone it would have to be brought from a distance, for I saw none of any importance during the first part of the march, and I question whether piles would answer in many of these swampy parts. I think it would be very difficult to find a foundation sufficiently solid for a railway on piles. There is no doubt the Government, as well as Sir Garnet, were led astray in this matter; whether intentionally or otherwise I can't say. I feel sure if Sir Garnet had not been led astray he would never have asked for a railway. But that has nothing to do with me, so I will go on to the second day's march on this side of the Prah.

"On the 22d we marched to a place called Acrofumu, and as to the road it was much the same as the day before, the only difference being rather larger streams and the path rather more hilly. We passed through a village or two, or rather, I should say, sites of villages, for there were no houses. Every bridge is guarded by a few native troops within a stockade. On the 23d we marched to a place called Moinsey, at the foot of a mountain, which we had to cross the following morning. There was a nice mountain stream running close to our camp, and here we overtook Sir Garnet and his staff. On the 24th, on leaving camp, we had this hill or mountain to climb, and it was quite two miles to the top of it, by a zigzag path, which made us breathe hard. We halted at the top, and should have had a fine view of the surrounding forest, but the fog prevented that, and all we could see were the summits of hills all round us, with here and there the top of a very tall tree below in the distance. I was in hopes we were coming on a table-land, but we had no such luck, for down, down we went again, up another hill, and down again. Now we are in a forest about as low as the other side of the hill. The jungle is quite as thick up to the top of the hill as it is down here, and the trees are quite as large. At the foot of the second hill we passed through the first Ashantee town we had seen. The name is Quesa, and it is about a mile and a-half from here. I shall say nothing about it, but a few words about this place will do for both, as they are much alike, and I don't expect to find much difference in any of them.

"This village—or town I suppose I must call it—is built of red clay and wood after the fashion of the old English 'whattle and dab' houses. The timber in them is not so stout, and I should think they don't last long, for the white ants soon make light work of the woodwork. They are unseen, as the clay is plastered on inside and out. They are built in blocks, or squares. For instance, where I am living there are five little huts or houses, and the corners are filled in with bamboo wicker work. There is one little door of admittance into the yard or square, but no doors to the huts, all of which are open to the yard. The floors of these shanties are raised, some 6in., others 3ft. The roof is high enough, for these houses are very steep, and thatched with palm leaves. Some of the places are higher and larger than others, according, I suppose, to the means of the owner, and the number of his wives. I saw a few Fantee houses below the Prah which were built— the walls, I mean—of solid clay, higher, and altogether more substantial looking places than they are up here.

"As regards streets, there is no such thing. The road runs through the centre, and there is a space of 20 or 30 yards between the houses on one side and those on the other, where fig, orange, lime, and other trees grow. With the exception of this open space these towns are built without regard to plan or the convenience of neighbours. The refuse runs out of one yard into the next, and so on, and the smell in some of them is dreadful. No wonder the people are unhealthy. I don't know what they live on, for I have seen no corn of any description, but some of our native followers go out and bring in yams, and there are plenty of unripe bananas and plantains all round. I don't think I ever saw such strong rank kind of banana and plantain trees as there are round here.

"There must have been a good many people living here to judge by the number of graves in the houses, in the open space, and in the jungle all round. They don't put the body in the grave and then fill it up with the soil, but they put the body in it and place sticks over the top, and a little earth over them. As soon as the sticks get rotten or eaten away by white ants the earth falls in, and leaves the body exposed, or the bones, for the flesh is soon eaten up by insects.

"The day we marched in here we had to parade at 5 p.m., and formed line along the road, front rank one side, rear rank on the other. Every one was wondering what was up, as it's not usual to parade so for the inspection of any one; but we had not to wait long before down comes an escort of West Indians, followed by some officer, and in their midst a native of some importance, the rear being brought up by another escort. We found out afterwards that this native was one of King Coffee's officers, sent down to Sir Garnet, what for I do not know. We heard before crossing the Prah that King Coffee would agree to anything that Sir Garnet proposed, if he would not march on Coomassie. They say the Ashantees will not fight with the white man. Whether they will or not we shall see in a few days now. There were two white men, one woman, and two children came into camp at Moinsey from Coomassie, and they say the slaughter there daily is frightful. They had been prisoners in Coomassie for four years, and one of the men and his wife were made to march from the Prah to Coomassie naked. You will know, however, better about these things by the time you receive this than I do now, for one can't believe all one hears, and I won't vouch for the truth of what I have said.

"On Monday, the 26th instant, the company I belong to was ordered to march at 5.44 A.M., together with 60 men of the Naval Brigade. We went to the next town, some three or four miles further on. The people there would not turn out, so we were sent to rout them out. We did not want to harm them if they would go quietly, but some of them would not do so. A couple lost their lives, and we brought two back prisoners. The remainder went peaceably away. One was despatched that evening with a note to King Coffee; the other is a prisoner here still, and he says he don't believe that the King knows even now that the white men have crossed the Prah. He says no one dare take the news to him, for his head would be off the next minute. You have probably heard before this of one of his officers who was sent to Prashue, who, rather than go back and tell the King what he had seen, blew his brains out on the spot.

"Long before you receive this we hope to have been to Coomassie, to have settled our business with this black King, and to be on our way to the Coast again. You will see before then whether we are to come direct to England or not. If we do it would scarcely be worth while to answer it. If we do not an answer would meet us somewhere on the road. We march to-morrow again. You see we can't go very fast now, on account of the supplies. It is no use to go on faster than our food and ammunition come up. I have heard different statements as to the distance from Coomassie. Now, I think myself that we are about 28 or 30 miles. That would leave it to be between 70 and 80 from the Prah, and 150 from the Coast.

"We get no cocoa up here, for the simple reason that none has got up so far, but we get tea instead. Before leaving England I could not bear the smell of cocoa, but now I can drink it as well as any one: it is far better than tea in the morning to march on.

"I am still very well, thank God; I wish I could say the same of all our men. There is no doubt this is an awful climate for Europeans. We have no deaths, but we have had over 200 admitted into hospital already; 70 have been sent back to the Coast, and there are several very ill in hospital now who will return to the Coast as soon as they can be sent with safety to themselves—at any rate they will advance no further. My section was 20 strong when we left the Coast, and now we are only 14—six have been sent back.

"I can't think of anything more to tell you now. I have received all three of your letters.

"I shall not write again to any one until I have seen Coomassie. So until after hat event I must wish you all good bye."

CHAPTER XIV.

HOUSING OF THE TROOPS.

WHEN the garrisons of the Gold Coast were augmented with the continuance of the war, the small amount of barrack accommodation available at Elmina and Cape Coast rendered it necessary to have recourse extensively to tentage and hired quarters. Camps were formed at Connor's Hill, Forts St. Jago, Napoleon, and Abbey, from four to seven men occupying each bell tent—a contrivance which at no time would hold with any degree of comfort more than three men, one at either side of the doorway, and the third opposite the opening and between the feet of the two former. The cubic space for each of the three inmates would be 171 cubic feet, with 51·3 square feet of floor space.

At Napoleon and Abbey the men of the 2nd West India Regiment supplemented their tentage accommodation by the erection of palm shanties or small huts, not unlike those made by their enemies the Ashantees, but by no means so well put together or so neat. Such palm leaf huts are a cool and agreeable lodging in fine weather, but afford little protection from the rain or dews of night. A square palm-leaf roof, sufficiently wide to protect from slanting solar rays, and supported upon bare poles, so as to allow of a free circulation of air all round, is far cooler than a tent, and admirably suited for messing under, or to sling a hammock in during the warmer hours of the day, but unsuitable for sleeping in at night, as the cold and damp land wind soon saturates the clothing of the incautious slumberer. One of the coolest and most primitive quarters I ever have been in was a native mud hut, circular in shape, with opposite doors, and a high conical grass roof projecting well beyond the summit of the walls, and thus allowing a free current of air all round. There was just room for a bed at one side and a table immediately opposite. I found it by no means an unpleasant habitation during the six weeks or two months which I occupied it. A good and properly constructed and roofed mud hut makes as good a residence as any for West Africa.

On Connor's Hill there was a small officers' convalescent wooden hut, and a longer one supported on brick pillars, by which means a free circulation of air was admitted beneath the floor. At a later phase it was equipped and used as an hospital for twelve patients. Several others of a similar description were erected in the same situation subsequently. These wooden huts on Connor's Hill were cool and pleasant habitations, as they caught the whole force of the sea breeze, and were well raised above the miasma of the filthy town beneath. The change was found of much benefit to convalescents from fever, or those suffering from general debility. It may be laid down as an axiom derived from African experience, that a change of *any kind* is always most useful, even from one end of an island to another, especially if the diet and living is somewhat different to that which you have been habitually accustomed to. The first bamboo hut was erected here by Captain Crease, R.M.A.; it was thirty feet long by fifteen wide, thus giving to each of the intended occupants a floor space of thirty-eight superficial feet. The six bamboo beds were arranged at either side, supported along the central passage between the doors upon long bamboo poles. The sides and ends of the hut were of bamboo, supporting a thatched roof, beneath the eaves of which was a space of two feet for purposes of ventilation, in addition to the doors and chinks between the bamboos; these were bound together by tietie, a species of vine. Matting was hung along the sides as a protection against the night wind and damp: during the daytime these mats could be raised to form a verandah all round. Upon a shelf which ran round the inside could be placed the kits and haversacks of the inmates. This hut afforded an excellent model for the bamboo ones subsequently erected at the various halting stations. These last were not, however, nearly so elaborate in their construction.

The Naval Brigade erected for themselves at Prashue a unique kind of hut; the sides were formed of sails, which might be drawn up and let down at pleasure. When drawn up completely there was a free circulation of air; when let down the malarious night air and rain were kept out. The advantage of this form of hut was the rapidity with which it might be built.

At each of the halting stations south of the Prah were erected in *echelon* six bamboo huts, capable of affording accommodation to 400 men. These were constructed of bamboo, thatched with palm leaves: the interstices between the former allowed ample means of ventilation. A long guard-bed, raised two feet from the ground, ran down either side, with a three feet passage down the middle. The ends were open under the eaves, and protected by a projecting ledge of bamboo; at the centre of either side were the doorways and two small windows. Each hut, calculated to hold 70 men, was sixty feet long, seventeen feet wide, and five feet to the eaves. The floors were of red clay, well trodden down and pounded. These huts were cool and airy during the daytime, but damp at night. Behind were the huts for the officers, much smaller, but of the same model; they afforded accommodation for three persons. These were also arranged in *echelon* to the prevailing wind. In front were the Control stores, tubs to contain water for the carriers' ablution sheds, and at the lower stations Crease's filters to purify the former previous to use; beyond basket ones. In the vicinity were latrine trenches for the men and officers, screened off from view by a few palm or plantain leaves: those used by the officers were covered in. At some of the stations the soil was received into small tubs, into which a little earth was thrown by each person using them previous to his departure. The contents were removed to a distance and emptied at night into a pit in the forest. This was an excellent plan. The latrine trenches also did very well as long as they were sufficiently long, deep, and narrow. Earth should be thrown up behind, and to each should be adjusted in front a long pole, supported upon forked sticks, for the men to sit upon, with a back rest of the same construction, and whenever possible a screen to protect the inmates from view. These latrines should be placed well away from all sources of water supply, and have fresh earth thrown into them morning and evening. In passing through the deserted Ashantee Camps I observed that they had particular spots which they appeared to have set apart for latrine purposes, covering over the soil with leaves on their departure. Sometimes a fallen tree was used as a seat; at other times a neighbouring hut appeared to be the favourite place of resort.

In the neighbourhood of each halting station was a clearing for a few cattle, an *abattoir* and bakery, where the portable ovens were set up. The near vicinity of water and a dry site were always required for these last. Cooking sheds were also erected. At the Control Stores were rations for the different parties passing daily, such as tea, sugar, rice, preserved potatoes, tins of Australian beef and mutton, boxes of medical comforts, small kegs of rum, salt beef and pork, ammunition, tents, hammocks, compressed hay for the mules and cattle, and many other articles too numerous to mention.

Near the halting places for the European troops were the shelter huts or shanties, constructed by the carriers and native auxiliaries of light sticks and poles, covered and lined with plantain leaves. These were arranged in rows and small squares, with small beds or couches a few inches from the ground in those of the principal chiefs and captains. Between them were the fires blazing in all directions. So damp was it in November, that I was obliged to have a fire burning upon the floor of the hut which I slept in occasionally. Others soon followed the same example, and found the advantage of doing so.

The original idea was to form a large depôt at Prashue of stores and supplies, and to make it the base for the start upon Coomassie. Long before the minimum number of carriers, 15,000, could be obtained, large quantities of stores had accumulated at Dunquah, upon which the two roads from Cape Coast and Ammaboo converged, at both of which stations they were being disembarked. All along the road had been cleared and widened by Engineer labourers, swampy bits raised in the centre and drained at the sides, other spots were corduroyed, and bamboo bridges were thrown across the streams. Beyond the Prah the men of the Irregular Native Regiments aided the Engineer labourers in making the road passable; in constructing sheds to shelter the European troops from the sun during the day. On other parts of the *route* the houses in the native villages were cleaned out and utilized for shelter. When the advanced guards of natives arrived they piled arms, set to and collected all *debris* into heaps, burned them and swept the whole place and the interior of the huts thoroughly clean, dug latrines, and fortified the post by *abattis* and a sunk fence, so that when the European troops marched in from their last station everything was in readiness for their reception, huge fires being lighted to cheer them up, and water collected to quench their thirst. At each of these stations a garrison of West Indian and Irregular regiments were left in the forward march, a precaution necessary in order to protect supplies, and have fortified posts to rendezvous upon in case of a reverse. The bush was cleared for seventy yards all round.

When the troops arrived at Akankuassie, they were obliged to take to their *tentes d'abri*, in consequence of the dirty condition of the native villages. The tents were left behind at Amoaful after the action, in order that the men might push on to Coomassie in light marching order. Their first bivouac was on the banks of the Dah, and on arrival at the capital of Ashantee, exposed to dew and rain on both occasions. To the *tentes d'abri* were made the following objections, viz., that they formed an insufficient shelter from the rays of the sun during the daytime, owing to the thinness of the canvas and proximity of the latter to the men's heads, and that they prevented the body from being raised from the ground. Their defects could be seen at a glance. Raised further from the ground they did better, especially when pitched under the shade of forest trees. Many officers made their *tentes d'abri* far more comfortable by using bamboo canes, instead of the regular tent poles, in order to raise them, sewing around the bottoms a width of the country cotton cloth, by which means an additional height of nearly three feet was obtained, the increased weight being scarcely a pound. In a tent of this last kind, one of the Special Correspondents informed me, that he and a brother journalist went through the six months' Abyssinian campaign with little trouble from exposure. Before occupying their *tentes d'abri*, the men spread a few leaves and twigs on the ground beneath their waterproof sheets, by which means their bodies were slightly raised.

At all the larger rivers they had ample opportunity for bathing parades, which were indulged in when occasion permitted, with much benefit to all: at Mansue in the Okee, at Prashue in the Prah, and in other deeper streams a plunge could be taken from the banks. A very picturesque bathing place at Mansue was spoiled by the beautiful bamboos overhanging it being cut down. Bamboos should be always preserved.

The camp at Prashue was a large space of about twenty acres in extent, on the site of an old clearing, in the small promontory made by the loop or bend of the Prah. The tents and huts were placed as much as possible under the shade of lofty trees, on four sides of a square, the centre of which was used as a parade ground. By the 1st January 250 tents were distributed between there and Barraco.

At Addah on the Volta, at the first break of day, Sir John Glover's camp was astir, the bugles of the Houssas rang out, and before the sun was up, the men were at work at their drill. Near their drill ground was the market, crowded with women selling fowls, cocoa nuts, kankie, maize, and fish. In the Houssa camp the bell tents were ranged in perfect lines, with a number of little palm-leaf shanties interspersed amongst them, the cooking being done by the women in the intervals. The interior of the tents were divided into little compartments by palm-leaf mats, the whole being an encampment of married people. A hundred yards distant from the Houssa camp was that of the Yorubas. These men were not under canvas, but hutted in palm-leaf shanties. The camp was divided into four quarters, each under one of the four chiefs, and built upon a regular plan. The walls of the little huts were neatly made of palm-leaves, light enough to allow of air passing through, but sufficiently thick to be impermeable to the eye. The roofs were thick, and each hut was divided into several chambers, surrounding little uncovered yards, where the family cooked and washed in privacy. The cleanliness and order in both camps was most apparent, every place being swept most carefully, and all refuse carried down and thrown into the river, 300 yards distant.

CHAPTER XV.

MEDICO-CHIRURGICAL LESSONS.

A LARGE amount of sickness, increasing rapidly with an insignificant mortality—a comparatively few grave cases of remittent fever and hæmorrhagic dysentery—many slight wounds, and few severe ones—a great tendency to debility, followed in some instances by a prolonged malarial dyscrasia, in others by speedy recovery, were, in a few words, the medical and surgical teachings of the Expedition. Out of 2,587 of all ranks employed (exclusive of native levies and West Indian regiments) there were 723 admissions into hospital and 71 deaths up to the 31st May, 1874 (War Office Return), a ratio per 1,000 for the period of—

    Admission . . . 279·5
    Deaths . . . 27·0

The rapidity with which the sick list increased may be seen by reference to the admissions on board the Encounter and Victor Emanuel. On the 16th January the health on shore was good, only five officers and thirty-two men being under treatment in the hospital ship, and very few for climatic ailments. On the 26th, ten days afterwards, the health of the men had become so deteriorated by their stay in the bush at the various encampments, that the sick in the hospital ship had increased to 160, in addition to six officers and eight European soldiers on Connor's Hill, and twenty-five men of the 2nd West India Regiment. At this time there were only twenty-eight patients in the Colonial and small-pox hospital out of a population of some 7,000—a ratio of 4 per 1,000 only. According to a short War Office Abstract, published some months after the termination of hostilities, the total casualties were—

    Among officers 95
    ,,   men 628

Of this number eighteen officers and fifty-three men had died up to the 31st May, 1874. According to these figures the percentage of total losses would be—

    Among officers . . . 31·98
    ,,   men . . . 27·41

WEST AFRICAN CAMPAIGNS.

The total losses may be again subdivided into those occurring from diseases, 511, viz:—

    11 officers and 33 men who died.
    50 officers and 248 men invalided.
    169 officers and men left on board ship.

and those resulting from engagements, 202, viz:—

    4 officers and 2 men killed in action.
    1 officer and 10 men dying from the effects of their wounds.
    6 officers and 49 men severely wounded.

Ten deaths had occurred among the officers and men who had arrived home up to the 31st May, viz:—

    1 man from the effect of wounds.
    2 officers and 7 men from disease.

A total mortality of eighteen officers and fifty-three rank and file; wounded or invalided, 650. Figures which would yield the following ratios per cent of strength:—

	Officers.	Men.
Killed or died from the effects of wounds	1·68	0·52
Died from the effects of disease	3·70	1·44
Invalided	16·84	10.08
Severely wounded	2·02	2·14
Died after arrival home from disease	0·67	2·14

The deaths among the officers according to corps and branches of the service, were as below:—

Cavalry of the Line	1	Medical Officers		5
Royal Artillery	2	Control Officers		5
Royal Engineers	1	Army Hospital Corps		1
Guards and Infantry	6	Royal Navy		7
West Indian Regiments	12	Royal Marines		1
Militia	1			

in all *forty-two*, traceable to the Ashanti campaign.

The 42nd

Embarked December 4th, 1873.		At Portsmouth, 17th March, 1874. Disembarked	
Field Officers	3	Field Officers	3
Captains	8	Captains	8
Subalterns	17	Subalterns	15
Staff	7	Staff	5
Sergeants	36	Sergeants	35
Pipers and Drummers	16	Pipers and Drummers	14
Rank and File	600	Rank and File	488
Total	687	Total	568

The regiment arrived at Portsmouth with only 11 sick; a few had died or been killed, and 119 had been sent away sick or wounded. According to Major Brackenbury, the following were the statistical results of the Expedition:—Three *European regiments*, out of a total strength of 1,578, yielded 71 per cent. of sickness. Fevers, 59 per cent.; dysentery and diarrhœa, 13; other affections, 28: mortality (including killed), 1 per cent; invalided, 43 per cent. The 23rd had the greatest proportion of sick; the Rifle Brigade was next in order; the 42nd had least.

The *Naval Brigade*, out of 250 strong, had 95 per cent. sick.

Fevers, 56; dysentery and diarrhœa, 36; other diseases, 8 per cent.; mortality, 2 per cent.; invaliding, 39 per cent.

1st *West India Regiment*, out of 552, had 46 per cent. sick.

Fevers, 29 per cent.; dysentery and diarrhœa, 3 per cent.; other diseases, 69 per cent.; mortality, 36 per cent.: no invalids.

2nd *West, Wood's, Russell's, and Rait's Regiments* (1,605 in all), had among them 64 per cent. of sickness.

Fevers, 21 per cent.; dysentery and diarrhœa, 17 per cent.; other affections, 62 per cent.; mortality, 2·86 per cent.; invaliding, nil. 10 per cent. of the irregular regiments were sent home for discharge.

As showing to a certain extent the after effects of climate, the following particulars as to the health of the 2nd Battalion Rifle Brigade are interesting:—

Average daily sick, 15th October to 15th November, 1873, month previous to embarking for the Gold Coast, 13·2.

Average daily sick, 15th October to 15th November, 1874, after return to England, and previous to proceeding to Gibraltar, 24·50.

Average daily sick at Gibraltar, 15th July to 15th August, 1875, 37·06.

Do.	do.	1st Bat. 4th Regiment, 17·32.
Do.	do.	31st Regiment, 15·80.
Do.	do.	69th Regiment, 22·29.

On August 23rd 48 men were patients under treatment in hospital.

In 1873, out of a mean force of 1,760 Sailors and Marines employed in the West African station, there were 3,456 admissions on the sick list; 211 men were invalided, and 50 died, a ratio of 1963·6, 119·8, and 28·4 per 1,000 respectively, and an increase compared with the preceding twelve months to the extent of 443·4 per 1,000, invaliding 76·4, and death rate 12·5 per 1,000. This great increase was altogether attributable to the operations on shore, in connection with the Ashanti war. The ratio in the febrile group rose from 4·1 per 1,000 in 1872 to 14·1 per 1,000 in 1873. The average number of men daily sick rose from 58·3 to 102·7 per 1,000 of force. Of 785 cases of various forms of fever, 280 were simple continued, 46 ague, 444 remittent; one case of simple continued fever, one of ague, and fourteen of remittent fever terminated fatally. The ships in which the largest number of cases occurred were the Barracouta, Bittern, Druid, and Encounter. The greater number of cases were in the Christmas quarter of the year. Every one of the men sent up country on the two separate occasions were afterwards attacked with fever, each case being, on an average, between five and six days under treatment. The cases of fever and dysentery occurred for the most part in officers and men who were employed on shore. Of forty-three cases of remittent fever on board the Argus, thirty-nine could be distinctly traced to shore influences.

Fevers,
Dysentery,
Diarrhœa,
Scorbutic Affections,

Ulcers,
Bronchial Diseases, and
Muscular and Articular
Rheumatism

appeared to be the principal causes of inefficiency, due to climate, food, and accident. By far the greater number of admissions for fever were caused by the seasoning climateric of the Coast, which every European suffers from sooner or later in Africa—attacks there not generally of long duration, and followed, when the strength has been previously unimpaired, by a rapid convalescence; but on the contrary, when the physical powers have been reduced by prolonged residence or defective diet, the fever tends to relapse, and is not unfrequently fatal if of the remittent type. Under these last-mentioned circumstances experience teaches that after a severe attack an officer is not of much value for active work until the system has been renovated by a change. When the chief elements of the paludal or febrific exhalations are present, viz., earth, water, and decaying vegetable matter in large amount, under the drying effects of great solar heat, the intermittent type of fever was the prevailing form, the chances being from two or three to one that the new-comer would be attacked with this form of the disease, into which degenerated, as a rule, all seasoning remittents when they occurred as the primary attack. This view is strongly supported by the returns from the European Army occupying our great tropical dependency, India, where, in five years, 122,418 cases of malarial fevers, dysentery, and diarrhœa were treated in the following proportions:—

Intermittent Fever	87,461 cases.
Diarrhœa	17,468 ,,
Dysentery	9,956 ,,
Remittent Fever	7,533 ,,

In that portion of the country, as in the Madras Presidency, where the climate is characterized by a little varying temperature throughout the year, a moist heat, and much rain along the sea coast, bowel complaints are far more frequent in occurrence, in the aggregate exceeding the admissions for fever, as evidenced below:—

    Intermittent Fever, . . . 7,773 admissions.
    Diarrhœa, ... 4,819 ,,
    Dysentery, ... 4,159 ,,
    Remittent Fever . . . 559 ,,

In Western Africa the same facts are observed. On the Coast, as a whole, febrile affections predominate, dysentery being rarely seen in the settlements along the more Northern seaboard; but when we come to the 126 miles of coast in the envirous of the line, some 5° North of which it runs, we find the great humidity of the atmosphere, and little changeable heat, predisposing to dysenteric and diarrhœal affections, which are a chief characteristic. Sometimes, especially in the wet season, the type is an irregular remittent of not a very long duration, and in which the prognosis is very frequently unfavourable. Under favourable circumstances a mild attack of seasoning fever left to itself, the patient the while taking some simple warm diluents or acid drink, to act on the skin, and some easily-digestible nourishment, rarely lasts longer than eight or nine days. One of the first intimations of the coming attack is high-coloured urine, which, on being voided, scalds slightly, and gives forth an odour not unlike that given off from freshly-prepared beef tea. Immediately before the attack, the new-comer imagines himself in rude health, has a voracious appetite, and scoffs at anyone who suggests the possibility of his having a fever; quite suddenly he feels heavy and feverish, and loses all inclination for his meals and work. These symptoms are followed by a dizzy headache and a succession of slight chills, the countenance assumes a yellow paleness, and very frequently there is violent emesis or a quick evacuation of the contents of the stomach. As the chills pass off a scorching fever follows, the tongue becomes parched, and the thirst and longing for cooling drinks is excessive: racking pains in the head, back, and loins preclude all attempts at sleep. The unhappy sufferer tosses about in restless anguish during the long and weary night, praying for daylight or some mitigation of his sufferings, while at the same time the brain appears to be stimulated to increased activity, a never-ceasing series of waking dreams following the one upon the other in rapid succession. At last, in the grey of the morning, or after several hours' suffering, the patient falls asleep; as at first the forehead, and afterwards the skin bursts out into a perspiration, a change followed by an immediate and delicious sense of relief. Only those who have gone through this exquisite torture, as many of us have, time after time, can appreciate the nature of the change. The patient awakes weak and debilitated, disinclined to eat, but on the whole much better. After an interval of twenty-four hours the fever returns for two or three alternate days, gradually decreasing in force on each occasion. Chills, followed by headache and a general sense of debility throughout most of the day, constitute the principal symptoms of these after attacks. In the very dawn of medicine it was observed by the great Hippocrates, that these tertian attacks often terminated spontaneously after from five to nine revolutions. Modern experience has confirmed this. Among others, Cleghorn, in his Diseases of Minorca, notices it. An officer who was three years and eight months on the Gold Coast many years ago, and who is now in rude health, fortunate man! quite recently gave the writer a short account of his first seasoning fever. He said, "I got on very well for six months, when I got very bad. I was delirious, and was the second person on whom they tried the quinine treatment. They gave me *one hundred and forty grains*. I became so deaf I could hear nothing, which was an advantage in the noisy situation where my quarters were situated. In ten days I was able to go to my office, but was not all right for a fortnight. It was a kind of remittent fever. Afterwards I got ague now and then. I always cured myself. The moment I felt the attack coming on I went to bed, between the blankets; made my servant pile all the clothes he could get over me; swallowed a drink of lime juice, as hot as I could bear it; remained rigid and immovable; had everything kept perfectly quiet. In a short time I fell into a profuse perspiration, went off to sleep, and awoke as jolly as a sandpiper; jumped into my bath, had a good wash, and was as fresh as a lark, never having taken a particle of medicine."

One of the Special Service officers who landed from the "Ambriz" in October, gives the following graphic account of his first attack of fever, which may be taken as a very fair type of the ordinary seasoning endemic. He wrote—"On the 19th (sixteen days after landing) I could not eat anything, but I tried to persuade myself it was all imagination. During the 20th I tasted nothing but a little arrowroot and port wine, and passed a most wretched night. I felt very ill on the morning of the 21st, and went early down to the beach, when I was sent on board the Simoom, was put into a berth, and for twenty-four hours had a very nasty time of it. Violent headache and vomiting, one minute quite warm, the next quite cold; however I did not mind, as I did not get delirious. On Tuesday evening (21st) felt very wretched, and the rolling of the ship wearied me greatly. However, in a day or two I felt much better, thanks to all the kindness I received on board. They then dosed me with quinine, and the consequence was, the second attack was a very mild affair. I was sick only for about an hour, and then it passed off, leaving me very weak. When I tried to get out of my bed on Friday (24th) I found how helpless I was, for I nearly fainted in my cabin from the exertion, so I quickly turned in again. However, from the 26th I slowly began to mend, every day feeling stronger. I felt so well on Saturday, 1st November, that I asked permission to leave the ship, and landed in the evening." In this case the duration of the attack, from the preliminary feeling of *malaise* to complete convalescence, was twelve days. This officer served during the remainder of the war, undergoing much hardship with Russell's regiment. With the exception of a short attack or relapse of fever on the 5th January, 1874, two months subsequent to the termination of the first one, he was well throughout.

In a case which came under my treatment in September, brought about by exposure when heated to the chilly and damp night air, the initiatory symptoms of a sharp attack of bilious remittent were a dry bronchitis with cough, and little expectoration, followed in succession by congestion of the base of the right lung, excessive irritability of stomach, bilious vomiting, diarrhœa, yellow suffusion, hæmaturia, tendency to delirium towards evening, albuminous urine, and exacerbations of fever in the afternoon, symptoms accompanied by great weakness, a drawn face, prostration. This officer had arrived from the West Indies on the 6th July, was admitted on the sick list 13th September, 1873, and discharged convalescent on the 12th October. He was sent to Connor's Hill for a change, rapidly improved in health, but was attacked by a crop of boils in the calf of the right leg. These became inflamed and painful, refusing to heal for a long time, and then only when freely cauterized with nitrate of silver. After a short trip to sea in the Sarmatian he returned on shore, went up to the Prah to join the Head Quarters of his regiment, was in a short time attacked with fever, sent back to Cape Coast, only to die. In this case the fever had been ushered in with bronchial symptoms; in others violent vomiting and pain in the back, or a feeling of weight in the epigastrium and inclination to vomit, relieved by an ipecacuanha emetic and plenty of warm water; or violent headache, bilious vomiting, and pain in the right side, ushered in the attack of fever. In a few, violent delirium was observed almost from the onset of the disease. Among those of the first batch of Marines who went to Africa in May, 1873, and were attacked with fever; chills, followed by obstinate and distressing vomiting, which resisted all remedial measures to diminish its violence, were the first symptoms— the matters evacuated being the ingesta, bile, or bile and a glairy mucus. In one the matters ejected resembled black vomit. This was followed by much prostration, high temperature, pains in the loins, headache, coated tongue, and confined bowels. In most of the cases which followed later in the war the attack was sudden and violent. In these fevers the dangerous complications were—

Affections of the head and cerebral congestion or effusion, denoted by headache, suffused eyes, dilated pupil, stertor, sometimes low delirium, subsultus tendinum, coma.

Excessive and continued irritability of the stomach, combinations of fever and dysentery associated with great debility, which last was scarcely apparent to the unhappy sufferer until the sinking and scarcely audible voice betokened the rapid approach of death.

Congestions of various organs contained in the abdomen, such as the liver, spleen, and kidneys. The first indicated by pain and fulness in the right hypochondrium, jaundice, irritable stomach; the second by the increased area of dulness in the left hypochondrium, tenderness on pressure, and dull aching pain in the side and right shoulder; the last by the violent pain in the loins, and dark brown or hæmaturic and albuminous urine, sometimes retained or altogether suppressed.

Thoracic complications, usually indicated by symptoms and signs of sub-acute bronchitis or pneumonia; less frequently more general congestion.

Cutaneous complications, such as boils, ulcers. Prostration, collapse.

Of the foregoing, cerebral congestion or effusion, irritability of the stomach, and extreme prostration, were the ones most to be dreaded. In complications of fever and dysentery the prognosis was unfavourable as a rule, and the difficulty of conducting the case to a successful termination much enhanced. It will be thus seen that in its mildest form African fever was an intermittent; when more aggravated, an irregular remittent; and when in greatest severity, a quasi-continued fever, assuming not infrequently many of the characteristics of yellow fever. This last form was not, however, the true "Febris Icterodes," but a severe non-contagious form of bilious remittent, in some years of more frequent occurrence than in others—in fact, a quasi-epidemic, appearing at intervals of some seven years, and usually preceded by a number of fatal cases of congestive remittent. Why it should be more prevalent in some years than others is still unexplained. During the war this form of disease was prevalent on the Bonny River, a favourite *nidus*. A case occurred on board the Volta, on her homeward voyage, in December, in a man of a very feeble constitution. It was described as "a slow, continued fever, lasting ten days; the patient dying on the tenth day, exhausted, and without a trace of black vomit." There were no remissions in this case, and in a few others which recovered: the fever lasted about four days, the patients becoming jaundiced. A number of deaths occurred from this form of fever on the homeward voyages of the African steamers during November, December, and January. The colouration of the skin appeared to be due to the absorption or retention of bile. The skin had a hot, stinging feel, and

L

was usually of a lemon yellow tinge. It not unfrequently happened that the colour did not become developed until after death had taken place. In one of the officers who died after leaving Sierra Leone, there was violent delirium shortly before death: the patient rose from his bed and nearly strangled one of the stewards before he could be restrained. The only officer of Sir John Glover's force who succumbed to the effects of climate, exposure, and fatigue, Dr. Bale, died of what was evidently a bilious remittent, ending in dysentery. It was described as "fever and jaundice ending in dysentery." Death was usually caused by exhaustion or cerebral congestion. One of the medical officers who died shortly after the close of the military operations, appeared to have passed away solely from the former cause. He had a little fever, and a slight amount of pneumonic consolidation of one lung: he seemed to have lost all rallying power. It is in such cases as this that careful and constant nursing, nourishing and easily assimilated food, and alcoholic stimulants, are of such value. Cases are seen where, in addition to the symptoms already touched upon, hæmorrhage from the gums, nose, and anus occur. A step further, and we have the epidemic West African paludal remittent. I do not think the disease contagious; the danger is the locality or ship: keep away from both on such occasions, and the chances are ninety-nine to one that you will escape an attack. At Sierra Leone this fatal disease has frequently been raging in the town along the banks of the river, while the officers in barracks, on a conical hill, only 375 feet above it, have been free from febrile attacks. Curiously enough, it has never been epidemic on the Gold Coast, at least within the memory of the present generation, and this is why that portion of the Coast had always the reputation of being the most healthy of the stations in West Africa. I am inclined to think this immunity has been due to the little intercourse and difficulty of communicating with the homeward-bound steamers from the Bonny and the Bights, the short stay of the latter off Cape Coast a few hours), precluding any attempt at sending clothes, &c., on shore to be washed or otherwise disposed of. But although this has been the case, the fever here, as we have already seen, may assume grave features. On one occasion more than one European who was attacked some years ago suffered from sloughing and gangrene of the scrotum during the course of the disease. Even when no actual attacks of fever occur, the health becomes sometimes much debilitated, as evidenced by the sallow complexion, diminished strength, and difficulty of performing more than the slightest exertion, symptoms much aggravated when the spleen is very much enlarged, a form of tropical debility which rapidly disappears on return to England, a wholesome and anti-scorbutic food, and pure air. The presence of serious organic lesions, especially if of long standing, will, of course, alter the case. Here the convalescence is often prolonged and not always complete. The rapid convalescence of the majority of the invalids on their passage home after the war proved the former conclusively.

Many of the officers and men had, on their return from the Gold Coast, attacks of ague; others after more lengthened intervals. Exactly five months after I had landed, I had an aguish attack in the afternoon; could not eat; felt disinclined to move; drank several cups of tea, which were no sooner down than they were rejected by the stomach; felt cold and chilly; then very hot, afterwards perspiring; had much headache, and spent altogether a miserable night. Next day felt very weak; on the third afternoon had a far more violent attack, which set in at 4.30 P.M., accompanied by much pain in the region of the liver, spasmodic cough, and very great headache, the paroxysm lasting as far as 11 A.M. During the next and following days I felt very weak indeed. A brother officer who had been about the same time in England was attacked in a similar manner—a comparatively mild paroxysm, followed by one more severe. In my own case the pain in the side continued for several days. Here, curiously enough, the sequence of the attacks was the reverse of that observed in Africa, where the primary one was the most severe. Of all the symptoms of African fever, the cerebral disturbance coming on with the hot stage is the most distressing. Atonic and painful boils are another of the sequelæ which follow West Coast remittents, either abroad or at home, sometimes blind, sometimes discharging a core, and leaving a small but deep ulcer, surrounded by an inflamed halo, difficult to heal, and for the time painful to a degree. A change of climate, or trip to the Continental baths on return home, appeared to be necessary, in order that a cure might take place. In some the eruption did not appear until after the arrival in England. Another symptom which several have suffered from, especially upon the setting in of the cold weather, was slight congestion of the kidneys and pain in the loins, irritability of the neck of the bladder, and a sensation of deep seated pain in the perinæum and inability to retain the urine for any length of time. This last fluid was secreted in large quantities, very acid, and of a pale colour, a series of symptoms causing sleepless nights, and much annoyance. Opiate suppositories, alkalies, iron, and the avoidance of sherry, beer, and other drinks tending to increase the flow of urine or the amount of acidity, appeared to be the most appropriate remedies for this troublesome condition of things. Some individuals who never suffered from fever while in Africa had it on their arrival in England, or shortly afterwards. Among the West Indian soldiers the febrile symptoms were either a febricula, mild or more severe irregular remittent. They generally reported sick in the hot stage, and on careful examination, congestion of the base of the left lung approaching almost to the condensation of a pneumonia was not unfrequently observed. The same want of rallying power was observed amongst them as in 1863, 64. It should, however, be remembered that the greater number were new to the Coast as well as alien to it, and required to pass through the ordinary seasoning fever, after recovering from which they became much hardier and more capable of withstanding the effects of climate. When performing the ordinary routine duty in quarters, their sick list was, as a rule, insignificant.

The febrile symptoms observed by the Naval surgeons were singularly alike; ordinary febrile symptoms for a day or two, then an exacerbation every night, accompanied by intense frontal headache and lumbar pains. Pulse varying from 84 to 96; temperature 101° to 103°; tongue white or whitish, with irritability of the stomach and bowels. Towards morning the skin became soft and cool, and the pulse slightly fallen, with a general sense of relief. The duration of the disease varied from four to fourteen days. Distinct rigors were rare, except in the more severe cases; and in these cases during the hot stage, before perspiration was established, distressing vomiting often occurred, resisting, as a rule, all sedative treatment, but disappearing when the free action of the skin was induced. In some cases attacks of fever were ushered in by diarrhœa, lasting from twelve to twenty-four hours, gradually followed by an accession of fever, and more rarely diarrhœa, accompanied with some tenderness in the iliac region, with a feeling of epigastric tenderness and uneasiness, the tongue coated and brown at the base, dry and red at the tip and edges. A very slow convalescence was occasionally observed. In the majority the remission was well marked, in others not so distinct. The extreme range of temperature was from 60° during a remission to 107° during the exacerbation. In several cases convalescence was considerably retarded by the occurrence of headache, assuming a periodic form of hemicrania or facial neuralgia, the more remote effects of the original miasmatic poisoning; whilst others suffered from an eruption of small painful boils over the trunk and extremities. In many cases of slow convalescence there was much debility, with loss of nervous energy remaining. In many of those discharged to duty, several attacks of mild fever, followed by debility, occurred. Serious head symptoms were an occasional complication, and one case rapidly assumed a typhoid character, with uncontrollable vomiting of green bilious fluids, and the passage of frequent dark watery stools, dark brown tongue, and hot, dry skin—in fact, remittent fever without the remission. The very mild cases had a distinctly remittent character, and were very amenable to treatment. When the febrile symptoms occurred in seamen who never landed, and who were in vessels anchored well away from the shore, the remissions were not marked, but the disease was very amenable to the administration of quinine when it could be borne. It was remarked that the longer on shore the sooner the attack might be expected on re-embarkation, and that the greater number of those who suffered from relapses were found to be amongst the men who were longest on shore; and physique and age seemed matters of no moment in the first instance, as the finest men were often the greatest sufferers, showing that the malarial poison was no respecter of persons.

Nothing seemed to have such an effect in bringing on an attack as getting wet, even if the clothes were changed a short time afterwards. In fact, when a man got wet, either by surf or rain, he was perfectly certain to be down with fever next morning, or the morning after. Exposure to the sun was also very likely to bring on an attack.

The men of the wing of the 23rd, who had been the whole time either off Cape Coast or at St. Vincent, had a wan, washed-out look, as if they had suffered from jaundice, and had been just bleached a pale lemon colour. The features were pinched and sharp, and the skin drawn like parchment over the bones of the face.

The period of incubation varied much. Some who never landed at all and were crowded together on board ship, as the men of the 23rd, suffered almost as much, if not more, from the relaxing nature of the climate, *ennui*, and disappointment, as those who landed and were constantly marching on shore. The ships of the squadron, according to Captain Freemantle, were very healthy as long as they were able to move about the Coast, and while the men were not employed on shore, the sick list of each ship averaging something under *ten*. After the men were on shore some time he always found that they went down with fever. The Druid was the first ship to leave the Coast, her sick list having got up to *fifty* after her Marines and seamen had been on shore. She left for Ascension, and returned with her ship's company *partially* restored to health. The Barracouta was very healthy until her crew had been engaged on shore at Essiaman and Abracrampa, where the men had to march up country in the sun and heat of the day. The ship's company then began to go down very rapidly, twenty-five being discharged in one day on board the Simoom. The ship was obliged to leave the Coast with forty sick, the number increasing day by day. She went to St. Helena and Ascension, coming back in six weeks with only eight sick on board. The men who had not been on shore had been employed by day and night coaling, clearing transports, and other very trying work for the climate. These various operations resulted in an increase in 1873 over 1872 of 76·4 per 1,000 in the invaliding, and 12·5 per 1,000 in the death rate on the West African squadron.

Of the first batch of Marines who went out, the majority were attacked with fever thirty and forty days after landing. A few were not attacked with the disease until they had been sixty days on shore. Thirty-five days appeared to be the average period of incubation. Three Marines were sent on board seven days after having been landed. This was the earliest manifestation of the fever. In one case the febrile symptoms did not show themselves until twenty-two to twenty-nine days after embarkation, average 5·7 days, before the onset of the attack of fever, after return on board. The Encounter landed 110 officers and men on the 6th November, eight days after arrival. On the 11th November, 11 were on the sick list; 17th, 21; 20th, 38; 21st, 46; 23rd, 56; 24th, 63; 25th, 73.

On the 8th January, a week after landing, out of 427 Europeans only 13 were sick at Prashue. On the 23rd, at Moinsey, sickness had much increased. The Naval Brigade had 40 out of 250 sick since leaving the Coast line on the 27th December; the Rifle Brigade 57 out of 650. On the 25th the Rifle Brigade, out of a total of 684 officers and men, had 591 present on parade—a loss of 93 in twenty-five days; 77 had been left behind sick, 9 were sick at Fomanah. Out of 1,800 men, the hospital states showed that 218 men had become ineffective since landing, a little over an eighth part of the force. The sickness according to corps since landing in the twenty-five days, had been in 23rd (half battalion) 38 men; 42nd, 51; Rifle Brigade, 78; Naval Brigade, 48 (ont of 250). Total, 215 men and 3 officers.

The first four of the Special Service officers who arrived in October were attacked with fever sixteen, seventeen, twenty, and twenty-two days after landing. The Rifle Brigade crossed the Prah on the 19th: nineteen days after the men were disembarked sixty-nine sick had to be left behind. A private of the Army Hospital Corps, employed at Connor's Hill, was on shore a month before he had fever. In his case it was excited by much exposure in the sun on a particular day when superintending the embarkation of some men from the bush. He had a nine-day attack; was sent to St. Vincent; had a second nine-day attack on board the Simoom; arrived at Netley in March, when he had a third attack, lasting in all eight or nine days. Since then he had been at his duty. A Blue Jacket gave the following very amusing account of how he came to get dysentery after being thirty-nine days on shore:—"Each of us carried a rifle, cutlass, seventy rounds of ammunition, water bottle, one day's provision, a filter among four; a blanket and waterproof sheet for the night was carried in the baggage. We started at 4.30 A.M. After a pint of cocoa, halted at 10 A.M., when we had a breakfast of tea and a biscuit; rested until 4 P.M., pretty well in the shade all the time. Sometimes we had dinner before starting on the second half of our daily march; pretty good—preserved meats, potatoes or rice, fresh meat now and then; we had not much in the way of grog allowance. On arrival at the Prah, made the bridge in three days. Stayed seventeen days, doing about four hours' work a day, felling trees, and clearing ground for the 42nd, rigging up huts for ourselves at the same time. Our first day's march beyond the Prah was twelve miles. Made our beds from branches, twigs, &c., surmounted by canopies of banana leaves. On the fourth day arrived at the Adansie Hills, which we crossed, and entered Fomanah. Eighteen miles from Coomassie left all our baggage, save the blankets. Next day it rained in torrents; most of us remained standing or walking about with our blankets around us. Rose at 3.30 A.M., and tried to make fires; the rain put them out, so we had no warm cocoa in consequence. We crossed the Dah at 6.30 A.M., reached Ordasu at 2 P.M.; at 3 P.M. followed up the 42nd, very slow work, stopping every twenty paces. We forded three streams and a swamp, and upon arrival at Coomassie were told off to the different huts. We were parched with thirst from the biscuit and meat, and want of water. We turned in at 11.30 P.M. in our wet clothes and no blankets. At 6 A.M. we were roused, inspected, and ordered to dry our clothes in the sun then shining. Having no change, we were obliged to shelter ourselves beneath the trees whilst our clothes were drying. We left on the 6th, not having had much to eat during the two days we remained. On the 5th, at noon, it came on to rain again. After leaving, we were obliged to wade through many swamps and rivers. Three days afterwards (thirty-nine after landing) was knocked over with dysentery, and was carried for dead to Cape Coast Castle." This brief description is most interesting, as giving as it were at a glance the various hygienic causes predisposing the body to the action of the morbific poison. An officer of the Royal Marines, who left for Africa on the 13th May, 1873, served during both phases of the war, was only on return to England attacked with fever, accompanied by delirium.

I landed in Africa on the 1st September, 1873, when the noxious exhalations from the soil was most perceptible, rising as they did from the damp ground with the bright sun; again on the 3rd and 4th; and again on the 11th. Got on pretty well until the 26th November, eighty-seven days after landing, and after being a month in the bush. I then had a sharp attack of ague. It is, therefore, quite evident from the foregoing facts, and also from the duration and intensity of the symptoms varying considerably (in some favourable cases the febrile symptoms entailing only two or three days' confinement, little more than would occur with an attack of coryza, to a fever lasting nine days or a month, including convalescence), that the age and susceptibility of the individual, the period at which he comes under the influence of the telluric emanations, the quantity imbibed, the fact of his having been exposed to the common exciting causes, such as chills or wettings, marching in the sun, or the ordinary predisposing ones, viz., debility, induced by insufficient, unappetizing, or unnutritious food, unsuitable housing, clothing, and any depressing influences, are the causes which prolonged or shortened the incubatory interval. It was quite possible that if an individual was able to avoid a bush life and its many hardships, live well in quarters, in pleasant company, with interesting work to do, especially if of an active kind, he might have escaped an attack of fever altogether during the short time the Expedition lasted. Such instances did occur even on shore. Very few of the officers on board ship who had not landed, and lived well, suffered from fever. In all malarial countries or places similar discrepancies are observed. From observations made upon the endemic fever of Sicily in 1810, the average period of incubation appeared to be twenty days; the minimum *thirteen;* the maximum *thirty.* Of ninety-one persons exposed for a fortnight to the paludal exhalations, only fourteen escaped an attack of fever: of the seventy-seven attacked, twenty-three died—a ratio of thirty per cent. It is well known that many a traveller has had ague from merely passing through the Pontine marshes. Individuals who have only slept for a single night in Essex have been attacked in a similar manner: experiences repeating themselves in Africa, as already seen, in every particular.

The effect of the predisposing causes was especially shown at the outposts, where the officers suffered more, owing to the discomfort, indifferent diet, and monotony. In such situations scorbutic symptoms became invariably more quickly developed. I am inclined also to think that the amount of hardship and exposure underwent would modify the gravity of the symptoms induced. The only three European officers invalided from the Gold Coast, in 1872, had isolated commands on detachment—away from the comforts, regular diet, and fair living of a mess, to which causes their illnesses were in great part attributed.

Does one attack of fever prevent the occurrence of another, or moderate the violence of the after paroxysm? I would say yes, from my experience. We know that the marshes of Sicily are nearly innocuous to the inhabitants, while they are very fatal to new-comers or strangers, who may go shooting in them, particularly after sundown. In the Romagna, immediately the sun touches the horizon, the shepherds enter their huts, close the door, crouch round the fire, and smoke vigorously. A friend who would not be warned, and tried an opposite plan, remaining in the pursuit of game in the short twilight, was quickly attacked with fever, and ultimately obliged to depart in consequence, for more genial climes. Here the seasoned natives did not get fever: probably a stranger would not after his first attack, if he adopted similar precautions; but, although not showing the outward signs of a febrile paroxysm, the residents of such places invariably present a cachectic appearance, with a sallow, leaden countenance, and upon examination the evidence of visceral engorgements, and very often a protuberant abdomen. Such persons carry with them into other latitudes the latent germs of the disease; they become ill upon very small provocation, and can scarcely be said to be at any time completely well, although they may manage to prolong their term of service to the end, especially if opportunities occur for a short voyage or change to another station. During an officer's first term of service in Africa he appears to suffer from sharper attacks of fever than he does afterwards: his rallying power appears to decrease with service and age. Men who live in Africa, and are fortunate to survive for any length of time, become so accustomed to fever that they look upon it as a kind of second nature—as one of those things which must be gone through and endured. It is only when some friend dies, or an epidemic arises, that the fact is brought home to them that their lives have been hanging the whole time upon little better than a thread. When I passed Sierra Leone, in September, 1873, only *five* of the Europeans who had been among the residents of 1861 remained; the remainder had either left or died. Four of those who remained were Colonial officials; the fifth a lawyer. From this it is evident that some few can resist the deteriorating effects of malaria for years. In this case those few were civilians, actively engaged in interesting pursuits, and who felt the place to be their home; they were also well housed, rarely exposed to vicissitude of climate, lived well but moderately, were of temperate habits, and to some extent adopted the habits of the country. When at anchor at the Gambia we dined at the house of an English merchant, hale and hearty, who had been trading there for *forty years*. He looked well and sprightly, while every one around was either down with fever, or showing evident signs of the disease, from which they were only just recovering. It should be remarked, however, that the better class European merchants at this station visit England or France once a year, at the fall of the rains, returning with the commencement of the dry or ground nut season.

The primary cause of disease on the coast of Africa is a morbific poison, term it what you will, leading to certain well-known symptoms, and when inhaled for a prolonged period, to equally well-known degenerations. The exciting causes, chills, exposure to the sun, wettings; the modifying ones, a scorbutic taint, and some unexplained peculiarity of constitution; the intensifying influences, exhalations from a newly turned up soil. Unaccustomed exertion in the moist and excessively humid climate appeared also to predispose to disease. I feel confident that the conducting vehicle in many instances was water, holding in solution the poisonous miasm—a poison we can still only recognize by its effects. It has often struck me that this particular virus, in its manifestations, may be likened to the poison which produces secondary syphilis. This is best seen by a tabular comparison of the manifestations and exciting causes of both:—

MARSH POISON.	SYPHILITIC POISON.
Primary cause, a specific germ.	Primary cause, a specific germ.
Period of incubation, generally a few days to six weeks.	A few days to six weeks. (I have seen the rash in twelve days.)
First outward manifestation, a specific febrile state, followed not unfrequently by boils and ulcers.	First outward manifestation, febrile symptoms and a specific rash.
May be delayed in its appearance under certain circumstances.	May be delayed in its appearance under certain circumstances.
Aggravated by mal-hygiene.	Aggravated by mal-hygiene.
May remain latent for a time under certain favourable conditions.	May be latent for a time under certain favourable conditions.
In the more severe forms leads to congestions and diseases of internal viscera, and an impoverished blood.	In the more severe forms leads to degenerations and deposits in the internal viscera, and to an impoverished blood.

It will be seen from this brief comparison that the train of symptoms in each is very similar. Of the exact nature of the ultimate virus of syphilis we are as yet as ignorant as we are of that which causes paludal fevers. We can go back a certain way in both, and then have to stop. In both diseases is observed a comparatively mild and more severe affection. The one we know to be due to sexual intercourse; that the chief elements of paludal or febrific exhalations, viz., earth, water, and decaying vegetable matter in abundance; the cause of the other virus was present on the Gold Coast, was patent to all. These are always inland from a Coast line, and it is in consequence of this that the night breeze in Africa is so much more dangerous than that blowing from the sea. Remove a European sufficiently far away from the influence of the former or the shore, place him under the best hygienic conditions possible, and he will not get intermittent or remittent fever. Captain Selwyn, Royal Navy, when reciting his experience on board the "Prometheus," on the Coast of Africa, says, when alluding to the treatment of paludal yellow fever, "as long as we had to combat the malaria of the Coast it was utterly futile to expect good results."

The greater prevalence of the fever up country and on the line of march was probably owing to the specific poison being there more powerful, because more concentrated, owing to the stillness of the atmosphere and the absence of a brisk breeze to render it more inert by diffusion. When marshes were not present *en route*, their equivalents were always to be found, which all experience has proved to be equally productive of specific fever of the paludal type, viz., a very retentive subsoil, not allowing water to easily percolate through it, an extent of forest which impeded thorough ventilation and the action of the sun's rays, excessive dampness with heat, and a total inattention to drainage and culture, the *whole of which* conditions were to be found on the Gold Coast; where, in addition, the excessive and almost unvarying humidity of the atmosphere, the rank luxuriance of the vegetation, and the extreme heat, causing a continuous evaporation from the soil and rivers, tended further to enervate the frame and predispose it to the noxious influences of the tainted atmosphere, rendered still more impure by the offensive effluvia arising from the decomposing refuse of the inhabitants in many places, as well as from numerous dead bodies—a combination of smells perfectly indescribable.

From the following percentages to strength, where in the case of the 1st West, Naval Brigade, and the European regiments, the figures relate to the period between the 1st January and the 28th February, 1874 (the dates of disembarkation and embarkation), it will be seen that remittent fever was the prevailing disease over attacks of dysentery.

Regiment.	Strength.	Fevers.		Diarrhœa and Dysentery.	
		Sick.	Died.	Sick.	Died.
23rd	270	30	0	9	0
42nd	656	42	·31	6	0
R. B.	652	57	·31	14	·61
1 W. I.	552	13	·36	1	·0
2 W. I.	560	25	·18	17	1·25
N. Brigade	250	54	0	34	1·20
Wood's	440	45	0	4	0
Russell's	500	5	0	4	0
Rait's Artillery	45	16	0	16	0

The figures are taken from Brackenbury. Years since the mortality from remittent fever at Sierra Leone was very high among the European garrison. Of 1,600 cases recorded, 760 died—nearly one in two. In the Niger Expedition of 1841, the steamer arrived in the river on the 13th August. Remittent and other fevers began to display themselves on the 4th September (twenty-two days). In seven weeks, 130 out of 145 Europeans were attacked, and fifty-three died—nearly a third of the force. In the seven weeks' occupation of the Gold Coast by the white troops, 511 out of 2,507, of all ranks, were attacked, the mortality being only a ninth of those falling sick, instead of a third, as in the Niger in 1841. I have alluded to these figures to show how disease and mortality may be reduced by hygienic measures carried out in the proper season.

The causes which lead to the development of malarial fevers tend also to produce dysentery. We have instances of this at home without going to Africa. In former times in Ireland dysentery stood next in order of frequency to continued fever, called by Boate the "Irish Ague." It was then endemic, and disappeared *pari passu* with the improvement and cultivation of the country. In the seventeenth century it was one of the great army diseases, and committed great havoc amongst the troops, many of King William's army falling a victim to it, in that "devilish wet swampy country," as the Emerald Isle was then styled by Walker and others. The English and Scots regiments were generally more affected with it. Several of the great epidemics were epidemics of fever and dysentery. It gradually disappeared with the improvement in the barrack and hospital accommodation, dress, and food of the soldier. In 1801 the disease was attributed to the "long continuance of dry, hot weather, followed by a change of temperature, and a considerable fall of rain." It arose at the end of the epidemic fever, as it did afterwards after that which prevailed in the autumn of 1818, so graphically described by Cheyne. Of ninety-eight cases analyzed and carefully noted by Dr. Cheyne, the then Physician-General to the Forces in Ireland, thirty-three arose during recovery from fever, fifteen while the fever was in progress, fifteen arose from cold or cold and wet, four from indigestion; the rest were doubtful, but nine had been in close communication with the sick. The dysentery frequently occurred at that period of recovery from fever when there seemed the greatest liability amongst the convalescents to relapse. "Dysentery often commenced with a rigor and terminated in a free perspiration. It was sometimes converted into a fever, while on the other hand, fever was frequently converted into dysentery; and lastly, during convalescence from dysentery, several persons sustained an attack of fever; in short," writes Dr. Cheyne, "these forms of disease were convertible the one into the other; so that the opinion of Sydenham, that dysentery is a febris introversa, that is, fever turned in on the intestines, received support from our observations; and it is not unreasonable to suppose that as these patients in my wards, in common with most of the poor of the city, had been exposed to the contagion of fever, this contagion, according to the condition of the system at the time of its application, or some other modifying circumstance, may have produced at one time fever, at another dysentery." This view is borne out by recent experience in Fiji, many of the natives being attacked with dysentery after they had jumped into the water while suffering from measles, and the high fever accompanying the outward manifestations of the exanthem. If we turn to the history of the disease on the Gold Coast, it will be found that this description applies very closely to the dysentery and fever which prevailed during the late operations. There were fevers and dysenteries, or either alone, or the one following upon the other.

The type of dysentery seen during the first phase of the war varied much. In this affection as well as in the diseases already considered, the symptoms betokened a mild, severe, or dangerous form, according to circumstances and length of residence. Of the fifty-nine cases admitted to Haslar Hospital on the return of the first batch of Marines to England, nineteen were suffering from dysentery; the prominent symptom being, according to Dr. Donnet, prostration of the mental and physical powers; no bodily pain, but a state of despondency, from which it was difficult to rally them, the expression of the countenance being that of extreme languor, the frequent looseness of the bowels being the cause of much distress. In these cases the evacuations were either fæcal matters in various degrees of fluidity, fæcal matters mixed with mucus, or in the graver cases, blood and mucus, with a wax-like matter, consisting principally of granular matter mixed with epithelial cells. During the later stages of the war, the more severe cases were accompanied by dejections of pure blood, coming on almost at the onset of the disease; or the symptoms would commence with slight griping, frequent desire to go to stool, passage of only a little mucus, followed by fæcal matter and blood. During the time Fort Napoleon was occupied by a detachment of the 2nd West, a number of cases of dysentery occurred amongst the men, mostly of a mild form, and readily amenable to treatment. In these cases the evacuations were chiefly liquid fæcal matter, slightly coloured with blood. When the dejections were scanty, slime and fæcal matter appeared to be in equal amount. In the only case which ended fatally, a patient who contracted the disease at Dix Cove, and was admitted almost *in articulo mortis*, the matter passed from the bowels consisted of mucus, blood, pus, and slime: the stools were very offensive. The unfortunate man, a West Indian Creole, was worn to a skeleton, and scarcely ever off the chamber utensil. In this case the *post mortem* examination revealed extensive ulceration of the internal coat of the large intestine. In some instances the more acute symptoms supervened upon a chronic persistent diarrhœa of varying duration, not unfrequently kept up by local irritation within the rectum. In others, as stated before, the first intimation of the presence of the disease was the frequent desire to go to stool, griping, straining, and small mucus dejections. I have also observed the primary symptoms to have been ushered in with much fever, indicated by a hot skin, accelerated pulse, temperature of $102°$ or $103°$, very severe pain in the abdomen, frequent desire to go to stool, and dejections of liquid fæcal matter mixed with blood and slime. When the disease had become at all chronic and severe, indicating much bowel mischief, the stools were most offensive, so much so, that it was almost impossible to remain in the immediate vicinity of the sufferer, more especially while evacuating the contents of the bowel. At such a time the odour permeated throughout the entire apartment. In the most severe form of all, sloughs were passed away from the colon, which after death was found to be gangrenous, sometimes perforated, death being preceded by sudden collapse and violent pain in the abdomen, indicating the passage of the contents of the bowel into the cavity of the peritoneum. In the Marines who died, the colon and rectum were found thickened and raised in several places into lardaceous masses; in others, ragged ulcers remained to show the site of the sloughs which had been thrown off. The ulcers varied from the size of a pea to half a crown. A scorbutic taint was evident in many of those who suffered from dysenteric symptoms on the Gold Coast; and the close analogy between the fever and dysentery, so much dilated upon by Cheyne, Pringle, and other writers, was observed. Sometimes the two affections would accompany each other, under the term "fever and dysentery;" or the one would follow or precede the other—a patient convalescent from fever being attacked with dysentery, or the reverse. A private of the Rifle Brigade, who marched to Coomassie, and was months afterwards treated for fever in the General Hospital, Dublin, attributed the onset of his dysenteric symptoms to a chill brought on while crossing the Dah on the return march. On reaching the opposite bank, he was obliged to do sentry during the night in his wet clothes. Next morning he was attacked with griping and other symptoms of dysentery. No doubt many similar instances occurred. Many of those who suffer from Gold Coast dysentery die on the voyage to England, mostly upon arrival in the colder latitudes. Getting on apparently well, they are, after some indiscretion in the matter of diet, suddenly seized anew with all their former symptoms, and rapidly succumb. Several instances of this kind have come under my notice. As a rule, however, the health rapidly improves on the return voyage, especially when the organic lesions are not profound; the purer air, better food, and entire change of scene working wonders. While dysentery is very common in the Gold Coast, and easily excited there, it is comparatively speaking unknown at Sierra Leone. The immunity appears to be due to several causes. These are the purity and abundance of the water which flows into the town from the mountain ridges; the better cultivation and higher state of civilization of the country and people; the facility with which all the necessaries of life are obtained; the abundance of fresh animal and vegetable food, and consequent absence of the scorbutic taint; the greater diversity of the climate, and the admirable position of the barracks; the comfortable quarters and good mess usually kept up, and the absence to some extent of those damp, chilly night winds, and the greater dryness of the atmosphere.

From the figures indicating the percentages of sickness during the march to Coomassie, it will be seen that the troops suffered from fevers in the following order:—

Rifle Brigade	57	per cent.
Naval Brigade	54	,,
42nd Regiment	42	,,
23rd Regiment	30	,,
2nd W. I. Regiment	25	,,
1st W. I. Regiment	13	,,
Average	37	per cent.

DIARRHŒA AND DYSENTERY.

Naval Brigade	34	per cent.
2nd W. I. Regiment	17	,,
Rifle Brigade	14	,,
23rd Regiment	9	,,
42nd Regiment	6	,,
2nd W. I. Regiment	1	,,

Average percentage of mortality from fever, ·19; from diarrhœa and dysentery, ·51.

Contrary to what was stated very confidently at the outset of the war, the West India regiments suffered least from fevers; the 1st least from dysentery and diarrhœa; the 2nd, much longer on the Coast, less than the Naval Brigade, but more than the European regiments. The large number of admissions from fevers, diarrhœa, and dysentery among the men of the Naval Brigade was probably due to the fact of their being longer up country, preparing the camp at Prashue for the European troops. Some of the men had also served in the previous phase of the war. The very low rate of mortality is remarkable, and may be fairly attributable to the excellent hygienic measures adopted to preserve health. The admissions would have been less if time had allowed of the soil being dried before occupation, and not disturbed so immediately before.

The climate of the Gold Coast presented all the characteristics of one in which liver disease would prevail. A hot and humid atmosphere, with chilly, damp night winds. One officer, who died while *en route* to England, had a liver enormously enlarged, and extending as far as the crest of the ileum. His symptoms were those of great exhaustion, irritability of stomach, and disinclination for food. In others, the chief symptoms were cough, dyspnœa on exertion, tenderness increased by pressure over the liver, the margin of which was lower than natural, roughened and creaking respiration heard over the lower portion of the right lung posteriorly, increasing pain and enlargement of the liver, and dulness at the base of the lung. A weak and thready pulse, rising to 130 to 140, swelling and fluctuation, coughing up of purulent matter, containing lung tissue and hepatic cells; profuse sweats and rigors indicated the presence of hepatic abscess communicating with the lung. After death a *post mortem* examination would reveal large single or multiple abscesses, the smaller ones varying from the size of a pea to an orange. Instances occurred where an enormous abscess existed with a temperature not above 100, little hectic, no rigors, jaundice, or irregularity of bowels. The early occurrence and continuance of prune juice expectoration, Eames considered of much diagnostic value, as suggestive of the inflammatory process having been continued through the diaphragm to the pleura and the lung. In the case of an officer suffering from symptoms of hepatic abscess, and admitted into Netley from the Gold Coast, the patient was expectorating daily ten or twelve ounces of purulent matter from an abscess situated on the convex surface of the right lobe. The liver was much enlarged, but not in any way tender. Professor Maclean diagnosed the presence of a deeper seated abscess from—

(*a*) The enlargement of the liver.
(*b*) The case having had a dysenteric history.
(*c*) Persistent high temperature, 101°–104°.
(*d*) Progressive emaciation.

The long needle of the aspirator, passed between the eighth and ninth ribs in the axillary line four inches deep into the substance of the gland, reached an abscess from which twenty-four ounces of pus was evacuated. Dr. Maclean considered persistent vomiting following upon hepatic symptoms significant of abscess pressing upon the stomach and duodenum, and making nutrition impossible, and that a large abscess may exist without pain as long as the peritoneal covering is not affected. I have more than once verified the correctness of this opinion. Of three cases of hepatitis admitted to the Royal Victoria Hospital, Netley, from among the invalids on board the Victor Emanuel, one was the sequence of remittent fever, the other of ague, and the third of an attack of dysentery contracted after fording a river.

Fayrer's experience confirms these two points. Although bilious attacks and sub-acute inflammations and congestions, the latter two indicated by torpid bowels, clayey stools, dyspepsia, and pain in the side, are not uncommon among the residents in Western Africa, hepatic abscess is a comparatively speaking rare disease. During five years and a-half I only saw one case, occurring in the person of an American sailor in a temperance ship. It was pointing externally in the epigastrium. During a service of seven years on the station in the Navy, Eames only remembered two cases. Amongst the black troops on the Coast in 1870 there was only one admission for hepatitis, six in 1871. A chill after being heated is probably the most frequent exciting cause.

In the earlier phases of the war, men of the 2nd West India Regiment suffered more than afterwards from bronchial affections, owing to the damp and inclement weather which then prevailed; in a few cases the tubercular dyscrasia was evidently present, the wet and cold exciting it into activity. There was a very constant tendency to pneumonia, especially at the base of the left lung. In these troops the prognosis is not by any means a favourable one when the congestion of the lungs is extensive. The same rule holds good in phthisical affections.

Ulcers of the lower extremities and foot sore were rather more common towards the close of either phase of the active operations. In some, the scorbutic taint was very pronounced; in others, a combination of the malarial dyscrasia and scorbutus. Among the European officers who suffered from these ulcers of the lower extremities (the parts nearly always attacked) the ulcers were mostly very troublesome, painful, and not easily amenable to treatment. Any one who was unfortunate enough to suffer from them was completely "pinned by the leg," and only able to hobble about. The tendency to spread, and slowness or entire cessation of the healing process, or again, the healing up to a certain point, and breaking out again as bad as ever, pointed to the presence of a constitutional change or deterioration of the blood or tissues. These ulcers sometimes followed upon an attack of purpura or land scurvy, or after much wading through swamps and water. Some attributed their presence in such instances to the poisonous quality of the water. Of a party of officers who left Dunquah on the 18th November to open the road, when it was very wet, and necessary to wade through many pools, the only one who did not suffer from ulcers afterwards wore a pair of long boots, by which means the legs were protected. A common exciting cause was a bruise or a scratch; at other times they appeared to originate in one or more boils. The resulting sore was essentially an irritable, painful ulcer, with inflamed and undermined edges, or a livid margin surrounding a mass of dark fungating granulations. These ulcers would heal and contract for a time, and then suddenly retrograde, and slowly slough away in spite of all care; or in other instances remain stationary, the margin of new skin becoming undermined and easily detached. The discharge was usually abundant and unhealthy looking, and the pain occasionally most agonizing. An enlarged spleen, congested or torpid liver, and sluggish portal circulation appeared in some cases to prevent a favourable termination. In one instance a trip to sea of ten days' duration, a raised position, and an entire change of diet, with careful bandaging, and spirit lotion, did a good deal to complete a cure, but on return to a residence on shore, things became shortly as bad as before; so that as a rule little more could be done on the Gold Coast than to prevent these ulcers spreading or becoming worse. The general appearance of the invalid, his previous history, present symptoms, and speedy restoration to health, and with

M

this the contraction and healing up of the ulcerated surfaces, and sudden relapse upon a return to the shore and a humid malarial climate, appeared to prove conclusively the presence of an all-powerful constitutional taint. These ulcers were confined almost exclusively to the lower extremities. In only one instance, where they followed a crop of boils after an attack of bilious fever, did I see them succumb to treatment after a thorough cauterization with solid nitrate of silver. In this case the officer was enabled to proceed up country, but had afterwards to return, suffering from a relapse of his former endemic remittent. The same tendency to remain stationary, or a very slow process of healing, was observed among the black troops. The application of a strong lotion of nitric acid, although most painful at the time, usually left a more florid and healthy surface. Alum lotion was almost a specific: where the ulcer would heal at all, it would do so after the application of this salt in solution. Spirit lotion was also a very good form of application. The application of lint, soaked in either of the two last lotions, morning and evening, a raised position of the affected limb, the application of a soft, wet bandage, evenly applied over it and the oil silk, a trip to sea, and good animal and vegetable food, might effect a cure if the patient would keep away from the influence of the Coast line until the healing process was complete. Warm linseed poultices merely soothed and relieved pain, doing little more towards the healing of the ulcer. A cold bread and water poultice was sometimes useful, as were also opiate, poppy-head, and camomile fomentations. The constitutional treatment would principally consist in the administration of alkaline tonics, to restore the normal condition of the intestinal secretions and correct acidity; occasional purgatives, to diminish the contents of the portal vessels, good, fresh animal and vegetable food, milk, porridge, and claret. In former times in Dublin, blood-letting in the early stage, and purgatives and opium during every stage of the complaint, with change of air, light tonics, the vegetable and mineral acids, sufficiently diluted, also the warm bath, had been a favourite mode of treatment for purpuric affections.

The appearance of these inflamed ulcers and boils, their slow and unsatisfactory progress, the negative result of treatment, and the evident presence of a constitutional taint, make them akin to those lingering sores which prevail in North Western India, and which in many instances seem to result from the combined ill effects upon the system of malaria, a scorbutic taint, and a water derived from a soil largely impregnated with nitrates. The cicatrices remaining are exactly similar in appearance.

In those who had had ague; cold feet, a cold bath, or a chill of any kind, brought on at once either an abortive or acute attack. On one occasion when I tried to do the heroic, a few days after landing from Africa, about Christmas time, I found it would not do. I went into a cold bath, had scarcely touched the water when my teeth began to chatter, and a paroxysm of ague came on in full vigour—a warning to others not to follow such a foolish practice. The water should be always tepid, at least for a time. The predisposition to these aguish attacks continues for a long period. It takes two or three years in a good bracing climate to wear out the malarial poison, provided that the visceral disorganizations are not extensive: when the spleen is very much enlarged and the dyscrasia profound, a much longer time is required. Some seem always liable to a recurrence of their former attacks upon very slight exciting causes. Damp and aguish districts should be always avoided. An officer told me quite recently that as long as he was quartered at a station situated upon a dry and elevated porous soil, he was quite well; but that when he was sent to another, to leeward of a long mud reach, on the South Coast of England, over which blew daily the sea breeze before reaching his quarters, he was constantly having ague. Warm clothing is absolutely necessary on the return to our cold northern climate.

A month or so after these earlier aguish symptoms occurred, urinary attacks were noticed in some officers. There was much irritability of the neck of the bladder, inability to retain the urine (which was strongly acid) for any length of time. There was also great weight and pain in the perinæum. Others, as the cold weather approached, were much troubled with cough and relaxed throat, or from inflammatory boils, or from periodical feelings of *malaise*, stopping short of the ordinary quotidian paroxysm—seeming as if the poison was losing its force with time, and unable to do more than show its presence by the annoyance which it caused. Frost and cold was severely felt; the former, in spite of heavy clothing, especially at night, when it appeared to penetrate as it were into the bones.

The malarial poison is best encountered in its early stage, and then most easily neutralized by remedies, and prevented from exercising its well-known disorganizing influences upon the viscera. Once these last are seriously affected, it is by no means an easy matter to restore them to their former normal condition. It is very doubtful whether this is even possible. I agree with Livingstone, that the best prophylactics are a generous diet, plenty of intellectual and ambulatory work to do, a good house, proper clothes, and the avoidance of a sedentary life.

An officer who served three years and eight months at a stretch on the Gold Coast, attributed his good health to the fact of his rising early, having at 2 o'clock P.M. a strong pot of soup made from good stock, such as fowls, rice, &c., and at night tea. He employed his leisure time in fishing, shooting, and sailing on the salt-pond, and plenty of other interesting work. He was not ill for six months. He then had his first attack of fever, which lasted fifteen days. He afterwards spent an occasional month at Accra, shooting every day in the sun, he and his companions starting in the early morning, and taking with them some sandwiches and beer. From these excursions he never felt any ill effects. My experience is against the idea that quinine will prevent the advent of fever, but quinine wine bitters given morning and evening may be useful as a mild stimulating tonic. On the Zambesi, Livingstone found that those who took quinine and those who did not were equally attacked, which led to its final abandonment. The men of the West India Regiment who occupied the camp at Napoleon were given daily a solution of quinoidine. I cannot say that it did them any particular good, or prevented them from suffering from mild attacks of fever and dysentery. A clerk in one of the merchant's offices, who had been taking very large doses of quinine daily, under the idea that it would prevent the occurrence of fever, was attacked with a severe form of congestive remittent, and died, the alkaloid having proved useless as a remedy. The general idea among the European residents in West Africa is this—that quinine has little power as a prophylactic against fever, and that when taken *de die in diem*, it loses its power as a remedy. When a febrile attack is coming on, it may cut it short or abort it. It has been always thought there that its frequent use destroyed its after curative power, which is believed to be, in the vast majority of instances, with suitable adjuncts, all-powerful. I have myself very rarely taken it except as a remedy, and as a consequence as rarely found it to fail in its specific therapeutic effects. These views are in accord with those recently enunciated by M. Seé, at La Charité, who affirms, as the result of his investigations, that quinine does not prevent malarial poisoning when taken as a prophylactic, or prevent its recurrence after a variable period; and that it is useless in some of the fatal forms, especially when the fever tends to assume the continued type; and that in other fevers, which present the characters of periodicity, and the occurrence of initial rigor, quinine has an equally beneficial effect. M. Seé considers its effect in ague to be due to its three-fold action exerted during this period, viz., its action on the heart diminishes the frequency and force of the pulse; it lowers the tension and produces dilatation of the peripheral arteries, and acts as a sedative on the spinal cord and vaso-motor centres; and lastly, exerts a direct cooling action on the system generally, whereby the febrile paroxysms are checked or moderated.

Some of those who took quinine mixture in the early morning at Cape Coast before going to work became sick in the stomach immediately afterwards; in others much dizziness, and a feeling of inability to work in the sun followed its use. The latter effects would be probably prevented by giving it in more moderate doses, and the former by administering it as wine bitters, or in warm coffee, a capital vehicle, which removes altogether the bitter, and to many, disagreeable taste. A late Naval officer of distinction kept his boats' crews very healthy in the African rivers by giving, the first thing in the morning, a cup of hot coffee and a little rum mixed with it. The heat and diffusible stimulant probably acted as a diaphoretic, and prevented the initial chill so frequently the exciting cause of ague.

Although quinine, when taken in small doses from day to day, did not appear in West Africa to prevent attacks of fever, it seemed certainly sometimes to modify or check altogether—in other words, prevent or cut off a coming febrile paroxysm, when taken in a sufficiently large dose immediately before. An old resident will, for instance, feel a number of symptoms coming on, such as frequent yawning, slight headache, disinclination for exertion, an occasional shiver or creeping sensation down the back or in one of the limbs, and an indescribable feeling which he knows but too well to be the premonitory warnings of his old enemy. If he at once takes a large dose of quinine in some hot coffee, the chances are greatly in favour of the paroxysm being cut off or aborted. This fact I have verified on more than one occasion. I am also inclined to think that quinine is useful if taken at the onset of a march through a swamp. It should not be forgotten that quinine is more effective in its curative or specific action, when the chylo-poietic viscera have been previously relieved by a purgative, or when the preliminary dose is given in combination with it. As long as the liver, spleen, and portal systems are congested and unrelieved by depurants, quinine and ferruginous medicines fail not unfrequently to exercise their usual well-known effects. A very good form of combination is a saturated solution of sulphate of magnesia, containing five grains of quinine and ten minims of diluted sulphuric acid to the ounce, with a little tincture of ginger—an ounce for a dose. Another excellent combination, especially where hepatic symptoms are present, is Livingstone's powder (quinine, rhubarb, calomel, and jalap). Quinine has also been combined with excellent effect with sulphate of iron and sulphate of magnesia when the spleen is enlarged. Warburgh's tincture has never had a fair trial in African fevers. That it would prove most useful I have no doubt, from the very strong expressions of approval given of it by many officers who used it in India. When quinine is given in fever, where cerebral complications do not contra-indicate, it may be combined with very small doses of morphia, one-sixteenth of a grain to a dose. The morphia appears to aid, by its sedative effect upon the vaso-motor nerves, and thus lead to an earlier relaxation of the skin, and a general soothing influence on the whole system. Lind, who was an accurate observer, and had an immense experience, recommended the administration of an opiate half an hour after the commencement of the hot stage of ague. He was of opinion that it shortened and abated the fit, relieved the headache (always an urgent symptom), and brought on a profuse sweat, with an agreeable softness of the skin, ending in refreshing sleep. Opium has this effect; it will cure an ague; but the frequent repetition of the remedy induces a far graver affection, and one most difficult to cure—opium-eating. I knew of the case of one officer who adopted this method of cure for ague in Western Africa; the remedy had its effect when used; but his whole system is now so disorganized that he can neither eat nor sleep with any comfort, his liver is altogether out of order, and to add to his misfortunes, he has come in for a fortune which he can no longer enjoy. Quinine in very large and continued doses is almost equally hurtful. Its mal-effects are seen especially in the nervous system, in the shape of deafness, ptosis, contraction of the fingers, &c. When the stomach is irritable and rejects the liquid solution, quinine may be best administered in pill. Six grains of the alkaloid, one of gum arabic, and two of glycerine, into two pills, morphia being added under certain conditions with benefit. For field service, pills will always be found the most portable form: they must be recently made. I have used quinine, combined with aloetic purgatives, in some chronic cases where the viscera have been more or less disorganized, with good effect, free purgative giving wonderful relief. When the three-fold action of a diaphoretic stimulant and anti-periodic is required, a solution of sulphate of quinine may be combined with sweet spirits of nitre, the liquor and aromatic spirit of ammonia, a purgative having been administered previously. The quinine is at first precipitated, but afterwards re-dissolved. In the subsequent convalescence, extract of iron and quinine, tincture of orange peel, and spirit of chloroform, is of great benefit. In obstinate agues, which resist quinine and the usual mode of treatment, arsenic may be employed with advantage. I have known it to cure where all other means have failed to afford relief. Its efficacy was well established by Fowler, of Stafford, in 1783, when out of 247 persons upon whom he tried it, 171 were permanently cured. At the onset of the febrile paroxysm, emetics are sometimes of service. At Mansue, the engineers and others working on the roads came at once for an emetic of ipecacuanha when they felt the fever coming on. Its use afforded much relief. Quinine is undoubtedly our sheet anchor in malarial diseases of the intermittent and remittent type, more especially when the remission in the last named fever is sufficiently marked to allow of its administration. The identity of the cause of the two diseases is shown by the degeneration, as it were, of the remittent into the intermittent or typical malarial fever. When, however, the fever assumes the form of a severe bilious remittent, with head symptoms, or approaches the continued type, quinine is, as a rule, of dubious benefit. Neither is it so effective in those chronic cases where the malarial and scorbutic cachexia are well marked, and the viscera of the abdomen are hypertrophied and congested. Where irritability of the stomach forbids its administration by the mouth, it may be either injected hypodermically, or given *per rectum* in combination with brandy and beef tea. I have seen more than one case rescued in this last manner, when the patient was almost gone.

In the opinion of the Naval officers employed during the earlier operations in the Protectorate, quinine was not a prophylactic against attacks of remittent fever. Quinine was administered regularly to the Marines landed at Elmina to guard the place; yet, within a month, all of the men returned on board ill with fever. Men who landed for a day and did not take quinine, fared as well as those who took it and escaped an attack. All the 110 officers and men who landed on the 28th of October, before leaving the ship took quinine; ten returned sick the same day, chiefly suffering from insolatio and gastric symptoms. Quinine was served out to the Marines who started for Elmina on the 12th June—five grains in half a gill of rum all round, the same quantity at daylight in port wine; all these men had severe attacks of remittent fever. After wet and damp nights it was always given to the sentries, with no better effect; bearing out the opinion already noticed as being held on the Coast, that the daily use of quinine causes such a tolerance of it to be created, that when attacked with fever, it requires enormous doses to produce any effect. With regard to its curative properties, Naval officers were of opinion that the enormous doses (as much as sixty grains) given by foreigners and American practitioners, were unnecessary. Some medical officers gave *five* grains every third hour during the remission, doubling the dose immediately before an expected exacerbation of the fever stage, and five grains three times a day directly the remissions ceased; reducing the dose to three grains three times a day during the latter days of convalescence—a practice found most satisfactory. Others preceded the use of quinine by purgatives, salines, and diaphoretics, giving a full dose of the specific remedy, fifteen to twenty grains, on the occurrence of a remission, followed by ten-grain doses every four or five hours after, for twenty-four hours, if there was no return of pyrexial symptoms; reducing the dose gradually to five and three grains, or substituting citrate of iron and quinine during convalescence; or quinine, strychnine, and cod liver oil. Even in cases of fever where the remission was not well marked, but which were evidently due to malarial poisoning, the use of quinine was of decided advantage. Quinine was also given at the onset of the disease, in combination with sulphate of magnesia, four grains of quinine to half an ounce of sulphate of magnesia, repeated every twenty-four hours, until the bowels acted well—a mode of administration found generally to relieve the head symptoms, and produce a remission. Quinine was then given in four-grain doses every fourth hour: salines, with antimonial wine, to relieve the heat of the skin. When relapse occurred, a mild purgative was administered, and then quinine, until convalescence was completely established, the dose being gradually decreased to four grains daily. In situations where dysentery prevailed, some mild purgative, such as castor oil or rhubarb, was substituted for sulphate of magnesia.

In the course of an interesting paper on the Australian blue and red gum trees (*Eucalyptus globulus* and *Eucalyptus rostrata*) the *Revue Maritime* gives the following extract from a letter written by the Abbé Charmetant, superintendent of the Maison Carré Orphanage, near Algiers, confirming the views already upheld and advocated of the expediency of giving these trees a really fair trial in the neighbourhood of some of our more insalubrious tropical and semi-tropical stations, and gives some information on the value of this drug.

"I must give you, writes the Abbé, a few particulars respecting our plantations of *Eucalyptus globulus* here at Maison Carré, which I am sure will interest you.

"This place, now our parent establishment, as you know, was some six years ago covered with a thick coppice of dwarf palms, which the stagnant water of the neighbouring harach rendered highly insalubrious.

"In 1869, 70, as the ground was cleared by grubbing up the coppice, large numbers of *Eucalyptus* were put in in clumps and rows along the fields and garden ground; these have given a park-like appearance to the domain, with a striking semblance of long-standing growth, as you have youself seen.

"The most remarkable result, however, has been that the intermittent fever, formerly so continually contracted by the pupils of the orphanage when engaged on field work, has gradually disappeared, and from being one of the most fever-stricken, the locality has become one of the healthiest in the vicinity of Algiers. Moreover, we have entirely discontinued the use of quinine in the exceptional cases of fever that now occur. For some years past we have used a *tisane* of leaves of *Eucalyptus globulus* taken from the young trees. We find—and the fact has been observed by many medical practitioners in Algiers—that this remedy is often efficacious in cases where quinine is of no avail, and what is more important, it has not, like the latter, the property of impairing the stomachic functions, and causing the disappearance of the fever to be associated with the distressing after-symptoms so well-known in Algeria under the name of '*la fievre quinine*.'"

Of blood letting I have no experience in African fever. Combined with the mercurial treatment, it was much in vogue on the Coast as elsewhere in former days: many died and many lived under this mode of cure. In some cases I feel sure the use of the lancet would prove of service, especially as a last resource, and when time did not permit of slower remedies. Take the following case, drawn from real life, as an example:—Many years ago a medical officer was called to see a European non-commissioned officer of the 1st West India Regiment, a full-blooded, thick-set man. He had been ailing for some days before he reported sick. The immediate symptoms were fever, intensely hot skin, coma, stertor—in other words, the closing ones of African remittent. The patient never rallied, and died some hours afterwards. A *post mortem* examination revealed congestion of the membranes of the brain and partial engorgement of the lung, yellowness of the skin. If this man had been bled to thirty or forty ounces, he would have probably recovered, or at least rallied sufficiently to allow of other remedies being tried. Quite recently a soldier was sent to hospital in Dublin: the death rattle was in his throat, and on examination, he was found to be suffering from pneumonia of so intense a form that respiration was scarcely possible. He was bled at once to forty ounces as a *dernier ressort*, and recovered. Cases like these seem to me to prove that, between life and death, the use of the lancet may sometimes turn the scale from the last into the first. According to Traube, the danger arising from serous exudations in important organs, as well as congestion of the brain and lungs, may be temporally averted by general blood letting, in consequence of the absorption of fluid into the vessels which it occasions—an experiment made so often as to leave no doubt on the subject; the very danger to be averted, if possible, in West African bilious or ardent remittent: hence the advantage of the practice under proper restrictions. The application of a large blister either to the occiput or spine, has been the usual application when symptoms of cerebral congestion supervene: when applied sufficiently early, I have seen it prove useful. A sinapism to the back of the neck, or the tepid douche, will sometimes remove those horrid phantasmagoria which render the hot stage of fever so painful to the sufferer. Warm lime baths are most refreshing and conducive to health in the intervals between the paroxysms, and during the first days of convalescence. The great principles to be remembered in the treatment of African fevers may be summed up in few words. Evacuate the contents of the digestive tract by purgatives, if necessary by emetics; seize upon the first interval or remission to administer the specific remedy to cut short or moderate the after paroxysm; relieve tension, heat, and pyrexia, by salines and sudorifics; encourage the secretion of the kidneys by warm diluents; assuage thirst by acid drinks in small quantities; treat local symptoms by local topical applications; support the strength by stimulants in moderate doses, nutritious broths, panadas, milk, eggs, and farinaceous powders, and guard against the tendency to death by

(a) Collapse.
(b) Exhaustion.
(c) Cerebral congestion or effusion.

In other words, the indications of cure are—
1. To moderate the violence of arterial excitement.
2. To support the powers of the system.
3. To obviate local inflammations and congestions.
4. To relieve urgent symptoms.

These are the principles which have always guided our treatment of febrile diseases in Western Africa; with careful nursing, which is half the battle, and must be often done by the surgeon himself, they have rarely proved unsuccessful. The prognosis in the milder forms of fever is nearly always favourable: the mortality in ague a little over 1 in 169 would point to this. In severe remittents it must, however, be always guarded. This can be easily understood when we look back to the history of this disease at Sierra Leone, when out of 1,600 cases treated years ago, 739 died, a mortality of nearly one in two.

Captain Selwyn, alluding to his experience while in command of H.M.S. Prometheus, on the Coast of Africa, mentions an interesting fact on the treatment of paludal yellow fever well worth mentioning. He says, "On both occasions when I commanded a steamer on the Coast of Africa, we had yellow fever on board. It was found at certain stages of the fever, particularly when complete exhaustion threatened to bring on a fatal termination, while the fever itself had been apparently overcome, that the administration of the strongest vegetable food we could get in the form of Scotch ale, invariably induced sleep and restoration of strength; while any attempt at giving strong animal foods, in the shape of jellies or broths, invariably had bad results. With regard to the ventilation of the ship, the only method we found successful was that of taking the men on deck, putting up a double awning, and sprinkling the inside of the latter continually with water, by which means a very strong current was set up, and very good results obtained. The bringing up of the yellow fever cases from the lower deck to under the awning diminished the percentage of deaths nearly one-half. A ship should go off the Coast for at least 300 miles, as only at that distance do the land breezes lose their specific effect." Such was Captain Selwyn's experience during two commissions. During convalescence from fever, good Dublin stout is of much benefit. In the acute stage brandy and sparkling Moselle are more useful. The state of the tongue, pulse, and the effect of previous doses, will indicate the necessity or otherwise for the use of stimulants, and the quantity required. Over doses are as much to be guarded against as infinitesimal ones. When the use of a stimulant affords a sense of relief, and the adding of a something which was felt by the sufferer to be wanting; when it gives force and volume to a weak or thready pulse, and when it does not increase the sense of discomfort and the general febrile condition, it is proving of service, and may be continued with advantage.

The treatment of dysentery depends altogether upon the stage and antecedents of the disease. In the acute and uncomplicated form, the administration of large doses of ipecacuanha (twenty or thirty grains), preceded by a draught containing a few mimins of tincture of opium, and a few grains of bicarbonate of soda, and the application of a sinapism over the stomach, the body being kept well covered while in the recumbent position, the head not raised upon a pillow, was, as a rule, most effective. No other remedy was tried with the men of the 2nd West treated at Cape Coast during the earlier phases of the war. The griping ceased, and the character of the stools changed almost immediately. As an example, showing how rapid are the effects of ipecacuanha, the following case may be cited:—The Brigade Office Clerk, a native of Sierra Leone, was admitted into the Garrison Hospital, Cape Coast, on the morning of the 17th October. He was suffering from the most acute pain in the abdomen, the beads of perspiration on his forehead, anxious countenance and drawn up legs, indicating the intensity of the griping; the pulse was quick and full, the skin hot, tongue coated, temperature 102°, tenesmus and desire to go to stool frequent; evacuations scanty, watery, and intermixed with blood. He was ordered twenty grains of ipecacuanha and warm stupes to the abdomen, to be followed by another scruple of the powder if the first dose was rejected. After a little time the first twenty grains of ipecacuanha was returned, but the second on being given was retained. When visited in the evening he was found to be much better, and on the following morning the temperature had fallen to 99°, a liquid stool having been passed without any mucus or blood; the griping had entirely disappeared, the skin had become cool and moist, and the tongue clean: on the third day he was discharged from hospital. My friend, Dr Finnemore, informed me that while at Mansue he had found ipecacuanha of much use when given either by the mouth or per rectum. Another valuable medicine in the premonitory griping and scanty mucus stools was the cholera mixture contained in the field companion, ten drops every quarter of an hour. Early one morning at Mansue I was suddenly attacked with slight griping, frequent desire to go to the rear, when nothing but a little mucus was passed after much straining. I at once lay down in my hut, got covered up with a blanket, took a small dose of opium, and sent for the cholera mixture, which I took in ten-drop doses frequently, and as soon as possible a little warm arrowroot and condensed milk. During the course of the day these premonitory symptoms disappeared. Dr. Fox, who was similarly attacked at Dunquah, followed the same routine treatment with equal success. Had these symptoms been neglected, much more severe ones would in all probability have followed. Here, fortunately, time permitted us to cut short the initiatory signs of disease. Had the symptoms been more urgent and severe, ipecacuanha would have been the remedy *par excellence*. The medicine, as long ago remarked by Pringle, appeared to exert its specific influence owing in great measure to its purgative qualities. I am inclined to think this premonitory griping is more frequently the initial symptom of the disease than supposed. A soldier of the Rifle Brigade, treated afterwards for ague in the General Hospital, Dublin, stated to me, that after wading across the Dah, and standing sentry in his wet clothes, he was attacked with griping, scanty mucus stools, followed by bloody evacuations and other well-known symptoms, necessitating his being invalided. In some instances acute dysentery supervened upon a chronic diarrhœa of long standing, connected or not with former dysenteric attacks. When such a diarrhœa assumed the form of the hepatic or white flux, small alterative doses of mercury and chalk, Dover's powder and ipecacuanha were of benefit. Small doses of castor oil, frequently repeated, or castor oil and opium, or the ordinary chalk and opium astringent, were of advantage in other cases. Sometimes local irritation in the rectum kept up the distressing symptoms. There was recently a very good illustration of this in the case of a patient invalided for chronic dysentery in the General Hospital. He died from an intercurrent attack of congestive pneumonia. The descending colon was found thickened, and the mucus coat of the rectum lined with cicatriced or open ulcers. In another soldier, who had never been abroad, an ulcer in the rectum just inside the sphincter, simulated all the symptoms of dysentery. In the former case starch and opium enemata would prove useful. In all cases of West African dysentery the most careful dieting, and an early removal to a purer air and more favoured locality, are, as a rule, the first essentials of a successful treatment. These are more especially necessary when the scorbutic taint complicates, as it so frequently does, the difficulties of the disease. Dysenteric cases should, if possible, be treated in isolated wards or tents so placed that the very offensive odour, sometimes unbearable, could not permeate through the apartments of others. Earth closets, or the lavish use of disinfectants, would prevent this to some extent.

Naval surgeons differed little in the general treatment usually adopted in fever and dysentery. In mild cases, simple effervescing draughts during the primary and exacerbation stage, sinapisms to the epigastric, hepatic regions, and nape of the neck, to relieve headache. During the remission, quinine, with five-drop doses of laudanum, when the bowels were too free, and stimulants, and as good living as obtainable, to hasten convalescence. Some commenced with free purgation, then salines and diaphoretics, until free action of the skin was induced. Sinapisms and turpentine stupes, with effervescing draughts to relieve nausea and irritability of stomach. Full doses of quinine during the remission, citrate of iron and quinine during convalescence, or quinine and strychnine, with cod-liver oil; and in all cases, even from the commencement of the attack, careful nursing of the patient's strength, with essence of beef and other medical comforts. Cold evaporating lotions were applied to the head, the hair in severe cases being removed. Cold drinks were given plentifully (chlorate of potash 31 to the Ol), tepid bath or tepid sponging. Diarrhœa was not treated actively unless there was much pain. Dilute acids and opium, or chlorodyne, were then found valuable. Turpentine stupes to the loins, fomentations to the hypogastric region, diluents, tonics and anodyne diuretics if the urine was suppressed. A case, complicated with serious head symptoms, brought on by exposure to the sun and the free use of stimulants, was completely relieved by a *general bleeding and blister to the nape of the neck*. Of sixty-seven cases treated on board the Barracouta, the average number of days on the sick list was 14·6.

These officers attributed the larger proportion of attacks among the Marines in July to the fact of their doing night guards, and occupying the badly-ventilated rooms in Fort St. Jago: other attacks to the fact of the men being landed, and on some occasions sleeping in the open air, as at Abbey, in October, or being wet with the sea spray. The march in the sun to Abracrampa, on the 28th October; wettings, and sleeping in wet clothes; overcrowding on shore; leakage of roofs during heavy rain; damp, impure and dirty tank water; salt or poor and insufficient fresh rations; want of fresh vegetables; bad bread at Elmina, heavy, and full of fungus; deficient hospital accommodation on shore shortly after arrival, want of proper latrines, bad cooking, rendering the poor provisions obtainable more distasteful; great humidity of the atmosphere preceding and following heavy rain, and the loss of the Nigritia and Yoruba, having on board provisions and medical comforts, combined with other influences, lowering the *morale* of the men.

As regards the actual time that must elapse from the first exposure to malarious influence to the development of febrile symptoms, no very accurate opinion could be formed; but it was evident that the longer on shore, the sooner the attack might be expected upon embarkation; also, that ships anchored at distances of a mile or mile and a-half from the shore, did not escape the effect of malarious emanations, but that the poison was so modified and diluted in transit, as to be comparatively inert and incapable of exerting any decidedly baneful influence upon a healthy ship's company. This was well exemplified on board the Merlin: none of the men landed; yet ten suffered from remittent fever, but of so mild a form that were it not for the beneficial effects of quinine, it could scarcely be called malarial.

The experience on board the Victor Emanuel alone proved the value of an immediate change, as has been already seen. Of 164 cases sent on board at Cape Coast, seriously ill, only thirty-one required admission into Netley on her arrival at Southampton. Only seven died during the voyage. Former West Coast experience has been the same, the rule having been to send at once to England or Madeira all convalescents from serious attacks of fever or dysentery, and who were found not improving under further treatment in Africa—a wise regulation, resulting in the saving of many lives. Of the two, dysenteric cases always yielded the most unfavourable result. On board the West African steamers severe cases of dysentery had few chances of rallying from a severe attack, owing to the want of comfort and proper attendance; while on board an hospital ship, replete with every comfort, and all the appliances for the proper remedial and dietetic treatment of the disease, the chances were much in favour of the recovery of the patient. In all steamers carrying passengers from such a deadly climate, the Board of Trade should, in the interest of humanity, require the owners to provide a proper hospital deck-house, and trained attendant, both being exclusively reserved for the use of the sick, who, if suffering from contagious diseases, might be there isolated.

In ships lying off these coasts the presence of decomposing animal and vegetable matter appears to impregnate the woodwork of the vessel, exposed to long-combined action of heat and moisture, with a poison or ærial emanation, capable of giving rise to continued or other paludal fevers, probably owing to the emanations being concentrated from the necessarily imperfect ventilation of a ship. Sometimes the resulting disease has been of a most virulent type. When such ships are cleaned out, the holds have been found to contain a mass of brackish mud and vegetable matter so offensive as to be almost insupportable. Captain Hosenson, R.N., relates an instance showing how a small hole in the kelson, not holding more than some pints of water, became so putrid, and gave off so much offensive gas when stirred up, that all hands had to rush immediately to the hatchway, while all the silver in the cabin above, and the white paint, became nearly black. It was such decomposing matter which rendered the old timber ships so fatal to the residents on board; the green timber, previously soaked in the mud reaches of the rivers, being impregnated with a deadly malaria so concentrated, that fifteen minutes exposure to its influence was known to give rise to an attack of West Coast yellow fever. On the 15th of November the Simoom had become so unhealthy, that officers not suffering from fever were taken ill on board, and cases treated failed to improve.

All the sick of the Marines landed in June were at first treated in the Military Hospitals at Cape Coast and Elmina—the former, a small building, containing twenty-seven beds, ten of which could only be used by natives; the latter, formerly the Colonial Hospital, was not much better; it contained twenty-one beds. When these became crowded, the European sick were transferred to the Himalaya, an hospital ship, to which the Marines were sent as soon as the acute stage of their disease was over, and they could be removed with safety.

As already mentioned, a chill was, on the Gold Coast, one of the commonest exciting causes of fever and dysentery. Of this we had many examples. An officer, for instance, who had been walking smartly, until the skin was profusely perspiring, got into his hammock on a damp evening in September, shortly before he neared the end of his journey. In a few days he was attacked with bronchial symptoms, which were followed by a severe form of remittent fever, from the effects of which he barely escaped after the most careful nursing. Another officer was thoroughly drenched while lying in his hammock *en route* from Accra to Cape Coast. He had an attack of bilious remittent, and died. Many of the Marines, who marched from Cape Coast to Elmina during the heavy rains of July, were afterwards seized with fever and dysentery. Another form of chill occurred during the close of the campaign, as, for instance, when the men were soaked during one or two thunderstorms, or after wading the Dah, and streams and swamps. After such chills on the return journey, the number of cases of fever and dysentery increased largely, many of the cases being of a severe type. Again, from bivouacking in the open during damp, chilly nights, following upon a day of extreme heat; or exposure to wet and rain in a bivouac after an exciting day of much exertion; showing that history had repeated itself, and that the same causes observed by the older military writers were again in operation. Exposure to the sun, as already stated, undoubtedly acts as an exciting cause of fever. I have observed many instances of this. It appears to act by deranging the biliary functions, thus throwing out of gear the normal routine of functions, whereby the fever poison could develop itself. Possibly such exciting causes may act by suddenly drying up the cutaneous secreting surface, up to then relieving the blood of the excess of malaria. The exigencies of the war required that in many places the oftentimes virgin soil should be turned up—either for the purpose of making clearings sixty yards all round the fortified posts, to widen the roadway, or, again, to form a site for camps. Here there was a fertile and well-known cause in the production of ague, mostly felt during the first or preparatory stage of the Expedition, and during the march beyond the Prah, where the roadway was being widened by the Royal Engineers. Up country the water certainly held in solution much vegetable organic matter, especially after the rains, when the streams, as already shown, received the overflow of the up to then stagnant swamps on their banks. I have observed the water on such occasions to be of a greenish hue, with a disagreeable taste and odour. At Fort Napoleon the drinking of this water by the men of the detachment favoured the production of fever, dysentery, and diarrhœa. Flint, a celebrated American writer, alludes to water holding in solution the malarious poison as a very common cause of paludal fevers. Another cause of fever was the long stay of the men upon the banks of the Prah, and in the bush before the onward march, and the disappointment and *ennui* consequent upon the belief that the military operations within the confines of the Protectorate had finished off the enemy—two effects aiding the already too debilitating effects of climate. This debility was one of the commonest predisposing causes to attacks of fever and dysentery. When weakened by exertion and fatigue, both diseases would come into play; this being the case, all causes of debility might be regarded as among the predisposing ones to attacks of fever and other malarial affections.

The monotonous and un-nutritious diet, *plus* the climate, caused the production of a cachexia and a depraved condition of the blood, and a train of scorbutic symptoms, denoted by tenderness and bleeding of the gums, feeble pulse, inability to perform any active exertion, want of appetite, purpuric petechia or blotches on the skin, especially the legs, thighs, and abdomen, which formed painful irritable ulcers, with livid raised margins or white edges surrounded by a bright red areola, the granulations purgating and bleeding, the slightest bruise or scratch opening out into one of these unpleasant visitors which persistently refused to heal. This constitutional taint considerably modified the course of the febrile disease, observed during the progress of the Expedition, and the nature of the treatment. "If we analyze," says M. de Méricourt, principal medical officer of the French navy, "the different causes of scurvy, we shall be able to divide them into two distinct groups. We shall have, on the one hand, those in favour of the miasm-theory, and, on the other, those who believe that scurvy is brought on by depressing influences variously associated, the food being at the same time insufficient and unvaried, and consequently unfit to maintain the body in its normal condition. Scurvy is a malady of nutrition; it may be classed naturally by the side of chlorosis and anæmia, and consequently it is neither miasmatic nor contagious: it is brought on by certain known causes. The prophylaxis consist in maintaining the populations, the bodies of armies and navies, in the best possible condition, compatible with social necessities and the exigencies of the service. It is particularly necessary to secure fresh provisions, and in the absence of fresh vegetables, to supply the men with lime juice. When in spite of proper precautions, the disease breaks out, the sick should be disseminated, not only with a view of removing them from the imaginary focus, but to place them in the best possible condition for the re-establishment of their health. Give a scorbutic patient comfortable lodgings, rest, a good table, and plenty of light and air, and he will assuredly be restored to health, as the etiolated plant, when placed in the proper conditions for its existence." Defective rations, particularly when there is an absence of fresh vegetables, are constantly associated with the various causes adduced as being capable of producing the scorbutic taint, viz., sorrow, nostalgia, fatigue and idleness, dampness and cold, salt and unwholesome food. The last six of these appear to be most productive of the disease when seen during the operations of the war in Africa.

Change of diet was probably in many cases a cause of dysentery; diarrhœa would be set up by the presence of a food used for the first time, and which, as such, evidently affected the stomach and bowels, which last would naturally get rid of a substance entirely foreign to them. A purging once set up in a constitution debilitated by the causes already touched upon, would rapidly end in dysentery. As an instance may be cited the case of the inhabitants of Cape Coast, who previous to the war lived almost entirely upon kankie, or fermented Indian corn. To relieve their distress a quantity of rice was sent out by the Government, and distributed amongst them. Diarrhœa and dysentery began immediately to prevail extensively. Even a change from one form of rice to another seemed to have a similar effect. A respectable Sierra Leone native, who had been accustomed to eat in that colony a large-grained, full-bodied rice, well seasoned with peppers and rich sauces, and fresh animal food, was attacked with dysentery at Cape Coast after living for a little time on East Indian rice (*minus* the condiments), salt pork, and preserved meats. To no other cause could his disease be attributed after a most careful inquiry. He wore a cholera belt, lay in a quarter in the Castle not exposed to cold winds, slept at night in cotton drawers, and was in good physical health, never having been exposed in the bush, or obliged to drink anything but condensed or good potable filtered tank water. Very hot weather alone would predispose to diarrhœa in those unaccustomed to it, and it is to be feared that up country the use of unripe pine apples and plantains was an occasional cause. Many officers attributed their attacks to the use of impure water.

The causes of fever and dysentery are here taken together; for although either appeared oftentimes as separate entities, or the one, as stated before, supervened upon the other, the term fever and dysentery became very common. The pathological connection with remittent fever has been proved by a large number of facts, the two diseases being found in the same localities, and both appearing to be due to the same terrestrial emanations, the two affections co-existing, preceding, or following one another in the same individual, just as ague may precede or follow upon remittent fever. A boat's crew has, for instance, been sent on shore, and on their return a portion of the men have been attacked with fever, another portion with dysentery. It may therefore be concluded that there is a malarial form of dysentery. In the case of one of the Simoom's Marines who died, the man had been ill for three weeks on shore from diarrhœa, brought on by eating salt provisions; fever followed of a typhoid type, with uncontrollable vomiting of green bilious fluids and the passage of frequent dark, watery stools, a dark brown tongue, and hot, dry skin—remittent fever without the remission. Of sixteen sailors and Marines seized with fever between the 18th and 30th June, at Cape Coast Castle, two were complicated with dysenteric symptoms, and one with hæmatemesis. Another contracted dysentery several days after he had been in hospital. A Marine who was on shore for fifteen days to assist the Control Department, was attacked with remittent fever, complicated with dysenteric symptoms, several days after he had returned on board. On the 28th October, ten of the 110 Marines and sailors landed returned the same day, two with diarrhœa and gastric symptoms, the remainder suffering from insolation. Repeated paroxysms of ague, attended as they are with extreme and increasing congestions of the internal organs, and especially the spleen, react upon its tributary, the inferior mesenteric, which returns the blood from the rectum and the descending colon. The mucus membrane becomes congested, more prone to inflammation and dysentery, which last, in this indirect way, may result from the marsh poison. Ague, the effect of malaria, may thus, in this indirect way, lead to dysentery. Occasionally the three-fold cause, viz., malaria, bad water, and unwholesome food, may cause it. As an illustration may be taken the following case:—An officer, quartered upon an island in the Sherborough River, near Sierra Leone, was obliged to drink water obtained from a surface well, loaded with impurities, in a neighbourhood reeking with the marsh miasm. His food chiefly consisted of salt pork, varied by an occasional fowl, so starved as to be almost devoid of nutriment. Sleep, at the same time, was scarcely possible from the presence of sand flies and mosquitoes. He was shortly seized with fever, followed by dysenteric diarrhœa, not amenable to treatment. An immediate change alone saved his life. On a subsequent occasion, and many years afterwards, the same results were observed to follow the same conditions—fever leading to an attack of dysenterica alba. In the fatal cases of dysentery the spleen was generally found enlarged, of a dark, purplish, claretty colour, and readily broken down by gentle force. In fact, the appearances witnessed in the spleen were similar to those observed in fatal cases of remittent fever, convalescence from the latter disease being in many the initial symptom of the former. This fact may explain the well-known good effects of saline purgatives in the treatment of malarial fever. When you consider what have ever been the best prophylactics against attacks of fever and dysentery in a malarial climate, you will find that those dietetic and hygienic precautions found in practice to keep the body in the best physical health and the blood pure, viz., a generous nutritious diet, a moderate use of wine, exercise in the open, attention to the state of the skin, and the constant use of an adequate quantity of anti-scorbutic fruit, such as grapes, oranges, lemons, and the various crucifera and olearacea, such as lettuce, dandelion, cochlearia officinalis, sorrel, oxalis rumex, &c., are equally beneficial in both forms of disease.

After two attacks of Coast or remittent fever, in the great majority of cases a man's general health became so much debilitated that invaliding is the only resource left: such was the experience of Naval surgeons, an opinion pretty generally correct. Relapses were more frequent amongst the sailors and Marines who had been longest on shore.

The good effects of a short trip to sea was well shown in the Encounter, Simoom, and Barracouta. By short trips to sea in December, the sick list in the first of these vessels was decreased very much, the little change having had a decidedly beneficial effect. The same may be said of the Simoom: officers and men who left in her for Ascension and St. Helena, very unwell in the middle of November, returned after their six weeks' cruise very much benefited—the rest, good food, comfortable berths, and non-malarious air doing a great deal. In some few the paludal poison appeared to re-assert its powers as they again neared the Coast, showing that it was still in the system. An immediate change to the bracing air of home, the good food, and the society of friends, is the only plan to adopt to restore to health sufferers from the sequelæ of African fever or dysentery. While on the Coast, little more can be done than to moderate the effects of the bad forms of either. It is a mistake however, to think that men must of necessity leave Africa because they have had fever. Taking the general run of officers, they do, as a rule, put in some how or other twelve months on the Coast, after which interval they should certainly have at least a twelve months in Europe before returning to duty. The fact of exceptions occurring to this very salutary rule does not disprove its correctness; in fact, I doubt very much whether an efficient European service can be carried out in any other way on the Coast of Africa. The climate appears to affect non-commissioned officers and men much sooner than officers: this was exemplified in the case of the Marines who landed in June, 1873. "It was remarkable," writes a Naval Surgeon, "how quickly these strong and powerful men broke down; even those who were not actually sick, after being landed for about a month, presented a careworn and debilitated appearance; and only very few, indeed, after that time, were fit for anything like active work. The officers kept their health and appearance better. This, I think, was entirely due to their being able to obtain better and more varied food." These observations I can fully corroborate, from after experience, and the appearance of the Marines, who were subsequently to this quartered up country, at Dunquah, Assayboo, &c. These men had a pale, washed-out look, and seemed devoid of all energy. "To keep white men," writes the same officer, "in any way healthy in such a pernicious climate, their diet should be good and varied, for food that one could go on eating in England for a long time, soon gets distasteful here. They should also have a fair allowance of beer or porter, which, I think, would be better than grog. They ought to sleep in large, well-ventilated rooms, and all the water used for drinking purposes should, if possible, be distilled." As a rule, before reaching Madeira from the Coast of Africa, patients suffering from fever and dysentery, who have been sent to England as a last resort, have recovered wonderfully, a state of progress maintained, as a rule, as long as the individual remains outside the malarial zone. In a year or two, according to circumstances, and the dose of the poison received originally, the effects of the latter appear to have exhausted themselves. This is the experience of the African Medical Service, which was very inefficient until re-modelled in 1859, upon the principle of alternating short periods of Coast duty with equivalents of leave in England.

The sooner invalids from Africa get home to English comforts and the pure bracing air the better. Previous experience proved this fact. Ten out of 174 officers and men sent home in the Victor Emanuel, suffering from various affections, only died, and thirty-one required to be transferred to hospital upon her arrival in England. Many years ago I left Africa in the depth of our home winter, worn down almost to a skeleton from the effects of fever and a previous attack of dysenteric diarrhœa. I had an attack of ague every alternate day, and was at the same time so sea-sick that it was only by lying down on deck, covered up with a great coat and rugs, that I could get on at all, and retain a little soup and biscuit on the stomach. Yet, before I arrived in England, and the keen intense cold, for the winter was a very severe one, I was so much better that I could get about the deck, and afterwards walk on shore. The cold I did not feel while warmly clad, but a chill brought on immediately a state of much misery. The effects of cold can be obviated to a great extent by warm clothing. Certain it is, that nothing oxidizes the malarial poison so rapidly as a pure, bracing air; nothing mitigates its effects so much as the comforts of home; and nothing renders its well-known sequelæ so endurable as the fact of knowing that one stands on one's own native soil once more. Many officers have had the opportunity of trying the experiment frequently, with always the same result. For some three to four months you suffer most after arrival. After that interval the effects appear to wear off gradually. A short trip to the Continental baths appeared to have been of service to several officers who returned from the Gold Coast. One of them, who was very much annoyed by a crop of atonic boils, which showed themselves shortly after his arrival in England, wrote to me from Germany that the use of the "waters" had completely cured him. Internal congestions, such as those of the spleen and liver, would, no doubt, be also relieved by such natural alteratives and depurants. Frequent exercise in the open air, while suitably and warmly clothed, the avoidance of sudden chills, or a residence in a damp, low-lying situation; nutritious and easily-assimilated food; a moderate amount of stimulants, and a course of ferruginous tonics, such as citrate of iron and quinine in infusion of calumba, or triple syrup, thirty minims three times a day, with an occasional purgative, are really the best restoratives—medicinal, hygienic, and dietetic.

The value of quarantine as a preventive measure will depend altogether upon the view we take of the contagiousness of the ordinary paludal remittent, or Coast yellow fever. Most experienced medical officers look upon the disease as neither infectious or contagious. That the ship itself may generate the disease has been proved a host of times, and that those going on board such ships may contract a similar form of fever is equally certain. Under such circumstances a vessel should be admitted to free *pratique* when a medical investigation shows that no case of illness of a suspicious nature exists among the passengers and crew. When necessary to bring patients or individuals on shore from an infected ship, the simple rule is to isolate them in a building well separated from all surrounding ones, to leeward, and with all appliances within its precincts for washing and disinfecting clothes and other materials. If after a moderate interval of time, and after all clothes have been fumigated and disinfected, no symptoms of disease appear amongst the inmates, they should be liberated. I have never known an instance of this form of fever having been introduced on shore from an infected ship. As such cases might possibly occur, a few simple quarantine rules become necessary as a measure of precaution.

Livingstone's last journals bear out many of the opinions expressed in the foregoing pages. He writes on January 27th, 1867, "A set-in rain all the morning, but having plenty of meat we were very comfort able in the old huts;" and on the 20th October, "Very ill; I am always so when I have no work: sore bones, much headache, then loss of power over the muscles of the back, no appetite, and much thirst." On the 1st January, 1869, he writes: "Moving is always good in fever;" on the 7th, "It is probably malaria which causes that constant surging in the ears. Ideas flow through the mind with rapidity and vividness in groups of twos and threes." In July, 1870, he gives a graphic description of African ulcer: "For the first time in my life my feet failed me. Instead of healing quietly as before, when torn by hard travel, irritable, eating ulcers fastened on both feet, and I limped back to Bambani on 22nd. The sores on my feet now laid me up as irritable-eating ulcers. If the foot was put to the ground, a discharge of a bloody colour flowed, and the same discharge re-appeared every night with considerable pain, that prevented sleep." On the 26th September he was still unable to report the ulcers healing. "For eighty-eight days I have been completely laid up with these, and it will be long ere the lost substance be replaced."

At Lagos and in the Bights the principal diseases of the population are fevers, remittent and intermittent, with a generally well-marked cold stage. In the black subjects the fever partakes more of the intermittent than the remittent type. The native remedies are principally the warm tea of two or three aromatic plants, and an infusion of some green herb, of which the dose is four or five pints, and which purges violently. Dracunculus and elephantiasis are common. Ulcers in the legs are very common, sound legs being the exception. Europeans, Creoles, and natives suffer equally, owing to the deteriorated condition of the blood and the congestion of the hæmorrhoidal and abdominal veins consequent upon enlarged spleen. Enlargement of the spleen is endemic, and the margin of the organ, in many instances, may be traced far over on the right side of the abdomen.

CHAPTER XVI.

WOUNDS AND INJURIES.

THE indifferent nature of the powder used by the Ashantees, and the use of slugs and stones, projectiles which quickly lost their velocity and penetrating power after discharge, and were easily stopped after penetration, and rarely effective beyond fifty yards, lent a peculiarity to the wounds received during the late Expedition, not usually seen in modern warfare. Owing to the foregoing peculiarities, the larger bones were not, as a rule, capable of being broken, and cavities were only penetrated when the generally-concealed enemy was within a short distance. The powder used during the earlier operations in the Protectorate was rather better, and the projectiles somewhat different to those used during the later stages, when the enemy was running out of his ammunition from a stoppage of the supply. As the latter became short, the charges of the coarsely-grained powder became smaller, and were sometimes mixed with fine earth to increase their bulk; stones of various kinds, bits of tin, &c., largely taking the place of brass, iron, and leaden slugs and bullets. The powder was the ordinary trade variety, similar to that used for blasting purposes. It was carried in a small gourd, in a loose state, or in charges in a leather bandolier encircling the waist. The wadding (a species of brown fibre not unlike jute), in a small pouch, and the projectiles in a purse or bag. Towards the close of September, one of the Ashanti muskets taken from the enemy was fired at a deal board thirty yards distant: the slugs penetrated about an inch; they would, consequently, go right through a half inch deal at that distance, and have still some force left. There was a great variety of muskets used. Short Tower marked flint fusils, and long Danish and French flint muskets. Some were new, others evidently very old. The projectiles were iron and leaden slugs, of various shapes and sizes, square bits of iron stone and pebbles. I have also picked up small revolver and larger bullets, and portions of the latter: all had more or less sharply-defined edges, which gave this additional peculiarity to the wounds inflicted, viz., that they bled a good deal at the moment, the angular slugs causing a kind of inciso-lacerated wound. The missile in the majority of cases, especially where it penetrated any distance, was difficult to extract. Wedged between small bones, a slug was almost immovable until loosened by subsequent inflammation and suppuration. On referring to the history of the war, it will be found that the fatal wounds were generally received at very short ranges into either the head, chest, or abdomen: the latter were nearly certain to be fatal. The abdomen was more easily penetrated, owing to the want of any bony covering. A slug which would penetrate here, would glance along a rib or be arrested in its progress by the cranium. A good cummerbund was not a bad protection for the abdominal walls. It really becomes a question of some practical interest whether it would not be of advantage to devise some kind of light, but tough leathern doublets for this peculiar bush warfare. When officers or men were killed, you usually found that they were separated from the rest, surrounded and cut off, or that they were a leading file along a narrow pathway, and consequently the first to receive the fire from an ambush close by, or were again potted at from behind some tree or thick bush. The Ashantees were adepts at the art of concealing themselves: we rarely saw a live armed warrior. On one occasion we were proceeding along the road beyond Mansue, when we were fired into from an ambush twenty-five yards in our front. The leading file was shot through the abdomen, the slug entering just below the ensiform cartilage, and penetrating to the spine. He died almost at once. The next was shot through the middle finger of the right hand; the third in the head and thigh, the slugs penetrating to the bone and through the limb; the fourth received three slug wounds in the head, reaching to the cranium; the fifth, an officer, two wounds in the left forearm. Here was the results of a single volley fired at men in single file, about a yard apart, and distant from the enemy in their front some twenty yards, a fourth of the distance at which the old Brown Bess used to be effective. In line at this distance, the Ashantees could then have made some effective use of their weapons, provided they had not been opposed to Sniders, one or two volleys from which would have sent them to the right about, as did actually occur at Elmina. Sometimes these wounds caused a severe nervous shock. An officer hit over the heart with a spent slug fell immediately to the ground. On examining the arm of another fired at from an ambush in a pathway the head of the humerus was found to be penetrated. It might be generally calculated upon that five of the leading file would be wounded when the head of the column was fired at from an ambush at either side of the roadway, one at least mortally. The Ashanti scouts generally cut a small pathway parallel to the main one. When the head of the column was sufficiently near they fired a volley, and disappeared immediately, getting in again at right angles some distance behind. Under these circumstances the volley at the head of column was a pretty sure indication of immediate work for the surgeons further behind, who, if the column was on the move, had little time for doing more than applying the most superficial of dressings while passing their patients to the rear. When a man is only wounded in the upper half of the body with slugs, or in the lower limbs, provided in either case no important organ, vessel, or bone is injured, he can generally manage to keep up with his comrades, as the progress through a dense forest with an enemy in front is necessarily slow. In the by-paths we traversed we found cots a nuisance except for sleeping in, and the larger hammocks little better, in consequence of the two bearers being unable to march abreast. In such situations a hammock without cross pieces, and slung upon a longer pole, would be more useful, one somewhat similar to those used by the natives.

Slugs, when losing their velocity, caused wounds varying in effect from a slight bruise to a severe contusion, causing much pain, inflammation, and swelling; in the latter case the skin and areolar tissue was usually penetrated at the spot where the slug touched the body: the feeling was that experienced after a sharp blow. Immediately upon the receipt of the injury, a circular swelling of the integument took place, of a red colour, changing to black, purple, and yellow. A circumscribed discolouration remained for a considerable time. The appearance of the swelling, and its size, was not unlike that of a Normandy pippin. With still greater force, the slug penetrated in direct proportion to its velocity. When it got between the muscles or between the small joints it was difficult to extract, as stated before, owing to its angular form. When in the vicinity of joints, especially those of the lower extremity, much pain was complained of, and free mobility impeded. In two or three cases I have seen the knee penetrated with a resulting acute inflammation of the joint. A slug hitting the rib would generally be deflected, and pass for some distance beneath the muscles. In many cases the slug penetrated the skin and muscles for about half an inch, and then fell out of itself. According to the Returns of the later actions of the war, viz., Borborassie, Amoaful, Bequah, and the Dah, bearing the signature of Dr. Mackinnon, the following were the numbers of casualties:—Killed, 10; wounded dangerously, 19; very severely, 34; severely, 86; slightly, 175; total, 314.

The conspicuous point in these Returns is the large proportion of slightly to more severely wounded. Out of a total of 45 wounds received by officers and men of the Naval Brigade, 22 are returned as dangerous or very severe; of 269 in the Military Return, only 21 are returned as dangerous or very severe; 163, or considerably more than one-half, are returned as slightly wounded; in the Naval Return only 12—about one-fourth. Whereas slight contusions are shown in the Army Descriptive Return in large amount, no mention of a contusion occurs in the Naval.

Only 16 wounded, 2 officers and 14 men, were landed from the Victor Emanuel on her arrival in Southampton water. One wounded officer died during the voyage. He had received a very severe wound of the upper part of the thigh, implicating the profunda artery. The fatal termination was due to disease of the heart of old standing. One officer had passed through an attack of pyæmia, and was very emaciated and weak. The right humerus had been shattered by a rifle bullet. Union had not taken place in two and a-half months. The other officer had received a slug in the right elbow joint. In one man a slug wound in the back of the neck had led to paralysis of the upper and lower extremities of the same side. The projectile entered just below the mastoid process. Good union had occurred in one case, where the humerus had been broken by an Ashantee slug, which passed through the arm; another had a severe gunshot wound of the lower jaw, accompanied by considerable laceration of the soft parts and division of a branch of the carotid, causing at the time a considerable amount of hæmorrhage, difficult to arrest, and to ultimate impairment of the use of the lower jaw and the power of mastication. One of the gravest slug wounds was at first sight apparently a trivial one, the missile lying just beneath the skin above the right clavicle. Paralysis of the arm of the same side immediately followed, showing that the cervical plexus of nerves was implicated; the paralysis gradually disappeared, but an aneurism of the sub-clavian supervened upon the injury; the slug was apparently firmly connected with the coat of the artery, so much so as not to admit of removal. In this case the assailant had been come upon in the bush as the 42nd were advancing; he jumped up, and fired almost point blank. The slug could be fairly laid hold of, together with the skin, but it could not be separated from the coats of the aneurism, which appeared prominently above the clavicle. In another case the slug lodged in the head of the humerus, which had to be excised. An officer received a wound in the left wrist, which cut the ulnar artery and nerve, severed some of the tendons, and caused contraction and loss of sensation in the little and inner side of the ring finger. Fair use of the hand had been obtained six months afterwards. One of the officers received a slug wound at Dunquah, in the left groin. The slug entered below Poupart's ligament, and was so painful in its effects as to prevent extension of the limb, which was kept flexed upon the abdomen. The missile could not be extracted, and still remains *in situ*. A sinus led down to it a year afterwards. A slug penetrated the abdomen of a West Indian soldier, just above the symphysis, and entered the bladder. The patient recovered. An officer of the 42nd had the outer table of the parietal bone depressed or grooved by a slug or bullet, which left a permanent depression without any untoward effects. A Naval officer, shot in the head, lingered for some days and then died. The Commodore appears to have been the only officer who received a penetrating wound of the chest and recovered. The angular nature of the missile would naturally, in a closed cavity, set up much irritation, and possibly render it less liable to become encysted. The brass slugs were most deleterious in their after effects. A wound from one of these caused the death of the late African traveller, Robert Lander. He received it in an affray with the natives, and succumbed to its effects shortly after his arrival at Fernando Po. One curious fact came to light during the war. The *post mortem* examination upon a Naval officer who died of fever, revealed a bullet lying immediately behind the descending aorta in the chest. It had been received in New Zealand, and was believed to have been extracted. A Company Sergeant-Major of the 2nd West was fired at by an Ashantee from behind one of their shelter huts at Dunquah. The slug just penetrated the sheath of the common carotid, without wounding the latter. At Abracrampa a sailor lost the sight of his right eye from a slug, which penetrated the cornea. From the situations of several of the wounds received it was evident that the mortality would have been far more if the missile had been larger, and its velocity greater. From the peculiar mode of warfare pursued by the enemy, and the fact of their firing from the hip, or while in a crouched position, with the muzzle well raised, the greater number of wounds were received in the upper two-thirds of the body. This was the case at Chamah, Elmina, Essiaman, Dunquah, Abracrampa, near Mansue, and at Fassowra. As the branches were struck by slugs, the leaves fell in numbers from overhead, and the stems and twigs were gashed and bent. An analysis of the wounds received in the various actions of the war forcibly illustrate this. Of 182 wounds received by the European and native troops engaged at Amoaful, fifty-seven were inflicted in the head and neck, sixty-two in the upper extremities, nineteen in the chest and back, three in the abdomen, thirty-six in the lower extremities.

Upper half of the body . . . 138 wounds
Lower half ,, . . . 39 ,,

The foregoing may be further sub-divided into—

Wounds of scalp 4
,, temple 4
,, forehead . . . 5
,, face 9
,, ear 5
,, eye 3
,, eyebrow . . . 1
,, chin 4
,, jaw 4
,, nose 2
,, orbit 3
,, lip 1

Total head and face, 45.

Wounds of neck	13	Total wounds of neck, 13.
,, shoulder	14	
,, scapula	1	
,, clavicle	1	
,, arm	18	
,, fractured	3	Total wounds of upper extremity, 65.
,, elbow	1	
,, forearm	17	
,, wrist	1	
,, hand	4	
,, finger	5	
,, side and chest	8	
,, chest, penetrating	5	
,, back	6	Total wounds of trunk, 22.
,, abdomen	3	
,, hip	7	
,, leg	9	Total wounds of lower extremities, 18.
,, ankle	1	
,, foot	1	

Many of the foregoing were contusions. Of the four deaths which occurred in the field at Amoaful, one died from the effects of a penetrating wound of the lung, heart, and abdomen; the three others were shot through the head, heart, and brain. Another soldier succumbed shortly after the receipt of a wound in the abdomen.

In the smaller affairs of Bequah, Borborassie, Dah, Aquamemmu, &c., two officers were killed, one shot in the abdomen, the other in the head and chest. In two of the wounds was the bone fractured, viz., the forearm and cranium. The latter case terminated fatally. One of the chest wounds was penetrating.

Gunshot wounds of the head		4	
,, ,, forehead		4	
,, ,, scalp		1	
,, ,, face		1	
,, ,, cheek		1	Total wounds of head and face, 23.
,, ,, ear		4	
,, ,, temple		2	
,, ,, jaw		3	
,, ,, nose		1	
,, ,, eyebrow		1	
,, ,, lip		1	
,, ,, neck		9	Total wounds of neck, 9.
,, ,, shoulder		8	
,, ,, clavicle		2	
,, ,, arm		7	
,, ,, elbow		2	Total wounds of upper extremity, 34.
,, ,, forearm		9	
,, ,, wrist		1	
,, ,, hand		2	
,, ,, thumb		2	
,, ,, finger		1	

Gunshot wounds of the side of chest	.	. 1		
,, ,,	chest, penetrating	. 1		
,, ,,	breast	. 2	Total wounds of trunk, 8.	
,, ,,	back	. 2		
,, ,,	loins	. 1		
,, ,,	abdomen	. 1		
,, ,,	penis	. 1	. Total wounds of penis, 1.	
,, ,,	hip	. 3		
,, ,,	thigh	. 10		
,, ,,	knee	. 4	Total wounds of lower extremity, 21.	
,, ,,	leg	. 2		
,, ,,	ankle	. 1		
,, ,,	toe	. 1		

In all 96. As at Amoaful, the low velocity of the projectile was shown by the preponderance of slight wounds. An incised or bayonet one was not received from the beginning to the end of the war. If the enemy had had a "statistical officer" he would have shown many incised wounds among his camp followers and slaves, several of whom suffered at the hands of the Kossoo auxiliaries. Their swords, wielded by their brawny arms, did severe execution upon the limbs and bodies of the unfortunate wretches with whom they came in contact. I have seen a blow from one of their weapons lay open the abdomen from side to side, exposing the diaphragm, solid viscera, and intestines. At each inspiration the latter were thrust out of the wound by the descent of the diaphragm, and at each forcible inspiration almost expelled *en bloc*. There was an almost entire absence of fat in the folds of the mesentery, and the pink vessels had a very beautiful appearance as they ramified over the protruded gut. Another had his instep and foot cloven in two; others of them various hacks over the chest, limbs, and head.

It will be seen from the foregoing remarks that the nomenclature adopted to designate the wounds received was as below, viz., contusions, slight wounds, severe, very severe, dangerous, a sub-division admitting of serious objection, because allowing too much latitude to individual opinion. On referring to the Returns it will be seen that wounds of the chin and lobes of the ear, and others of a similar nature, were returned indiscriminately as slight and severe. On further comparison it will be found that very different ideas were taken of the terms severe, very severe, dangerous.

Examples of *severe* wounds from the Returns:

Severe flesh wounds of various parts, such as right orbit, thigh, abdomen, eye, non-penetrating of chest, &c.
Gunshot wound of left arm (amputated).
,, ,, of clavicle and abdomen (since dead).
,, ,, left forearm with fracture.

Examples of *very severe* wounds:

Gunshot wound of right arm with fracture (two).
" " of right arm and knee.
" " of right shoulder.
" " of head.
" " of loins.

Examples of wounds returned as *dangerous:*
Gunshot wound of left thigh, involving profunda artery.
" " of chest (penetrating), (four).
" " of head and neck.
" " of right chest (non-penetrating).
" " of lower jaw.
" " of left arm with fracture, and of chest (penetrating).
" " of right side of head (since dead).

As the ultimate effects of a wound must be determined by the after-results and the certificate of a medical board, there can be no object in keeping up any minute sub-division of injuries received in action, only such as would illustrate the effect of the engagement to the public in the first reports. A wound has been always considered a mark of honour, because it cannot be either counterfeited or bestowed by favour. I think, then, the object should be to simplify rather than elaborate classifications of this kind, and adopt one which would not admit of being exalted or lowered according to the fancy of the returning officer or the position of the recipient. The term dangerous is objectionable, as no one can predict with certainty the ultimate effects of any wound. I have known a mere bruise, overlooked in the hurry of making up records after an action, result in months of acute suffering. Officers and men sleeping for days in their clothes, may not know that they were wounded until the after discolouration, pain, or stiffness called attention to the concealed contusion or laceration. In the case of an officer wounded in the arm, where the humerus was broken by a slug, the only outward sign was a mere trickle of blood which, upon a darker garment, would have almost escaped notice. Many officers suffering acute pain and much discomfort, have kept at their duty rather than disappear from the scene for a time or go to the rear. Several instances occurred during the late operations on the Gold Coast.

Bryant, one of the latest surgical writers, defines a wound as a division of the soft parts of the body by any mechanical force applied externally. When the "solution of continuity" is produced by a sharp-edged instrument, the wound is said to be "incised;" when with a pointed one, "punctured;" when with a blunt one that tears, "lacerated;" when with any implement that bruises, "contused." He further adds, "When the parts are only divided, the wound is called a 'simple one;' when associated with the introduction of foreign bodies, accompanied by hæmorrhage or pain, 'complicated.' ".

Le Gros Clark writes, "A gunshot wound is said to be *simple* when the skin and muscles alone are implicated; *compound* when a large artery is cut, a bone broken, or a visceral cavity entered. Yet deep textures may be severely injured without breach of surface, as by contusion."

Adopting the same simple divisions in military nomenclature, we might with much advantage record all gunshot injuries under two heads, and return officers and men after an action as being *wounded* or *severely wounded*, embracing among the first all solutions of continuity or injuries to soft parts, and confining the latter term to wounds where, in addition to the injury to the skin and muscles, a large artery has been cut across, an important nerve severed, a bone broken, tendons divided, or a cavity or articulation penetrated or injured. The result would be far greater accuracy and less confusion of ideas. This division is also indicated by M. Legouest in his "Traité de Chirurgie d'Armée." At page 132 he says:—"*Les plaies par armes à feu peuvent être divisées en plaies simple et en plaies compliquées;*" and further on to the difficulty of at all times tracing "*une limite précise entre les unes et les autres.*" Prince Gortschakoff returned his losses after the attack on the Redan, 18th June, 1855, as

Killed 797
Wounded 3,179
Contused 849
Slightly wounded, but not sufficiently to quit the ranks . 960

Of the gunshot injuries received in action beyond the Prah the most severe appear to have been—

5 cases of wounds of arm or forearm, with fracture (one forearm amputated).
1 case of wound of the clavicle and abdomen.
1 case of wound of the left thigh, involving the profunda artery.
1 case of wound of the right side of the head, with fracture.
5 cases of penetrating wounds of the chest.

And some dozen or two others involving the head, shoulders, loins, breast, and neck, &c. Of 159 Europeans and men of native corps wounded at Amoaful, whose injuries are recorded by Dr. Mackinnon in his published Return,

1 officer was hit in four places.
20 officers and men in two places.
135 „ „ in one only.

Of the effect upon locomotion of these various wounds we may have a general idea from the composition of the first convoy starting for the rear subsequent to the action. It consisted of forty-one hammocks with their occupants, and twenty-one wounded men capable of marching, but otherwise ineffective. The convoy left Egginassie for Insarfoo at

2.30 P.M., one hour after the cessation of firing. Of the 202 casualties resulting from engagements—

    4 officers and 2 men were killed in action.
    1 officer and 11 men died from the effects of their wounds up to 31st May, one of the latter after his arrival at home.

Taking the strength as 2,587 of all ranks employed, this would yield a percentage of mortality from the effects of wounds, among

    Officers . . . . . 1·68
    Men . . . . . . 0·52

Whether it was that they were more temperate in eating and drinking, or that their systems, owing to the large amount of vegetable food which they consumed at their meals, were less liable to take on the scorbutic taint, or that the poison of malaria did not to any great extent affect them, they showed, in the natives, very marked healing powers. This has often been observed. I might give many examples. A musket bullet struck a native (while bending forward to avoid the fire) a little above the posterior-inferior angle of the right scapula, passed through the spine of this bone, underneath the trapesium muscle, making its exit immediately above the clavicle, and severing the lobe of the ear. The man recovered without a bad symptom, the treatment being of the most simple character, viz., attention to cleanliness, water dressing, and subsequently the application of compound tincture of Benzoin, to stimulate the wounded parts into more active cicatrization. The ear was not interfered with, but allowed to heal under the scab formed. It made "a beautiful recovery." Another received a dozen slug wounds while in a semi-bent position, one larger than the rest lodged at the side of the spinal process of the dorsal vertebræ, another was firmly wedged between the bones of the carpus. The first I removed by cutting down upon it; the second resisted all legitimate efforts undertaken for its extraction. The wounded wrist became swollen and painful, much suppuration followed, with accompanying irritative fever. He afterwards picked out the slug himself, and ultimately returned to duty with a rather stiff wrist, but with fair mobility of the fingers. Another had his fingers blown off. He refused all surgical interference, went his own way for the time, but re-appeared subsequently with the extremities of the metacarpal bones covered with a good cicatrix, the broken ends of the phalanges having sloughed away. Many similar examples might be quoted to illustrate the facility with which wounds in the natives healed almost spontaneously. The natives, in their treatment of these injuries, first picked out the projectile, if possible, and then allowed the wound to heal under the scab or crust formed. Where the individual was an important personage, his wounds were bathed by his slaves in the first instance. Many of the badly wounded crawled into the bush to die. It was a curious fact, worth remarking upon, that during the various reconnaissances we made through the bush below and beyond Mansue, in the track of the main body of the retreating enemy, we never came across in their extensive camps a single wounded man, and only found one of their abandoned sick. He was lying in a shantie, with a large gangrenous sore on the foot, which was much swollen. They had left beside the poor wretch an earthen pot full of wild yams. A fire was smouldering by his side. A pitiable spectacle of deserted misery! Immediately after the action near Dunquah, 3rd November, the enemy abandoned his camp, but sent back next day for all his sick and wounded, who were removed. On being visited a few hours afterwards, a woman, in the last stage of starvation, and just breathing her last, a man in a dying state, and a small boy, were found remaining. Those who were unable to walk were either carried upon men's backs, supported upon either side and behind, or in litters or long baskets made from the mid-ribs of the palm leaves; or again, in country cloths slung to a long bamboo.

The effect of wounds occurring in African warfare depended upon the number received by any one individual, and the part of the body wounded. A Houssa had a portion of his head blown away in an ambush. He sank insensible to the ground, and lingered until the following day. An officer, in whose case the pellet lodged in the brain, lingered for some weeks. Scalp wounds bled a good deal upon the moment of being inflicted, and the parts were subsequently much swollen for a few days. When the chest was penetrated, or the abdomen, with a large projectile, or with more than one slug, there were the usual symptoms of shock, varying in amount with the extent of the injury and internal organ pierced. In a case where the bullet pierced the left chest from behind, making its exit to the left of and a little below the nipple in front, breaking the humerus in its passage into space, the symptoms were those of intense shock; weak, small, fluttering pulse; cough, frothy bloody sputum, and hæmorrhage from the lung. The man died in a few hours. A native who received several slugs in the abdomen, suffered a good deal from shock and the effect of intestinal hæmorrhage, the blood passing away per anum. In these last cases the symptoms were more or less collapse, followed by the usual signs of peritoneal inflammation and effusion, viz., hot skin, quick, full, and hard pulse, furred tongue, tender and tympanitic abdomen, drawn-up legs, anxious countenance, &c.

A slug wound not involving any serious complications would follow the following course as a rule:—On the moment of infliction there would be a certain amount of hæmorrhage. Shortly afterwards the surrounding parts would begin to swell and become painful—an intensely sore

O

feel rather than acute pain. The patient would be unable to lie upon the affected parts. You would then have in succession a thin, ichorous discharge, sero-purulent matter, and portions of slough coming away, followed by healthy pus and granulations. A dark brown cicatrix would finally remain, puckered, depressed, or scarcely below the level of the surrounding skin. It would gradually become white with age. The treatment of gunshot wounds pursued in Africa was, as a rule, simple and effective as long as no vital organ was penetrated, or the constitution impaired by the scorbutic or malarial dyscrasia. Flesh wounds not involving the joints of the lower limbs or impeding locomotion, did not require absolute rest or confinement to the hut. I have seen them heal readily under nature's plaster—a scab: in other cases, after the application of a little emplastrum adhesivum. A bandage was only required where it became necessary to support the parts in order to prevent bagging of matter or the formation of sinuses. The principles of treatment might be summed up in a few words:—Arrest hæmorrhage, remove the projectile if possible; at once when detected by the probe; if not easily found, and not causing any very urgent symptoms, allow it to remain, as unnecessary interference might make the artificial wound worse than the original one. Clean the parts with a little cold water, and apply a little lint steeped in the same harmless fluid, and do not obstruct nature in her spontaneous efforts at a cure. If the patient is on the move apply over the lint a little oil silk or gutta percha tissue, and confine it to the skin by a few strips of adhesive plaster. Dress the part daily, and observe the most perfect neatness and cleanliness. I have seen very many wounds cured rapidly by this very simple process. After Amoaful, upon arrival at Insarfoo, the course adopted was very similar. The wound was probed, the slug removed, and a little cotton steeped in carbolic oil at once applied; some wet lint was placed over this, and then a little oil silk, the whole being confined by strips of plaster, and if necessary a bandage. The men were then allowed to walk about until forwarded to the rear. An amputation of the forearm was performed on the field. In the case of broken parts they were co-apted, dressed, and confined in splints and bandages. Arteries were tied, or the bleeding arrested by styptic colloid, pressure, or the field tourniquet. Little more was done for severe chest, abdominal, or head wounds than to treat the more urgent local and constitutional symptoms, place the patient at rest in the shade, and give restoratives and cordials until the convoy was ready for removal to the rear in hammocks, the usual dressings being confined by a broad bandage. The latter were in some instances not removed until the arrival of the men at Fomanah or Prashue. In severe wounds, after the usual preliminary probing and primary dressing, the rule was to treat symptoms as they arose, relieve pain by local and constitutional sedatives, sustain the vital powers, and promote calm and sleep by rest, quietude, and, if necessary, soporifics and antimonials. When secondary hæmorrhage came on, all dressing and bandages had to be at once removed, and the usual means for arresting it adopted. The great object was to get all to the embarkation base as quickly as possible, and away from the malaria of the Coast; hence, time only permitted of the more simple and effective treatment while *en route* to the much longed-for goal. With regard to the important questions of the relative advantages of resections, primary and secondary amputations, little was learned, owing to the limited opportunity for study. One officer who received a bullet through the head of the humerus remained in action until killed, with his arm in a sling; another did not require resection until arrival in England. Under these circumstances such cases would certainly not appear to require immediate operation on the field. As there were only one or two amputations performed, an opinion on this subject could be scarcely expressed, excepting this, that when the hammock journey was a long one, the bones much injured, and the appliances for keeping the parts at rest indifferent and ineffective, the question might naturally arise under such circumstances, would not much after risk and disappointment be saved by immediate amputation? Esmarch's bandage does not appear to have been used during the operations. For resections it would have been most valuable, allowing, as it does, so free a view of the tissues and bones.

CHAPTER XVII.

EXPEDITION AGAINST THE CONGO PIRATES.

In March, 1875, Sir W. N. W. Hewett and Captain Hopkins went to Punta de Linha, about twenty-five miles up the Congo, and there held a "palaver" with the princes of that place. Captain Hopkins, our Consul in the Bights, had a thorough knowledge of the habits and customs of the natives. The princes visited were desired to give the names of the chiefs who attacked the *Geraldine*, but they would not say a word about the matter, and were most insulting; and when reproved by the Consul for their conduct, simply laughed in his face. One of their practices was, when they caught a white man, to tie him to a tree in one of their villages, and there keep him until he was ransomed. The Consul remonstrated with Capeta Macatalla, a chief, about this, when he immediately threatened to serve the Consul in the same manner if he ever caught him. When an attempt was made to seize the fellow, his followers charged bayonets, and made as though they would run the Consul through. This occurred at an English factory, in the presence of the Commodore and several officers, a gunboat also lying close by. Already there had been too many lives taken by these pirates, and a large amount of property lost. The factories in the Congo belong to English, French, and Dutch firms, the principal establishments being at Banana, Punta de Linha, and Emboma, most of them having credit in England. It is with English goods they are supplied, in the shape of cotton goods, knives, guns, gunpowder, and rum; and it is only by a quick return of produce that merchants in England can expect to be paid. As a considerable trade is done in ivory, palm-oil, palm and ground nuts, rubber, beeswax, &c., it had become a serious matter for our merchants to have a stop put at once to the plundering and murdering of British subjects. Some of the creeks were navigable for gunboats, but difficult to turn in; most of the villages were within range of the boats' guns, and many close to the beach. The whole of the Delta of the Congo was inhabited by a tribe called Misseloughs, who were always ready to pillage any merchant vessels in the river which were unfortunate enough to take the ground. The towns and villages were situated, some on the main banks of the river, but a great many in the mangrove swamps, only to be approached by creeks, whose banks were soft mud; many of them so buried in the bush that their presence was only inferred from hearing the natives talking. Lined with dwarf palms and mangrove bushes close to the water's edge, a concealed enemy might present a rifle almost close to the assailant before he was aware of it. Her Majesty's ship *Spiteful* arrived in the River Congo in August, from the Cape of Good Hope. Captain Medlycott at once commenced operations by establishing surveying parties to proceed up the different creeks, to ascertain the depth of water, the direction they took, their width, &c., and the localities of the different villages. Captain Medlycott, accompanied by Captain Hopkins, was away upon this service in the steam pinnace, with a steam cutter in attendance, for about twelve days, over 100 miles of unexplored creeks having been traversed in that time, the result of which was a correct chart of the whole of the Delta of the Congo.

The following particulars reached this country of the Expedition. It will be remembered that the cause of the Expedition was an attack, at the beginning of the year 1875, on the English schooner *Geraldine*, while she was lying stranded in the river; the cargo was plundered and four of the crew murdered:—

Acting under instructions from England, an Expedition to punish the marauders was determined upon, and early in the month of August H.M.S. *Spiteful* was despatched to map out the various creeks. On the morning of the 30th of August the following ships proceeded up the Congo:—The *Active*, the *Encounter*, the *Spiteful*, the *Merlin*, the *Foam*, the *Ariel*, and the *Supply*. At six A.M. on the following day the boats of the *Active*, the *Encounter*, and the *Spiteful* left their ships, and proceeded in tow for the entrance of the Chango Creek. Having proceeded about four miles the landing place leading to Chango was reached, where the Marines, numbering 150, under the command of Captain Bradshaw, were disembarked, and led by native guides to beat up the pirates' quarters. Three villages were destroyed, but no enemy was seen, although they declared their presence by keeping up a dropping fire from the dense jungle. Commodore Hewett, accompanied by his staff, led the way up the creek. On the 2nd of September the gunboats, with the boats of the larger ships, opened fire along the northern bank of the Congo on several villages. The landing party found in the private houses the remains of the plundered merchantman. The enemy continued firing from the bush, but only one man was wounded. All the villages on the northern bank of the river were destroyed as far as Melilla Creek. The men returned to the gunboats. On the following morning the Commodore proceeded up the creek, and opened fire on other villages. The firing having been discontinued a landing was effected, and the party marched some distance through a richly-cultivated country, burning the villages on the line of march, and arriving at the town named after the chief Armanzanga, who had been marked out for severe punishment. The town was of considerable size, and a teasing fire was kept up by the natives from the bush. The town was completely destroyed. The party under Captain Bradshaw having burned all the villages at the head of the creek, rejoined the gunboats. Early on the morning of the 4th September the *Spiteful* and

Encounter steamed further up the river, the *Merlin* and other boats going on to Punta de Linha, where Sir William Hewett gave the chief forty-eight hours to give up the murderers of the *Geraldine*. No notice having been taken of this offer, on the morning of the 7th the landing-party went ashore under a heavy fire from the natives, but quickly cleared the place, and committed the town and all its surroundings to flames. On the 8th all the boats returned down the north bank of the river till off the supposed position of Manoel Vacca's Town, where the men were landed under cover of a heavy fire from the gunboats. On entering the town it was found to be deserted. Having razed it to the ground, all re-embarked on board the gunboats and returned to their respective ships. On the 9th the squadron rested, and on the 10th the gunboats and boats entered the creek called Sherwood, where the King came on board the *Merlin*, as also did King Myanzia. Being informed that our sailors had not come into the river to make war, but to punish the wicked, they went on their way rejoicing. On the 11th hostilities were continued by a party of blue-jackets and Marines, with the boats of the *Spiteful*, under the command of Commander Medlycott, against a town called Polo Bolo. The town was soon destroyed, and only one man on our side was severely injured. On the morning of the 12th Commodore Hewett, attended by the three gunboats, started for the settlement named Emboma, situated seventy-three miles above the mouth of the river, where on the 15th he held a palaver with seven kings, who expressed themselves much pleased with the work which had just been completed, and stated that the commerce of the river was certain to be increased when it became known that peaceful traders could pass up and down without risk to life and property. Sir William Hewett returned down the river on the 17th. Thus ended what cannot but be considered a most successful Expedition.

The fatigue of the march is described by a correspondent as having been terrible. He writes:—

"Often for long distances, through deep offensive mud, sometimes knee-deep, sometimes wading breast-high through creeks. The navigation of the boats of a certain creek became so difficult that Captain Bradshaw's galley, the leading boat, could only get on by lopping the overhanging boughs. The order was given to jump out and wade through it, Captain Bradshaw himself leading the way, the men holding their rifles and ammunition over their heads. They waded thus for a mile before dry ground was reached and a village destroyed, and then, to get at the town of a principal chief, Armanzanga, they had to cross a broad stream, three feet deep and full of alligators. This sort of marching was the rule, and hard work enough. Nevertheless, not a man fell out. The burning of Armanzanga's town, and especially of his two-storey house or palace, was expected to have a good effect on the natives, owing to the long distance over which his authority and influence more or less extended. They never thought it possible that our men would risk fever and the other dangers of crossing streams and swamps, but now they seem to realize that they are no longer safe in their most secluded creeks. In Melilla Creek the natives made a great show of resistance. They lined the banks, opened fire on the boats, and kept it up with some show of spirit. It was here that Mr. Dixon, the engineer of the *Ariel*, was wounded, and their slugs penetrated the iron plates with which the larger boats were protected. The first Expedition on the 31st of August to Chango comprised the gunboats and all the boats of the squadron, twenty-five in number; the two companies of Marines were commanded by Lieutenant Crozier. A rocket and field-force party was under Lieutenant Nesham, and a second party under Lieutenant Rolfe; and another firing party under the gunner—all officers of Her Majesty's ship *Active*. Captain Bradshaw, of the *Encounter*, commanded the whole. Commander Medlycott, of Her Majesty's ship *Spiteful*, was second-in-command of the boats. On the 6th of September, when they operated in Luculla Creek, on the other side of the river, the boats of the squadron proceeded with the whole landing party in single file, owing to the narrowness of the creek, and they could not get within 500 yards of the head of the creek, where there was a village abandoned, as they afterwards found. After wading through mud and water, they burnt this village and pushed on to the next, one of considerable size and the residence of a powerful chief, along a track through dense bush and tall bull-grass. The chief did not stay to welcome them in his house. They found two sea chests with keys remaining in the locks."

"The chief's treasure was left behind here; the town was committed to the flames. The natives were gathered round in numbers, but concealed in the bush as we marched back. It was here the poor Portuguese guide was killed. The Marines kept up a fire into the thickets to clear the bush of natives, and there were no other casualties on our side. On Saturday and Sunday the men were resting; not so the Commodore. Accompanied by Captain Bradshaw, he proceeded in the *Merlin* to Punta de Linha, and called a meeting of the merchants, asked their co-operation in suppressing piracy in the river. Only one, named Shimbosh, was willing to co-operate with the Commodore. He furnished some native guides, who proved very useful, and a Portuguese merchant sent one of his *employés*, who, poor fellow, was killed a day or two afterwards." At Macatalla Creek, where they burnt several villages, we find it noted that for four miles the way was through tall bull-grass, intersected by morasses and streams, the mid-day sun pouring down as only a tropical sun could do. At Manoel Vacca's place, the chief who was imprisoned at Ascension ten years ago, and the reputed head of the pirates, it was given out that he intended to make a sharp resistance, and had a battery of guns in a commanding position, but this did not prove to be the case. The natives decamped and the village was burnt, but of the existence of the battery and the guns there was no further report. Our casualties were very small— only one killed and six wounded. Perhaps one of the most unfortunate was Mr. Dixon, engineer of the *Ariel*. He had just finished his watch in the engine-room, and came on deck for a mouthful of fresh air, standing on the gratings abaft. He had not been there a minute before he was shot through the back of the neck. He had, however, recovered. The trifling list of casualties by no means represented absence of danger. The natives were concealed in every bush, and lined the sides of the various paths and creeks. They were tolerably well armed, and it was only by incessant vigilance and strict discipline that the ambushed enemy were discovered and dispersed and the parties kept from straggling. Perhaps a still greater subject for congratulation than even the small list of casualties was the almost total absence of sickness. It was reported that after all the operations in the Congo the several crews were in better health than on an ordinary cruise, and this was attributed to the admirable arrangements planned in concert by Commodore Hewett and his chief medical officer, Dr. Fegan, C.B., and so well carried out by the officers under them."

Commodore Sir William Hewett's despatch gives a detailed account of the Expedition. The following are extracts from it :—

"I, however, feel satisfied that the moral effect produced on these savages by three gunboats appearing in creeks which it has hitherto been believed no man-of-war could ascend, and the unexpected attack made upon them in their remotest habitations, will combine to render the punishment inflicted effectual to prevent a repetition of such outrages—at any rate, for some time to come; and I believe the object of the Expedition will have been none the less fulfilled even if it should be found that there has been comparatively little bloodshed. The Misscloughs, or the natives who live on the islands forming the Delta of the Congo, are by no means cowards, and although they have never attacked us on the march, on most occasions they hung about our rear, and, according to their usual tactics, commenced a dropping fire as the force re-embarked and the boats began to move out of the creeks; and although—thanks to the inferiority of their arms and ammunition—they have not proved themselves on the present occasion very formidable, I believe with a less imposing force and fewer precautions they would have been found by no means a contemptible foe. As it was, their slugs, fired not further than thirty yards off, frequently fell thick about us, in spite of the heavy bombardment of the bushes by the gunboats and the fusilade from the small arms, and had it not been that the principal boats were fitted with protecting plates of sheet iron, backed with wood and raised about 2½ feet from the gunwale, the injury we should have suffered would have been very great. The chief features which characterize the country we have been operating in are dense bush and almost impenetrable mangrove swamps, and both officers and men deserve great praise for the manner in which, in a trying climate, they overcame the many difficulties that constantly presented themselves. In the absence of reliable information I am unable even to form an approximate idea of the loss of life sustained by the natives, but I have authority for stating that the shells from the gunboats did considerable execution, and it is to be presumed that the rockets and rifle bullets were not without their effect. The casualties on our side in action amounted to five wounded, three severely and two slightly (return enclosed); but it is with the deepest regret that in addition to those I have to report the accidental death of Manoel Fernandez, whose services were kindly placed at my disposal by Senor Valle, a merchant of Punta de Linha, to guide the Expedition to the village Lucella, a noted pirate on the south bank of the river above Scotchman's Head. He was shot by an able seaman of the *Spiteful* under the following circumstances:—The galley of the *Spiteful* being the last boat of a long string at the landing place at the head of Lucella Creek, the crew were ordered out to clear away the bush in the immediate vicinity, with their rifles unloaded. Isaac Bow, A.B., S.G., 1st class, one of her crew, having gone about 150 yards from the boats, heard men hailing to "stop him," and on looking round he saw a man rushing through the thick bush, about 100 yards off, in a direction away from the boats. He hailed him two or three times to stop, and waved his cutlass backwards. No notice, however, was taken of his hails or signal, and the man running faster, and the stick he had in his hand seeming to be a gun, Bow loaded his rifle and shot him in the belief that he was firing on an enemy. The unfortunate deceased being an old man had lost his nerve, and was afraid to disembark with Captain Bradshaw when he first landed; about three-quarters of an hour afterwards, however, it would appear that he changed his determination on remembering that he had some information to impart, and he indiscreetly left the boats without any escort and thus met with his sad fate.

"The boats engaged in these operations were—the *Active's* steam-pinnace, No. 1; the *Active's* steam-pinnace, No. 2 (brought up from the Cape), in charge of Sub-Lieutenant A. C. Middleman; the *Ascension's* steam-launch, in charge of Sub-Lieutenant P. M. Scott, who was also in charge of 7-pounder field gun; the *Encounter's* steam-pinnace, in charge of Lieutenant G. M. Richardson; the *Supply's* steam-cutter, in charge on different occasions of Navigating Lieutenant T. H. Flood, of the *Spiteful*, and Navigating Lieutenant T. G. Fenn, of the *Supply*, the *Spiteful's* steam cutter. Pulling-boats—the *Active's* launch, in charge of Mr. J. Miller, boatswain; the *Active's* first cutter, in charge of Mr. S. H. Benson, assistant-paymaster, a volunteer, there being no executive to appoint; the *Active's* second cutter, in charge on different occasions of Sub-Lieutenants H. C. Reynolds and T. B. Triggs, who were also second in command of the *Active's* company of seamen; the *Encounter's* launch, in charge on different occasions of Lieutenants H. G. Archer and D. M'N. Riddell; the *Encounter's* first cutter, in charge of Mr. L. Bayly, navigating midshipman; the *Encounter's* second cutter, in charge of Mr. W. R. Dodridge, assistant-paymaster, a volunteer, there being no executive to appoint; the *Spiteful's* pinnace, in charge on different occasions of Lieutenant Snowden and Lieutenant Gardiner (the latter also in command of the *Spiteful's* company of seamen No. 2); the *Spiteful's* paddle-box boats, No 1, in charge on different occasions of Lieutenant Gardiner and Mr. August, gunner; No. 2, in charge on different occasions of Sub-Lieutenants E. M. Domville and J. B. Benett, who were also second in command of the *Spiteful's* company of seamen No. 3; the *Merlin's* cutter, in charge of Mr. Vincent, boatswain; the *Foam's* cutter, in charge of Mr. Crump, gunner; the *Ariel's* cutter, in charge of Mr. Gilmour (acting); the *Ariel's* gig, in charge of Navigating Sub-Lieutenant C. E. Pritchard.

"Besides the medical officers mentioned by Captain Bradshaw (Mr. J. N. Stone, of the *Supply*, and Mr. Patterson of the *Active*); Mr. James B. Drew, surgeon, showed most praiseworthy zeal in leaving his ordinary duties at Ascension to serve with the Expedition as a volunteer, medical officers being short. The uninterrupted health of the squadron during the time it has been employed in this unhealthy river may be attributed to the care with which Fleet-Surgeon Henry Fegan, C.B., considered the precautions that should be adopted to secure its preservation, and I have to acknowledge the many valuable suggestions he has submitted to me.

"The following is the list of killed and wounded during operations in the River Congo between the 31st August and the 11th September, 1875:—*Active*—King Jack, native guide, gunshot, right cheek, slight; Manoel Fernandez, European guide, gunshot right side and chest, killed; William Ellis, gunner, Marine Artillery, gunshot, right hand, severe. *Merlin*—Charles Heckford, A.B., gunshot, right leg severe; George Rumball, ordinary seaman, gunshot, right leg, slight. *Ariel*—Mr. Robert Dixon, engineer, gunshot, neck, severe."

The following remarks appeared in *The Times* on the same day as the publication of these despatches:—

"We are happy to see, moreover, that he calls the attention of the Admiralty to the valuable assistance afforded him by the preparations of the medical officer. The surgeons seldom have their services duly recognized on these occasions; but it is not too much to say that it is medical science which alone renders these African Expeditions practicable. Not many years ago, our ignorance of the real nature and cause of the fevers which render the African coast so pestilential would have exposed a force to insuperable dangers either in such a slight Expedition as the present, or in such an undertaking as the Ashantee War; and there is no occasion on which the arts of preventive medicine become of greater value. It is possible now to avoid dangers which would formerly have been unconsciously encountered, but would have been absolutely fatal; and, though the climate of the Coast must always be pregnant with peril, it can be endured for a sufficient space of time."

CHAPTER XVIII.

HISTORICAL SKETCH OF THE AFRICAN MEDICAL SERVICE.

The infancy of the African Medical Staff commences with the year 1631, when the Gambia became a settlement; and on the 27th February the first Charter was granted to the Company of African Merchants who, to preserve their new acquisition, and Forts of Cormantine, James Fort, and Tococary (erected in 1640, 1662, and 1665), from the depredations of the French, Dutch, and Portuguese, were obliged to employ armed retainers, and with them chirurgions and their mates. In 1662 these merchants and their retainers had become incorporated by Charter, under the title of "Royal Adventurers," who shortly extended their influence by the capture of Cape Coast Castle, into which was thrown a garrison of 200 men, with a due proportion of officers. Twenty years before, the Portuguese were finally driven from the Gold Coast, from whence they had exported slaves, ivory, and gold for more than two hundred years—since 1142, when Baldeza first " took slaves from Guinea."

When the "Royal African Company" was established in the reign of Charles II., with the exclusive right of trading between Sallee and the Cape of Good Hope; Whydah, Pram Pram, Dix Cove, and Winnebah, were founded in the years 1680, 1690, 1691, and 1694; the garrisons came under their jurisdiction, and were often put upon their mettle in driving off the French under M. de la Roque, and the Dutch under De Ruyter, and the numerous pirates who then infested these seas. In 1701 the French took possession of Assinee, and in 1719 the Ashantees made their first advance towards the Coast by the conquest of Donkera. In 1724 the Company established and garrisoned James Fort, the same year that the Prussian Fortresses were sold to the Dutch; the French were driven from their factory at Albreda, which was burnt. So numerous at this time had become the "Rovers of the sea," that in 1730 the merchants of Haire and Nantz sent an armament to exterminate these freebooters, who had established themselves in Pirate Bay, Sierra Leone. In 1732 our factories at Bruloe (Gambia) were destroyed by the enemy, and ten years later the Ashantees made their next advance towards Fantee, by the subjugation of the Akims. In 1743 Captain

Stubbs explored the Gambia, and in 1752 the trade to Africa, to supply a sufficient number of negroes at a reasonable rate, was made free to all His Majesty's subjects. 1755 was a very *fatal* year at Cape Coast Castle, which was attacked by the French in 1757, who were gallantly repulsed by the garrison, so shortly before reduced by disease. In 1758 Goree was taken by the British; and in 1763 the Senegal and its dependencies vested in the "Company of Merchants trading to Africa." In 1765 the African Company ceded its Forts to the Crown, who at once raised a regiment to garrison them, styled the "Corps of Foot serving in Africa." The regiment consisted of a lieutenant-colonel commandant, three captains, three lieutenants, three ensigns, and a regimental agent, but no regimental medical officers—the garrison surgeons appointed to the different settlements taking charge of the detachments of the corps. Captain Joseph Wall, the afterwards celebrated Governor of Goree, held a commission in the regiment many years afterwards.

In 1780 the French succeeded in destroying Seccondee, and in expelling the British garrisons from the Senegal. In 1785 the English and Dutch captives were exchanged on the Gold Coast, where the Akims had already revolted under Ofoosoo. M. de Beauvois examined Benin and Wari, and our settlement at Sierra Leone was founded 19th February 1787, upon the arrival of 342 settlers from England, the new company being interdicted from dealing in or employing slaves. In 1792 sixteen vessels arrived, having on board 1,131 Nova Scotians, who in two years afterwards had their new settlement bombarded and plundered by a French squadron, whose ships ascended the river as high as Bunce Island. In 1799 the "Asia" arrived with the first detachment of troops, consisting of forty-five soldiers from the West Indies, who, with a few Maroons, succeeded in quelling an insurrection amongst the lately-arrived Nova Scotians. In 1801 the Colony was formed and regularly garrisoned, and our troops engaged in their first brush with the Timmanees, who to the number of 400 had invaded the settlement. About this time the great sacrifice of human life at which our European regiments were maintained in the West Indies, drew attention to the necessity for some remedial measures, and the employment of native soldiers, who were "more temperate, suffered less from exposure to the sun, were capable of garrisoning unhealthy posts for years, where Europeans would die in a few months, required less nights in bed, could garrison several stations, settled in the colony when invalided, were given a lower rate of pension, and required few recruits from a distance, no recruits being obtained from Africa between the years 1817--28, whereby a large saving in transport resulted." Recruits were drilled in nine months, and served on an average thirty years. Their utility thus became obvious, and year after year they were increased, so that in 1800 they amounted to between 4,000 and 5,000, and were finally augmented to 12,000 men, by which augmentation the white troops were relieved from laborious and unhealthy duties, and the casualties among them rapidly diminished in consequence, and the necessity for so large an establishment, as may be seen from the following table, an interesting and suggestive one of former days:—

LEEWARD ISLANDS.

Strength of the Forces.			No. of Deaths.		
Artillery, v. Artificers.	Troops of the Line.	Black Troops.	White.	Black.	Total.
601	19,676	2,405, 1st April, 1796, to	6,484	75	6,858
774	11,633	2,373, 1st July, 1797,			

THREE YEARS LATER.

893	7,304	4,099, 1st Feb., 1800, to	1,221	286	1,615
850	7,585	4,574, 1st Jan., 1801,			

The 30th Regiment landed at St. Lucia 776 strong, in May, 1796; by the end of the October following there were only sixteen fit for duty, and by March it had scarcely a man left!

In 1807 and 1808 the garrisons of our Forts on the Gold Coast were busily engaged in defending themselves against the Ashantees, who invaded the town, destroyed Winnebah, drove the Anamaboes into the sea, and attacked the Fort. On the northern coast the land forces under Lieutenant-General Sir Charles Maxwell laid siege to and captured the French Fort of Goree and the Senegal, where was left a European garrison, with its regimental surgeons and assistants, who remained until the Peace of 1814, and the restoration of the conquered settlements in the treaty agreed upon, and ratified 13th May, 1814. Colonel Macarthy had administered the government as Lieutenant-Governor from 3rd September, 1812, to 1814. In 1805 Mungo Park had left the Gambia in April, accompanied by forty-four Europeans, with the view of penetrating into the interior: by October all but four of his companions had died.

In 1809 Captain Columbine and Messrs. Davies and Ledlam were appointed Commissioners for investigating the state of the Settlements, two years subsequent to the abolition of the slave trade. Consequent upon the result of this commission, African Governors were empowered to "commission vessels and to make seizures of slaves." In 1811 Attah, King of Akim, killed the Ashantee messengers, the prelude to difficulties and war. The Ashantees were defeated by the Fantees at

Apam, and the latter repulsed from Accra. In 1816 Cape Coast was blockaded, the Ashantees, and our troops again drawn into collision with them until the conclusion of peace in 1817. In the Niger Captain Tuckey lost nineteen out of fifty-four of his crew; and at Sierra Leone, in 1815, a severe epidemic visited Freetown, resulting in the loss of many lives, yellow fever being very fatal in 1817, the first authentic notice of this disease as occurring in the colony, where it was exclusively confined to the shipping in harbour. During the two following years the European force had dwindled down to fifty-four. Of these eighteen died, and the remainder returned to England.

In 1821, upon the Company of African Merchants being abolished, the Gold Coast Forts were re-transferred to the Crown, and placed under the Sierra Leone Government, where Sir Charles Macarthy acted as Governor and officer commanding the troops. Previously to this, at the conclusion of the great war, a large reduction had taken place in the West Indian regiments; all but the 1st, 2nd, 3rd, and 4th Regiments being disbanded. The latter regiment, composed of men principally anxious to remain in the service, was retained on the establishment, and sent to Gibraltar towards the end of 1817, where it was supposed the men would be extremely useful in relieving British soldiers from such duties as subjected men to exposure during the heat of the day. The deaths, however, during their period of residence—one year and ten months—were 119, a rate of 62 annually, out of a strength of 1,000 of all ranks, four times as high as the mortality amongst the Europeans at Gibraltar during the same period, but little over the average mortality among these troops in the West Indies in 1819, viz., 63 per 1,000, the average of eighteen years being 44 per 1,000. This was thought to show that the constitution of the negro was unfitted for any climate of which he was not a native. The diseases from which the men of the regiment suffered at Gibraltar were as below:—

Diseases.	Admissions.	Deaths.
Fevers	62	0
Diseases of the Lungs	518	17
,, ,, Liver	1	1
,, ,, Stomach and Bowels	151	20
,, ,, Brain	6	1
Dropsies	5	3
Rheumatic Affections	143	0
Venereal ,,	7	0
Abscesses and Ulcers	88	3
Wounds and Injuries	62	0
Punished	47	0
Diseases of the Eyes	7	0
Other Diseases	4	0
	1,100	95

Unknown causes, principally Disease of the Lungs	24
Total mortality	119

In 1822 Brigadier-General Sir Charles Macarthy took charge of the Gold Coast. The stations on the Gold Coast were principally garrisoned by an average effective of 524·8 native troops, in medical charge of three or four military surgeons. Yellow fever prevailed extensively at Freetown, and carried off many Europeans, seventy-seven dying between December and June. In 1823, out of forty-one European officers serving on the Coast, ten died and eight were invalided. On the Gold Coast the Ashantees had for a third time invaded the Protectorate, advancing as far as Dunquah, where they were first encountered in 1823 by the Governor. The Royal African Corps, which had been raised in London at the conclusion of the war with France, numbered forty-four officers, chiefly reduced Peninsular veterans, or their sons, and 600 rank and file, with a surgeon and two assistant-surgeons, aided by hospital assistants at some of the stations. The Head Quarters was at Sierra Leone, and a half battalion at the Gambia. Previous to the transfer, the Gold Coast, under the African Company, consisting of nine principal merchants in London, Liverpool, and Bristol, subject to the supreme control of the Board of Trade, was garrisoned by their troops, consisting of 30 civil and military officers and 120 native privates, with a staff of five medical officers, the senior at Cape Coast Castle. The mean average effective on the whole Coast was 738, principally blacks. With a portion of this small force, a few Europeans, and some men of the 2nd West India Regiment, and Militia, numbering in all about 1,000, Sir Charles Macarthy took the field, and encountered the enemy at Essiamacou, 2nd May, 1824, where he was killed, with the principal medical officer, Staff Surgeon Tedlie, and eight officers of the 2nd West India Regiment. The enemy next advanced to the heights in rear of Cape Coast Castle, from which they were driven on the 24th July, 1824, by the aid of a small contingent of European troops, numbering 225, 221 of whom, or 98 per cent., died during the year.

In 1825 a large contingent of European troops was sent to Sierra Leone to augment the Royal African Corps, which now consisted of 511 non-commissioned officers and men and 20 officers. The men were crowded together into sheds at the foot of Tower Hill, and 300 of them stationed on the Isles de Los. A detachment of the Corps while at anchor at the Gambia, en route to Sierra Leone, consisting of 91 men, lost in three months 73 of their number, or 63·17 per cent. The following medical officers were appointed to the regiment:—Surgeon—William Fergusson, 24th November, 1825. Assistant-Surgeons—John Bell, 4th July, 1824; James Cahill, M.D., 24th November, 1825. Dr. Fergusson, afterwards Governor of Sierra Leone, had entered the service as an Hospital Assistant, 20th December, 1813; became Assistant-Surgeon, 13th May, 1824; Surgeon Royal African Corps, 24th November, 1825; Staff-Surgeon, 1st Class, 27th September, 1839, just before his regiment merged into the 3rd West, an event which occurred in 1840. He died on board the *Funchal* at sea, 11th January, 1846, after thirty-three years' service. In 1830 the regiment had only a surgeon and an assistant-surgeon, Mr. Foules, gazetted in 1829. Its last medical officer was Assistant-Surgeon John Ed. Burton, M.D., appointed 11th May, 1835.

With the arrival of a new governor and commander of the troops, Major-General Turner, came a Deputy Inspector of Hospitals, Dr. Barry, who was succeeded by Dr. Nicholl. These officers served at a time when the sickness and mortality was very great. Out of sixty-two officers on the Coast, fifteen died and eight were invalided. The mortality in the squadron reached a ratio of 61·8 per 1,000. Remittent fever prevailed largely amongst the shipping, the deaths to cases treated at Freetown being in the proportion of 1 to 2·73 amongst the white troops, at the Isles des Los 1 to 7. The 9th company, however, detained on board a transport in harbour, owing to want of room in barracks, from February to August, lost none of its men until they were disembarked. The mortality was increased by General Turner's armed Expedition up the Sherbro, from the effects of which many men, as before narrated, sickened and died. General Turner died on the 7th March, 1826, a few months before the completion of Tower Hill Barracks, which had been commenced by his order in 1825. On the Gold Coast the Ashantees were defeated at Dowdowah, near Accra, so that between disease and warfare the duties of the few officers of the African Medical Staff were of the most arduous description. In addition to the Deputy Inspector of Hospitals, and regimental surgeons stationed at Sierra Leone, was an Apothecary to the Forces, an assistant surgeon at the Isles des Los, and second class staff surgeon and assistants at the Gambia and the Gold Coast. An idea of the duties may be surmised from the fact, that between the years 1822-30, of 1,658 Europeans sent from England, 1,298 perished from climatic causes, 360 were invalided, 123 of whom died on the passage to England, 57 of the remainder being discharged as unfit for the service on arrival. Of 180 qualified for garrison duty, 53 were only found fit ultimately for the service. With the augmentation of the black troops in 1827 a corresponding reduction in the mortality occurred, and from this year no fresh importation of Europeans took place. In 1827 Clarence Town, Fernando Po, was established, and garrisoned by 30 Marines, the greater number of whom died. In 1828 the average annual strength of Europeans quartered at Tower Hill barracks was 231·75, ten of whom only died, probably owing to the more airy and better situation of the barracks, and the substitution of fresh for salt rations. During 1829 the Medical Staff were constantly employed during the epidemic of fever which again prevailed at Sierra Leone; in the December quarter no less than forty-eight cases having been admitted into the Garrison Hospital from H.M.S. "Plumper." Her crew had just returned from boat service up the Rio Pongos. Twenty-four of those admitted died. In 1830 the white troops were removed, and from thenceforth the military surgeons serving in Western Africa were chiefly employed in the care and treatment of native or West Indian troops. An immediate decrease took place in the mortality. Out of an annual average effective of 302·75 black troops, 218 men were treated in hospital, and only five died, or 1 in 60·55. While endeavouring to garrison these highly malarial settlements with white troops, the admissions to hospital averaged 2978·00, and the deaths 483·0 per 1,000 per annum.

In 1827 the forts and settlements on the Gold Coast had been granted to the Company of Merchants, and the garrisons and medical officers withdrawn; the Deputy-Inspector of Hospitals replaced by a First Class Staff Surgeon, and the General Commanding by a Colonel on the Staff. Between 1824 and '34 the West African settlements had no less than nine different Governors, the mortality amongst them being so great as to call from Theodore Hook the witty sarcasm, that Sierra Leone had always two Governors, "one going out alive, and the other coming home dead."

In 1832 a Detachment and Assistant Surgeon was first sent to Waterloo, on the frontier of Sierra Leone. In 1833–34 epidemic catarrh gave much trouble, and 1837 the medical staff were again called upon to cope with epidemic yellow fever, which commenced in the "timber ships" in harbour and extended to the town. The disease commenced in the same season and with the same symptoms as that of 1829, viz., pains in the loins, calves, and forehead; in several diminished temperature; tongue covered with an ash-coloured fur, or preternaturally red; eyes watery and suffused, on the fourth or fifth day the skin assuming a dusky, yellow tinge; great irritability of the stomach, and as the fever advanced, black vomit, like decomposed blood serum, and just before death delusive ideas of feeling better. In 1840 Livingstone sailed for Africa, and the Royal African Corps, since 1830 a native regiment, became the 3rd West India, disbanded in 1870, after more than fifty-four years' service as an African or West Indian Corps. While these events were occurring on the Leeward coasts, we had been extending our fortified posts on the Gambia. St. Mary's was purchased in 1816, and Bathurst town built and garrisoned; M'Carthy's Island in 1820, and Fort George built upon it in 1823; Barra ceded in 1826, Albreda being still held by the French. The garrison then consisted of about 150 of the Royal African Corps, and a Colonial Militia. At Bathurst, 1 lieutenant-colonel, 2 majors, 6 captains, 4 first lieutenants, 4 second lieutenants. Staff—1 adjutant, 1 paymaster, 1 quartermaster, 1 surgeon. Strength—6 colour-sergeants, 12 sergeants, 18 corporals, 12 drummers, 252 privates. Fort Bullen— 1 captain, 1 lieutenant, 90 non-commissioned officers and men. M'Carthy's Island—3 captains, 5 lieutenants, 1 surgeon, and 200 non-commissioned officers and privates. Several discharged soldiers were located at the different posts, especially at Fort Bullen. In 1836 the garrisons on the Coast appeared to have been reduced to a minimum.

Station.	Corps or Detachment.	No. of Companies.	Officers.	Rank and File.
Sierra Leone .	1st W. I. Regiment .	1	1	55
,,	2nd W. I. Regiment .	1	1	86
,,	Royal African Corps .	2	10	143
Gambia	,, ,, ,,	4	6	315
Isles des Los	,, ,, ,,	...	...	12
	Total	8	18	611

Ten companies of Artillery Militia, consisting of 19 officers, 42 non-commissioned officers, and 390 privates, were distributed in Freetown, Wilberforce, Kissy, and Wellington, in after years replaced by a corps of infantry, dressed in grey tunics, with red facings, white accoutrements, and armed with rifles. The men were drawn by ballot, and the officers appointed by the Governor. The colonial surgeon was surgeon to the corps, which was paraded with the regular troops in 1861 both in quarters and the field.

In 1841 Dr. Madden visited West Africa. The command of the troops was vested in a Colonel on the Staff, who was also Governor of Sierra Leone, where a first-class Staff Surgeon officiated as principal medical officer—Dr. William Fergusson. Under his orders were three Assistant Surgeons. In 1842 Prince de Joinville arrived in the frigate Belle Poule at Sierra Leone, and new colours were presented to the 3rd West India Regiment (the old African corps), on the parade ground, Falconbridge Square, by Mrs. Macdonald, the wife of the Governor. In 1843 the Gambia was made an independent settlement, and in the following year the Crown resumed possession of the Gold Coast, but these changes did not appear to involve any immediate increase in the African medical staff, which in 1845 numbered one first class staff surgeon, one second class staff surgeon, and two assistant staff surgeons. A new system of garrisoning the Coast Settlements now came into operation. The Head Quarters of the three West India regiments were retained in the West Indies, a company or two of each being detached for service on the Coast, forming, in effect, a depôt battalion, with garrison rosters and messes, but separate regimental commands. Out of a population of some 38,000 in Sierra Leone, there were not more than 105 European residents.

Yellow fever began again to prevail at Sierra Leone, and became epidemic in 1847, seven Europeans dying in one house, the first cases occurring in June, up to which date very little rain had fallen. It was observed that when the rains fell in their usual volume, remittents were the prevailing fevers; when irregular, and at their termination, yellow fever. In the year ending the 3rd March, 1848, only 88·46 inches of rain had fallen; to the 3rd March, 1849, 141·15 inches; 31st March, 1850, 140·63 inches. In 1846 Mr. Foulis succeeded Dr. Fergusson as First Class Staff Surgeon and Principal Medical Officer at Sierra Leone, his commissions dating Hospital Assistant, 5th December, '26; Assistant-Surgeon, R. A. Corps, 4th June, '29; Second Class Staff Surgeon, 2nd July, '41; Staff Surgeon, First Class, 11th July, '45. He died in 1847, and was succeeded by Mr. Robert Lawson, who became Assistant-Surgeon on the General Staff, 15th May, '35; was promoted Second Class Staff Surgeon, 15th December, '45; and First Class Satff Surgeon 27th October, '46, on the eve of his proceeding to Sierra Leone, where he served until the outbreak of the Crimean War, joining as a Deputy Inspector of Hospitals, having been promoted 8th December, '54, in little over nineteen years' service.

In 1847 a great boon was granted to the West African settlements in the shape of a man-of-war monthly mail to and from the Coast. Previous to this letters were sent by merchant ships, which were very irregular in their sailing. In 1851 the Cape of Good Hope line of steamers touched at Sierra Leone, and in 1852 the first of the new line of African steamers, the "Forerunner," arrived at Sierra Leone with Governor Kennedy, 12th October, 1852. With 1847 came a considerable increase to the medical staff, in consequence of the occupation of the Gambia and Gold Coast, upon their becoming separate Governments. At Sierra Leone was a first class staff surgeon and assistant surgeon; at the Gold Coast, a second class staff surgeon and four assistant surgeons; at the Gambia, a second class staff surgeon and five assistant surgeons, an establishment very little altered or reduced for several years. In 1850, the mean average strength of the black troops was 285·7, increased in 1851 by the raising of the Gold Coast Artillery Corps, for the purpose of garrisoning the forts. The regiment consisted originally of 17 officers and 200 men, 120 stationed at Cape Coast Castle in medical charge of the regimental surgeon, who was gazetted to the Corps. A similar number garrisoned Accra, and smaller detachments the remaining stations, in medical charge of staff assistant surgeons. The regiment was raised by Major Hill, its first *ex officio*

Commanding Officer, and afterwards Governor of Sierra Leone and Newfoundland. The corps was subsequently increased from three captains, three lieutenants, and four ensigns, to a major-commanding, six captains, seven lieutenants, and three ensigns. The regiment served in the first and second Crobboe Expeditions, and Ashanti Expedition of 1863, when it was disbanded, owing to its having mutinied in the previous year. Seventy of the mutineers were sent to Sierra Leone for trial, and two of them executed, one at Tower Hill Barracks, and the trumpeter, who sounded the "assembly," at Cape Coast Castle. A medical officer, Staff Assistant-Surgeon Crow, was a member of the General Court-martial convened at Sierra Leone. The following medical officers had been gazetted to the regiment, and served with it on the Gold Coast:—

1851—Assistant-Surgeon James Davis, 9th September, '51.

1853—Surgeon Thomas Kehoe, M.D., 15th March, '50; Assistant-Surgeon, 19th June, '46.

1854—P. H. Roe, Surgeon, 27th May, '53 ; Assistant-Surgeon, 3rd September, '47.

Mr. Roe served in the regiment during 1855 and 1856, and in conformity with the warrant of this corps, which granted a step of rank for three years' consecutive service on the Gold Coast, became on the 23rd October, 1857, a Surgeon of the First Class. In 1858 he served in this capacity as principal medical officer of the Gambia, and in conformity with the terms of the Royal Warrant, 1st October of the same year, became Surgeon-Major in little over eleven years' service. He retired on the half-pay of his rank 13th December, 1859, and afterwards commuted his pension. He was the last regimental surgeon. In 1859, after a season of very irregular rains, yellow fever made its appearance at Freetown in April, and during the three months ending 30th June, carried off thirty-five Europeans. One hundred and six Europeans died from January to December, including 65 seamen; the Roman Catholic bishop and four priests dying in one house. The garrison was comparatively healthy. In the Gambia the disease was also very fatal, three officers of the medical staff succumbing to its effects at M'Carthy's Island and Bathurst. The average strength of black troops was 356, yielding 193 admissions and 5 deaths—the very low ratios of 542 and 14·02 per 1,000, as against a millesimal ratio of admissions and deaths during the ten years ending 1836, of 812 and 30·1 respectively.

Officers who joined the African Medical Staff, 1841-58:—

1841—William Ferguson, W. S. J. Boyle, T. H. O'Flaherty, W. Duncan.

1843—W. Foulcs, H. L. Cowen.

1844—James Dickson.

1845—J. W. Mostyn.

1847—Robert Lawson, M.D.; Charles Godwin, M.D.; A. R. Ridgeway, M.B.; Thomas Park, Henry Temple, W. D. Marchant, T. B. Phillipson.

1848— C. Alex. Gordon, M.D.; A. J. Dolee, P. Henry Roe, J. H. Smith, M.D.; John Waller, W. F. Daniell, F. A. Ringdon, John Robertson.
1849—Thomas Kehoe, Andrew J. Waters, David C. Pitcairn.
1850—John Berry, W. R. Thompson, M.D.
1851—Fitz M. T. Denis.
1852—R. G. Fitzgibbon, J. Hendley, H. C. Rinkyn.
1853—R. W. Frazer, M.D.; Robert Bradshaw, E. H. Brien, Ed. Akers.
1854—James Davys, W. C. Hewatson, M.D.; Thomas Partridge, Charles F. Abbott, W. Tydd Harding, W. M. Skues, M.B.
1855—G. Power, M.D.
1856—Wm. Skeen.
1857—P. A. M'Dermott, Aug. Morphew, Wm. Page, Fr. Oakes, Curtis Martin, T. C. Beale, James Lauder, W. B. Trestrail, F. S. G. Gunn, John Bradshaw, Thomas B. Teevan, H. S. E. Shrooder, James H. Horton, William Davis.

Fifty-eight officers in eighteen years, an average of 3·2 annually. A large number lie buried in Africa; nine are still actively employed, viz., Surgeon-General Gordon, C.B., Principal Medical Office, Madras; Surgeon-Major Hendley, Bengal; Harding, Gibraltar; Skues, 26th Cameronians; Skeen, 65th Foot; Martin, 58th, Brigade Depôt; Morphew, 27th Regiment; Oakes, 56th Foot; Gunn, 99th Regiment.

Up to the year 1858, there had been no printed regulations for the African Medical Service. Since 1840 it had been recruited as the General Staff as vacancies occurred, and the officers were relieved as opportunity offered. The average service in the junior ranks was five or six years, promotion going on the station, as was then very much the custom. During the intervening years the Corps had been distributed as below:—

Years.	Sierra Leone.	Gambia	Gold Coast.	Total.	Years.	Sierra Leone.	Gambia	Gold Coast.	Total.
1841	4	-	-	4	1850	3	4	2	9
1842	1	-	-	1	1851	4	4	4	12
1843	3	-	-	3	1852	3	2	4	9
1844	4	-	-	4	1853	3	4	2	9
1845	4	-	-	4	1854	5	4	3	12
1846	3	-	-	3	1855	2	7	7	16
1847	4	1	1	6	1856	2	6	5	13
1848	2	6	5	13	1857	3	6	4	13
1849	2	5	3	10	1858	2	5	7	14

In 1858 it was determined to make the service more effective, and in the new medical regulations published in 1860, it was laid down that each medical officer volunteering for the West Coast of Africa would be required to serve at one of the stations on the Coast for twelve months, each year of such service counting as two towards promotion and retirement, with an equivalent of leave, the Senior Assistant-Surgeon being entitled to the promotion as vacancies occurred, either by death or the transfer of the Senior Surgeon to a West Indian regiment, and all officers who did not volunteer originally from the General Staff might be transferred to the latter or a line regiment after three years' service on the Coast. In the Dress Regulations it was laid down that officers of the medical department, serving in Africa, were to wear the shell jacket, as prescribed for officers of infantry. At this time the garrisons of the Coast were distributed as follows:—On the Gold Coast, the Gold Coast Corps; at Sierra Leone and the Gambia, detachments of the 1st West India Regiment, relieved in 1860 by detachments of the 2nd West India Regiment. No cases of corporeal punishment occurred, a striking contrast to the years 1819–36 inclusive, when the annual average amounted to 44 per 1,000 of strength.

	Average Strength.	Admissions	Deaths.
Gambia	314	205	8
Sierra Leone	356	193	5
Gold Coast	279	162	7

MEDICAL STAFF.

	On Leave.	At Sierra Leone.	The Gambia.	Gold Coast.	Total.
Surgeons	2	1	0	0	3
Assistant-Surgeons	1	1	4	4	10

The 1st, 2nd, and 3rd West India Regiments had each a surgeon and three assistant-surgeons serving in the West Indies. In consequence of representations made as to the injustice of requiring medical officers who had served for a prolonged period in Africa being required to serve immediately afterwards in the West Indies, the regulation as to the transfer of surgeons to West Indian regiments only took place in few instances, and the rule became a dead letter by the final removal of medical officers from these corps; from which date, and the disbandment of the Gold Coast Corps in 1863, the African service became a staff corps, with its own rules for promotion. The station and hospital became the unit, and not the regiment; and the senior medical officer communicated on all official matters through the Fort Adjutant; not with the officer commanding the regiment, but the officer commanding the troops. The sick were still treated regimentally, and the medical officers were usually honorary members of the regimental mess. A purveyor's clerk, in conjunction with the Commissariat, supplied all hospital requisites excepting medicines, which were indented for periodically and remained on the station, supplies being sent on detachment when necessary. The patients in hospital were treated, dieted, and clothed exactly as at home, and the returns were the usual monthly, quarterly, and annual ones required by the Army Medical Department. The senior medical officer officiated as principal medical officer, and when sick seamen or marines were treated in the garrison hospital, a separate return was forwarded to the Admiralty. All invaliding documents were confirmed on the spot by the senior medical officer and officer commanding the troops. The sick attended at hospital at 7 A.M. In 1861 Sherbro Island was ceded to the British, and with Bulama to the northward occupied and garrisoned, a medical officer in each instance accompanying the troops, and officiating as magistrate and Commissioner of the Local Court of Requests, as well as civil assistant-surgeon. In 1862 Lagos was ceded to the British, an island situated at the confluence of the Ogar, Oshwa, and Osso. It was occupied by a detachment of the 2nd West India Regiment in December, 1862, in medical charge of Assistant-Surgeon Rowe, now Administrator of the Gambia. The station is about 500 miles south of Cape Coast Castle.

	Average Strength.	Admissions.	Deaths.
Sierra Leone	317	252	9
The Gambia	209	254	4
Lagos	105	198	3
Gold Coast	313	144	9

The deaths from tubercular diseases had averaged during the four years 1859–62, 12·66 per 1,000 at Sierra Leone, 17·64 per 1,000 at the Gambia, and 7·44 per 1,000 on the Gold Coast.

On the 19th February, 1863, the Head Quarters of the 3rd West India Regiment returned to the Coast, and after the absence of many years the old Royal African Corps came again under the medical charge of the African Staff. The 4th and 5th West India Regiments were raised principally by volunteers from the others, and the former Corps proceeded at once to the Gold Coast to replace the Gold Coast Artillery. Colonel Conran, as Colonel on the Staff, commanded the troops on the Coast, the Head Quarters being on the Gold Coast, where the force had been largely increased in consequence of troubles with the Ashantees, who had invaded and retired from the Protectorate. The year 1862 had been a very fatal one at the Bonny, and at Fernando Po no less than 78 Europeans had succumbed to disease. The 2nd West returned by detachments in 1863 to the West Indies. The average strength of the troops on the Coast amounted to 1,323 all told. The average number constantly non-effective from sickness varied from thirteen at Lagos to twenty-eight on the Gold Coast. On the 22nd November, 1864, Colonel Ord arrived at Sierra Leone, with instructions to make certain inquiries respecting the state of the settlements. He was accompanied by Major-General O'Connor, C.B., and Deputy Inspector-General of Hospitals, Dr. Elliott, C.B. The Head Quarters of the 3rd and 4th, and detachments of the 1st and 2nd, were serving on the Coast, the latter two embarking in August for the West Indies on the cessation of the military operations on the Gold Coast. The African Staff had been increased to five surgeons and thirty assistant-surgeons, twenty-three serving on the Coast and thirteen on leave in England. Three of the former died on the Gold Coast; 1,638 non-commissioned officers and men were serving in the settlements, 757 on the Gold Coast. In 1865 the staff-sergeants' quarters were erected at Tower Hill Barracks, and the new road completed, chiefly by fatigue parties of the 3rd West India Regiment, then commanded by Colonel Chamberlyne. In 1865 the 3rd West garrisoned Sierra Leone and the Gambia, and the 4th West and a detachment of the 5th, the Gold Coast and Lagos, 1,506 in all. Dr. Daniell, who had entered the African medical service eighteen years before, was now senior staff surgeon in the Army. He died in the following year. In 1866, in consequence of Colonel Ord's report and the recommendation of a Parliamentary Committee, the colony of Sierra Leone was united by a Charter with the other Forts and Settlements on the West Coast, under a Governor-in-Chief. On the 19th February, and between the 1st April and 2nd October, no less than 100 Europeans, 45 residents, and 55 strangers, died of epidemic fever, which again extensively prevailed. One officer of the medical staff died, and another was invalided to England, and the garrisons withdrawn from the Sherbro and Bulama, and replaced by armed police. The Military Head Quarters were in 1867 changed to Sierra Leone, where Colonel Yonge, 1st West India Regiment, was Commanding Officer and Administrator-in-Chief. In compliance with the new orders for the reduction of our military establishments, the average effective had fallen to 1,005. In the West Indies, Staff-Surgeon Major Bacot, and Staff-Surgeons Dunlop and Crisp, and Staff Assistant-Surgeons Doran, Morris, and White, were shown on the Army List as attached to the 2nd, 3rd, and 4th West India Regiments, shortly before returned from Africa. In the following year they reverted to general duty. These officers had never served on the West Coast.

At this date the distribution of the Medical Staff was as below:—

Gambia, at Head Quarters, one surgeon and two assistant surgeons; M'Carthy's Island, two assistant surgeons; St. Mary's, one assistant surgeon; Sierra Leone, at Head Quarters, one surgeon and two assistant surgeons; British Quiah, one assistant surgeon; Bulama, one assistant surgeon; Sherbro, one assistant surgeon.

Gold Coast, Cape Coast Castle, one surgeon, two assistant surgeons; Accra, one assistant surgeon; Anamaboe, one assistant surgeon; Winnebah, one assistant surgeon; Lagos, two assistant surgeons.

In May, 1869, cholera broke out at M'Carthy's Island and Bathurst, Gambia, and furnished twenty-one cases and fourteen deaths amongst the troops. On the 6th May the detachment was broken up into three parties, one being sent to Cape St. Mary's, eight miles; another to Fort Bullen, three miles distant, upon the opposite side of the river; the third remaining at Bathurst. The detachment at Fort Bullen escaped the disease entirely. The mortality among the black civil population was very great, the deaths in eight weeks amounting to 1,700 in a population not exceeding 5,000. In 1870 a great reduction was made in the West African garrisons. In the end of May the Head Quarters and three companies of the 1st West India Regiment, under the command of Lieutenant-Colonel Anton, left the command for the West Indies, the force was withdrawn from the Gambia, and in June from Lagos, the average strength on the Gold Coast and Sierra Leone falling to 438 black troops. The Medical Staff was reduced in a corresponding degree, and for the first time embodied and shown in the *Army List* as a separate corps, under the heading "African Medical Service." Two surgeons and five assistant surgeons were employed on the Coast. The five senior surgeons were re-transferred to the General Staff, and six of the sixteen assistant surgeons. At Lagos the Houssa Corps raised to 360 non-commissioned officers and men by Commander Glover, and drilled and disciplined by Surgeon-Major Rowe, replaced the regular troops. The nucleus of this body had been formed from a number of carriers, who proceeded into the interior with Commander Glover, in 1856. They were year after year increased and disciplined, principally by a system of fines, which formed a reserve fund for the sick and their families.

Between 1860 and 1870 the following officers joined the service under the provisions of the Medical Regulations of 1859, and the Royal Warrants of 1867 and 1873:—1860—C. O'Callaghan, James W. Crow, M. L. Burrows, B. Hinde, E. W. Ward, J. B. Thomas, George Calvert. 1861—Albert A. Gore, W. H. Jones, C. H. Harvey, Alex. Long, Aug. Fr. Elliott, M.D. 1862—Frank Simpson, F. M. Skues, M.B., A. B. Eaton, M.D., E. M'Carthy, S. Rowe, A. J. Belemore, Allan N. Fox, W. M. Duggan, Joseph Gray. 1863—Michael Quinlan, William Jay, C. B. Mosse, P. B. Kearney, E. G. Ley, M.D., Robert Waters, Robert Wm. Hooper, John Wm. Heather, M.D., Aug. Stewart, M.D., Gordon Hammond. 1865—T. B. Moriarty, M.D., P. O'Connor, George A. Wright, M.D., T. W. Wright, D. D. Heather. 1866—Alexander Johnston, M.D., W. Verdon, M. Finucane. 1867—T. Ougten, W. Rutherford. 1869—John A. Buscarlet, E. A Roe. Forty-two: of which number fifteen died on the Coast, or shortly after returning to England; four were invalided on half-pay, and eight were transferred to the General Staff, previous to promotion. The greater number had been volunteers from the General or Regimental Staff of the Army. A year after the conclusion of the Ashanti War of 1873-74 there were serving on the African Medical Staff the following Officers:—

SURGEONS-MAJOR, RANKING WITH MAJORS.

C. B. Mosse, C.B., 18th Jan., '67.
Aug. Fred. Elliott, M.D., 4th July, '70.
Samuel Rowe, M.B., C.M.G., 4th July, '70.
Allan N. Fox, M B., 4th July, '70.
Edwin G. Ley, 1st April, '74.

Thos. W. Wright, 3rd August, '74.
Alex. Johnston, M.D., 23rd Nov. '74.
J. A. B. Horton, M.D., 1st April, '75.
W. B. Davis, M.D., 1st April, '75.

SURGEONS, RANKING WITH CAPTAINS.

Alex. Jennings, M.D., 20th April, 1859.
Frank Simpson, 1st Aug., '71.
V. S. Gouldsbury, M.D., 30th Sept., '63.

Jas. S. Conyers, M.D., 31st March, '68.
Fre. Hen. Spencer, M.B., 30th Sept., '73.

Uniform—Scarlet. Facings—Black Velvet.

SERVICE OF THE CORPS.

Epidemics 1807, '13, '16, '21, '25, '28, '37, '47, '59, '66, '69, '72. Military actions and Expeditions—Attack of the Timmanees upon Freetown, 1801. Cape Coast, 1807. Capture of Goree and Senegal, 1809. Winnebah, 1812. Cape Coast Castle, 1816. Dunquah, 1823. Destruction of Junca Cunda and Canni Cunni Tenda, Gambia, 1864. Capture of Stockaded Maritime Town of Tubar colong, near Albreda, Gambia, 3rd June, 1866, by 4th West India Regiment, with a loss of 4 killed and 13 wounded, from among 6 officers and 150 men. Battle of Essiamacow, 20th of May, 1825—Mr. Tedlie, S.M.O., killed. Sherbro, August and September, 1825. Battle of Dodowah, 1826. Capture of Fort Bullen, and Action of Barra Point, 11th November, 1831. Battle of Essow, capital of Barra, 17th November. Destruction of Stockades on the Rio Nunez, 1844. Expedition up the Sherbro, June and July, 1849. Detachments of 1st and 3rd West India Regiments in H.M.S. Alert. Destruction of Bambacoo, and Action on Quenella Plains, eighty miles up the Gambia, 6th and 8th May, 1849—Mr. Kehoe, S.M.O., wounded. Attack and Defeat of the Pirates on the Islands of Basis, Rio Jeba, 12th December, 1849, by British and French naval and land forces, under Commander Fanshaw. Expedition, 1st and 3rd West India Regiment, to Malaghea, 22nd May, 1855: British loss, 71 men killed and wounded, out of 151, including among the latter Mr. Bradshaw, S.M.O. Invasion of Assin Country by Ashantees, March and April, 1852. Defence of Christiensberg Castle by 131 men of the Gold Coast Corps, 1st September, 1854, from Danish Accra Rebels, and Bombardment of Labody. Expedition against Danish Accra, October, 1854. Cochrane's Crobboe Expedition, September, October, and November, 1858, and Action of Crobboe Heights, 18th September. Destruction of Mandingo Town of Talafu by detachments of 1st, 2nd, and 3rd West India Regiments, June, 1853. Repulse of Mahomedans of Gambia, under Omar Hadajee, at Gambia, 17th July, 1855—29 men killed and 53 wounded, from among 240 British troops. English and French attack on Mahomedans of Upper and Lower Combo, Gambia, forcing Pass of Baccow, and storm of Koubro Stockade, with a heavy loss in killed and wounded, including Mr. Hendley, S.M.O. Governor Hill's and Commodore Wise's Expedition of 500 Europeans, fifty miles up the Great Scarcias, January, 1858. Second Expedition of 400 Europeans and 240 1st and 2nd West, February, 1859. Expedition against the Dunquah Rebels, Gold Coast, June and July, 1859. Baddaboo Expedition, River Gambia, and Action of Saba, February, 1861. Quiah Expedition, November, December, and January, 1861–62; and Actions of Massongha, Madonkia, Robeah, Ribbee River; 2nd West India Regiment, and Seamen and Marines of "Torch" and "Falcon." Cochrane's Expedition to Eastern Akim; Gold Coast Corps and 2nd West India Regiment, April to July, 1863. Ashantee War of 1863–64. Occupation of Mansue and Prashue. Destruction of Epe, on Lagos River, by 2nd West, 12th March, 1863—1 killed and 16 wounded, out of 123 men engaged. Sir Garnet Wolseley's Expedition against the Ashantees, 1873–74. Actions of Elmina, Essiaman, Dunquah, Fassowah. Occupation of Prashue. Battle of Amoaful, and Capture of Coomassie, 180 miles from the sea. Officers who were serving on the African Medical Staff held the appointments of Secretary to the Principal Medical Officer, Medical Charge of 23rd Foot, 2nd Field Hospital, Wood's Regiment, and on the Volta "Chief of the Staff." It only remains to add, that owing to the nature of the climate, and the frequent sickness and invaliding of others, the officers of the African Medical Staff were often called upon to perform duties foreign to those of their profession. Two of their number were raised to the office of Colonial Governor, and other officers have attained to the highest rank in the Army Medical Service. The historical registers, army medical reports and general literature of the profession, contain many interesting contributions from their pens; and their devotion to duty in the field has more than once called forth commendation from the Military and Colonial authorities during their long and arduous service in that most deadly and trying climate.

www.ingramcontent.com/pod-product-compliance
Lightning Source LLC
Chambersburg PA
CBHW021827230426

43669CB00008B/895